WHO IS MY NEIGHBOR?
AND WHY DOES HE NEED ME?

JOHN HAY & DAVID WEBB

Who Is My Neighbor? (And Why Does He Need Me?):
Biblical Worldview of Servanthood

Published by
Apologia Educational Ministries
1106 Meridian Plaza, Suite 220/340
Anderson, Indiana 46016
apologia.com

Manufactured in the USA
Second Printing: April 2015

ISBN: 978-1-935495-09-3

Cover Design: Sandra Kimbell
Book Design: Doug Powell

Printed by Bang Printing, Brainerd, MN

Unless otherwise indicated, Scripture quotations are from:
The Holy Bible, New International Version © 1973, 1984 by International Bible Society,
used by permission of Zondervan Publishing House.

Other Scripture quotations are from:
Holy Bible, New Living Translation (NLT) © 1996. Used by permission of Tyndale House
Publishers, Inc. All rights reserved.

The Holy Bible, King James Version (KJV)

The Holy Bible, New King James Version (NKJV) © 1984
by Thomas Nelson, Inc.

The Holy Bible, English Standard Version (ESV) © 2001 by Crossway Bibles, a division of Good
News Publishers. Used by permission. All rights reserved.

New American Standard Bible® (NASB) © 1960, 1977, 1995 by the Lockman Foundation.
Used by permission.

The Holy Bible, New Century Version (NCV) © 1987, 1988, 1991 by Word Publishing.
Used by permission.

International Children's Bible, New Century Version (ICB) © 1986, 1988 by Word Publishing

Contemporary English Version, (CEV) © 1995 by American Bible Society

For Helen Garrity, my beloved friend, spiritual mentor, and fellow Christian educator.

For my darling wife, Peggy, who taught me that there's more than one way to say "I love you."

TABLE OF CONTENTS

Table of Contents

HOW TO USE THIS BOOK

Thank you for choosing the What We Believe series and the third volume, *Who Is My Neighbor? (And Why Does He Need Me?)*. As with every Apologia textbook, you will find this Bible curriculum easy to use for your whole family. The text is written directly to the student, making it appealing for children from six to fourteen. The material is presented in a conversational, engaging style that will make the study of God's Word exciting and memorable, thereby creating an environment where learning is a joy.

Each lesson contains a great deal of information and is formatted to allow children to learn at their own pace. The course is designed so that you may customize the amount of time you spend on each lesson, depending on your child's interest level and attention span. We do, however, recommend that you present the lessons in order, as each lesson builds on ideas previously discussed. Although most of the lessons can be covered in two-week segments, some will go a little more quickly, while others may take longer. Older students can read and do the activities on their own. Younger students will enjoy an older sibling or parent reading along with them.

Please note that the Bible verses in each lesson are taken primarily from the New International Version (NIV), although a number of translations are employed. For the sake of clarity, the authors have also made extensive use of the New Living Translation (NLT) and the New Century Version (NCV) as these versions use vocabulary more accessible to younger students. We recommend, however, that your child use your family's preferred translation for the purpose of memorizing selected passages.

NOTEBOOKING

Notebooking is a fun tool that enables students to personalize and capture what they have learned in an artful keepsake. In each lesson in this book, you will find a number of passages under the heading "Make a Note of It." In these sections, students are asked to write about what they've learned or about an experience they've had that relates to the lesson. As children think about their lives in light of the lesson, the spiritual truths of the text will come alive for them and make real-life application easy.

For this purpose, Apologia publishes companion notebooking journals for each book in the series. These full-color, spiral-bound journals include all "Make a Note of It" assignments as well as puzzles, activities, mini books, reading lists, lesson plans, and additional pages for taking notes. Students are encouraged to personalize these journals by filling them with their own words and illustrations.

For younger students—and those who learn best while their hands are busy—we have compiled a 64-page companion coloring book for each of the volumes. Lovingly illustrated, each page depicts a story or teaching from the textbook to reinforce the lessons.

LESSON STRUCTURE

Each lesson in *Who Is My Neighbor? (And Why Does He Need Me?)* contains several key components.

The Big Idea. Each lesson opens with an introduction to the main topic of the lesson and a brief overview of what students have learned up to this point.

What You Will Do. This section states the learning objectives for the lesson.

Short Story. Each of the lessons contains a short story featuring characters about the same age as your children. These stories provide a glimpse into the lives of characters with differing worldviews and integrate concepts taught in the lesson that follows. As the story's characters work through their differences, minister to one another, and seek counsel from the Bible and their parents, students see what a worldview looks like in action.

Think About It. These thought-provoking questions dig deeper into the short stories and can be used to check students' comprehension. You may choose to supplement or adapt these questions to better suit a child's age and reading level. More than reciting information back about the story itself, these questions probe students' understanding and provide great dinner-table talking points.

Words You Need to Know. Important vocabulary words in each lesson are defined in the Words You Need to Know section. Students should write these definitions in their notebooks. These are words that will be used and examined during the lesson and throughout the book. As students familiarize themselves with these words, not only will church services become more meaningful, but students will be better prepared to express their faith to others.

Hide It in Your Heart. Although the Bible is quoted extensively throughout the book, each lesson identifies two specific Bible memory verses for students to write in their notebooks. The first of these expresses the main theme of the lesson. By memorizing this verse, your student will learn that the theme of the lesson is biblical and something God desires us to know. The second pertains to a character trait that students will be encouraged to internalize and demonstrate as a result of the lesson. These verses are ideal for Bible memorization or copy work. The verses have been chosen carefully for the clarity of the concepts they communicate, but you may prefer to use your family's favorite translation of these verses.

Integrated Learning. Throughout the text we have provided interesting articles with an age-appropriate approach to interdisciplinary topics related to the main text. Some of these topics are specifically related to elements in one of the short stories, while others are tied directly to the lesson. These articles are designed to help students to pursue the book's ideas and concepts across the fields of art, math, science, history, and more. The beauty of the integrated learning approach is that it gives students a broader understanding of the main subject while exposing the student to new interests, skills, and experiences.

What Should I Do? This section highlights a specific godly character trait that students should demonstrate as an appropriate response to what they have just learned. Here students are given tools to consider how the lesson applies to their own lives. Consciously practicing godly character traits will create growth.

Prayer. The main body of each lesson concludes with a prayer that helps children to acknowledge the gifts of God and thank Him for all He has done. You may also choose to adapt these prayers for use as a family.

Encounters with Jesus. The final portion of each lesson is a story, adapted from Scripture, about a person who encountered Jesus during His ministry on earth. Explain to the student that although these stories are based on actual events depicted in the Gospels, we have imagined these events from the unique perspective of one of the participants while providing cultural details to help students better understand what is happening in the story. In some cases we have provided culturally appropriate names to individuals who are not given names in the biblical account. In other instances we have created peripheral characters to help us tell the story in an engaging way. Through these stories students can explore how Jesus showed God's love to individuals in their time of need, thus providing an example for students to follow as they meet people in need.

Take a Closer Look. These discussion questions encourage children to think about how Jesus' deeds impacted the people He met. The questions also help them to consider how they might serve as Jesus' "hands and feet" in a similar situation today.

House of Truth. Four of the lessons end with the addition of a new part of the House of Truth. Intended to be a hands-on memory aid, the House of Truth is a visual model constructed one step at a time. As new concepts are learned, the foundation, walls, and roof of the house are constructed, giving children a concrete way of thinking about their lives within the kingdom of God. In *Who Is God? (And Can I Really Know Him?)*, we erected the foundation and first wall of the House of Truth, the Fellowship Wall. In *Who Am I? (And What Am I Doing Here?)*, students completed the second wall of the house, the Image-Bearing Wall. In this volume, children will erect the third wall in the House of Truth, the Servanthood Wall. The fourth wall will be added in the final volume of the series.

Students can draw the House of Truth in their notebooks or build it with items you have on hand, such as LEGO blocks. A three-dimensional model of the House of Truth is available for purchase from Summit Ministries. This colorful, durable model is designed to be constructed block by block as each affirmation of the biblical Christian worldview is developed in the lessons. The model forms a visual, tactile framework to help children understand these truths and integrate them into their lives. You can purchase the model at www.summit.org.

LESSON PLAN

Each lesson is designed to be flexible and adaptable to your family's needs. Organize the lessons into a schedule that works for you and your child. Here is a sample lesson plan to consider based on a schedule of three weeks per lesson, two days per week:

WEEK ONE

Day One:
Read "The Big Idea" and "What You Will Do"
Read the Short Story and discuss
Discuss the questions in "Think About It"

Day Two:
Study "Words You Need to Know"
Memorize "Hide It in Your Heart" verses
Read sidebar articles and do activities
Write or draw in notebook about what was studied

WEEK TWO

Day Three:
Read and discuss first half of the main lesson
Notebook the "Make a Note of It" activities
Write or draw in notebook about what was studied

Day Four:
Read and discuss second half of the main lesson
Notebook the "Make a Note of It" activities
Write or draw in notebook about what was studied

WEEK THREE

Day Five:
Read and discuss "What Should I Do?" for character development
Read and use the prayer for spiritual development
Write or draw in notebook about what was studied

Day Six:
Read the "Encounters with Jesus" story
Discuss the questions in "Take a Closer Look"
Construct or draw the next phase of the House of Truth

ADDITIONAL TEACHING MATERIALS

Some lessons contain activities that require advance planning. A list of materials for these activities has been provided with each activity. Nearly all the materials are household items or are easily obtained. You will find the Apologia website to be a valuable source of information and materials to help you in teaching this course.

WHY SHOULD YOU TEACH WORLDVIEW?

When a particular worldview is held by a large number of people, it becomes highly influential, swaying many through media, entertainment, education, and corporate behavior. Some of the more widely held worldviews of the twenty-first century include secular humanism, socialism and Marxism, New Age, postmodernism, and Islam. Not to be excluded is the biblical Christian worldview, the focus of this curriculum.

People develop their worldviews based upon beliefs they perceive to be true. Obviously, not all beliefs are true. If they were, we would not see the wide diversity of behaviors that stem from different interpretations of the same reality. For example, the beliefs of secular humanists that permit abortion cannot be equally true with the beliefs of conservative Christians that do not permit abortion. Nor can the beliefs of cosmic humanists that identify all existence as part of a universal consciousness be equally true with the beliefs of Christianity that affirm that creation is dependent upon one transcendent God.

Diverse beliefs about reality fill the marketplace of ideas in the emerging global village. Many ideas are competing for dominance, and this competition is producing conflict and confusion in cultures long held together by traditional worldviews. Christian-based cultures are awakening to find mosques standing next to churches and Bible-based laws swept from the books by a simple majority vote of humanist legislators and judges.

Within this global arena of conflict and change, Christians are faced with at least two critical questions: "How do we know what is true?" and "How must we live our lives in relation to the truth we come to know?" This curriculum is designed to address questions like these. It is based on the biblical Christian worldview, which affirms that truth is absolute and knowable through the revelation of God. It affirms that knowledge of God is the beginning of wisdom and the key to understanding the world around us.

You have the privilege and responsibility of leading a child not only in the paths of truth, but also to a knowledge and fear of the One who is the Truth, Jesus Christ. With the lessons contained in this, the third book in the What We Believe series, you will lay several essential foundational truths upon which the biblical Christian worldview is built. Lay these stones of truth well. Pray that God will continually reveal and confirm the truths of His Word in the hearts of your student and that your child will respond in obedience to them.

We think you will find this to be an important course of study. Many eternal truths are presented that can change the way students look at the world every day. Minor points of doctrinal difference have been avoided in order to focus on the larger issues that make up our faith.

As Christians we are asked to be ready to give an account of the hope that is in us. We hope this book brings your faith into clearer focus and your family ever closer to the Lord.

COURSE WEBSITE

The Apologia website contains additional resources to help you teach this course. Visit www.apologia.com/bookextras and enter the following password: familyofGod. Be sure the password contains no spaces. When you hit "enter," you will be taken to the course website.

NEED HELP?

If you have any questions while using Apologia curriculum, feel free to contact us:

Curriculum Help
Apologia Educational Ministries, Inc.
1106 Meridian Plaza, Suite 340/220
Anderson, IN 46016
Phone: (765) 608-3280
Fax: (765) 608-3290
E-mail: BiblicalWorldview@apologia.com
Internet: apologia.com

DOES ANYONE REALLY NEED ME?

> TWO ARE BETTER THAN ONE. . . . IF ONE FALLS DOWN, HIS FRIEND CAN HELP HIM UP. BUT PITY THE MAN WHO FALLS AND HAS NO ONE TO HELP HIM UP!
>
> ECCLESIASTES 4:9-10

THE BIG IDEA

Can you imagine living completely alone? Not just alone in an apartment or house, but alone in the world? Several years ago there was a movie about a man who finds himself alone on an island after his cargo plane crashes in the South Pacific. While searching through packages from the plane, looking for anything he can use, he finds a volleyball manufactured by Wilson Sporting Goods. Lonely and desperate for companionship, the man draws a face on the volleyball, names it Wilson, and begins talking to it as if it were a person. A few years later, when he loses Wilson during an attempt to escape from the island, the man grieves deeply over the loss of his "friend."

Everyone enjoys being alone sometimes, but you couldn't live long in this world without other people. That's because God created you and everyone else to live in relationship with one another. He made us to need each other, to love each other, to share our joys and sorrows with each other, and to help each other. Why do people have such a strong need for companionship? It's because we were created in God's image. Remember, God has never been alone. Before the world and before time, the Father and the Son and the Holy Spirit lived together in perfect harmony as the one true God. And so when God made people in His own image, He intended that we, too, should live in harmonious relationships with one another.

He created Adam and Eve to love one another unselfishly and to help one another. They were given the responsibility of caring for and ruling over the entire earth and everything in it. Of course, such a job was too great for two people to do alone. So God also commanded Adam and Eve to fill the earth with people through family and childbirth (Genesis 1:28).

RED SUN RISING

In 1927, the country of China became involved in a civil war that lasted for decades. On one side was the Chinese Nationalist Party, also known as the *Kuomintang* (pronounced KWOH-min-tahng), led by Chiang Kai-shek (CHANG kī SHEK). The Kuomintang had already been in power for several years. On the other side was the Chinese Communist Party, led by Mao Tse-tung (mou tsay-TOONG), who wanted to get rid of the existing government and put power into the hands of the poor people.

The climactic events of the war took place from 1947 to 1949, a period Mao later called the War of Liberation. During these years, Mao and his revolutionaries slowly took control of most of mainland China, forcing the former leaders to take refuge on the island of Taiwan. On October 1, 1949, Mao declared that he had won the war. He quickly set up a new government in Beijing and changed the name of the country to the People's Republic of China. Numerous Chinese posters, badges, and songs proclaimed, "Chairman Mao is the red sun in our hearts."

Once in power, Mao began to change the way the country was run. He arrested and executed many people who had stood against him or spoke out about his new policies, and he sent many others to labor camps or prisons. He set about transforming the nation's economy, including the way food was grown and shared, a plan he called the "Great Leap Forward." But Mao's changes caused huge food shortages, which led to the largest famine in human history. Between 40 million and 70 million people died because of Mao's decisions during the thirty-three years he was in power.

Today, China still follows some of Mao's ideas, and many honor him as a great leader. But it has taken China as many years as Mao was in power to recover from the consequences of his policies.

Then together, loving and serving one another, God's image-bearers would be able to fulfill all His commands for His creation.

Now as you know, God created Adam and Eve a very long time ago. But the work He gave them to do and the responsibility He gave them to serve and love one another still apply to us today. Just as Adam needed Eve to be his companion and helper, you and I also need others as companions to love us and help us do all God commands us to do here on the earth.

But in order to serve, you and I must be more concerned about others than ourselves. This is not always easy. After all, most of us like being served instead of serving. Yet Jesus said, "The greatest among you must be a servant" (Matthew 23:11, NLT). Indeed, God Himself showed us how to serve one another. He did this by sending Jesus to serve us. God's Son was the perfect servant—He cared more about us than even His own life. Once you understand Jesus' willing heart for serving others and you choose to follow His example, you can become the amazing person God created you to be!

WHAT YOU WILL DO

» You will learn that God wants each of us to depend on one another.

» You will recognize your calling to serve others as Jesus served.

» You will learn to serve others in confidence, trusting that God will be with you.

DANGEROUS JOURNEY

As darkness fell over the Yuan (YWAN) River valley, the villagers of Kam Tin (KAM TEEN) all closed their window shutters in an attempt to make their homes invisible to enemy planes. Chang Ting carefully closed the shutters of her family's old, gray stone house, hoping to block out the turmoil of the outside world. Then she lit two candles, one for the kitchen and one for the children's bedroom.

"You may read until your father comes home," Ting said. "But do not open the shutters under any circumstances."

Chang Mei (MAY) and her little brother, Chang Li (LEE), giggled as they each chose a favorite book and climbed onto the bed to read. They enjoyed the coziness of a room lit only by one candle, although as the days grew longer and warmer, they often longed to light a lantern and open the shutters wide to allow the cool evening breeze into their room.

At the door there came a single knock, followed by three rapid knocks.

This told Ting that her husband, *Wei* (WAY), was home. She opened the door hurriedly, and just as quickly she closed it once he was safely inside.

"What did you learn, Wei?" she asked anxiously. "Can we leave? Oh, Wei, I'm so worried."

"My precious Ting," Chang Wei said in a hushed voice, not wanting to alarm the children. "The news is not good. I understand from Mr. Lee that the soldiers of the revolution have advanced to the outskirts of Tai Wai (TIE WHY). If Tai Wai falls, it may be only three or four days before Mao's soldiers reach our village. I greatly fear that anyone who resists them will be . . ."

"Will be killed? Oh, Wei, we must leave, if only for the children's sake. Did you speak to the mayor? Mr. Fong has always been a friend."

"Yes, yes, I talked with him," Wei replied. "He promised me he would do everything possible to arrange papers and passports for us by Friday."

"Friday?" Ting asked with alarm. "But that may be too late. I saw two revolutionary soldiers in our market today. Are you certain you can trust Mr. Fong? How do you know he's not working with the revolutionaries?"

"Dearest Ting," Wei said as he put his arm around his wife, "there are some people you just know are good. You can read it in their hearts. Mr. Fong has faithfully served our village all these years. He cares nothing for his own safety but is concerned only for the children of Kam Tin. He told me not to worry about him, that he has plans of his own. But for now, it seems he is determined to arrange papers for our escape."

"Papa!" cried Mei as she burst into the small living room. "You're home! We've been very careful to keep the shutters closed and use only candles. Did you see any light coming from the windows?"

Chang Wei lifted his daughter off the floor, spun her around, and hugged her. "No, the house looked very dark. Now, tell me about your day."

Just then, Li grabbed his father's leg from behind. "I caught you in my trap," he said, laughing. "It's so dark in the house, you didn't even see me sneak up behind you."

"You are indeed sneaky," his father said, trying to be cheerful. "Perhaps we shall all need to be sneaky in the coming days."

"What do you mean, Papa?" Mei asked.

Chang Wei told everyone to sit down at the kitchen table. As the candles threw pale, flickering shadows onto the walls, he began to tell his family of the dangerous journey they would be making two days hence. "Do you understand, my little ones, that we are not playing a game when we close the shutters and use only candlelight after dark?" he asked.

"Yes, Papa," Mei replied. "We sometimes hear the planes, and we've heard bombs exploding far away. Is the war coming to our village?"

"I'm afraid so," her father replied, making no attempt to hide his sadness. "And because your mother and I do not support Mao Tse-tung and his revolution, we must leave this place. But we must do so in secret. No one can know, not even your friends at school. Do you understand?"

"Yes, Papa," Li answered. "But how can we leave without anyone knowing?"

"We shall leave late Friday night," Wei said. "There is a new moon that night, so we will be helped by the darkness. We will cross through the rice fields north of town, then walk hidden among the trees beside the road leading to Mr. Wong's house. He will have his hay wagon ready to carry us into Shan Teng (SHAYN TENG). There he has made arrangements for someone to give us food and a map and instructions for the next part of our journey."

"But Shan Teng is already in the hands of the revolutionaries," Ting said with some alarm.

"That is why we will arrive hidden in the wagon. And we will leave the same night on foot," Wei explained, smiling, trying to keep everyone calm. "There's an old trail that leads into the mountains, over the pass, and down to the sea. If all goes according to plan, a fishing boat will be waiting to take us across the channel to Lang Tin (LAHN TEEN) Harbor. That's where we will board the freighter."

"A freighter!" Li said excitedly. "You mean one of the big ships with a smokestack that can cross the ocean?"

"That's right," Wei replied, tousling his son's hair. "A big ship with a smokestack."

"But where are we going?" Mei asked, her dark eyes sparkling in the candlelight.

"On a very long journey, far away. We are going to America."

"America!" Li squealed. "That's where Uncle Ping lives!"

"That is right, Li," his father replied. "He lives in San Francisco, as will we. Now off to bed, the two of you. Tomorrow you will help your mother pack."

Ting carefully tucked Mei and Li into their beds, blew out the candle, and closed the door. "I am frightened," she whispered to her husband. "How do you know Mr. Fong will have our papers and passports ready? I don't trust anyone in our country these days. What if we encounter soldiers? And the children, what if—?"

"If we do not leave now, it may be too late. We must take the chance."

Early Friday morning, Chang Wei hugged his wife and children. With grave seriousness, he said, "I'll be back this evening just before dark. Have everything ready to go. And children, today at school, you must act as if nothing is out of the ordinary. Do you understand?"

"Yes, Papa," Mei and Li replied together.

For Ting, the day was a frightful one as she gathered supplies for their journey while trying to avoid anyone who might ask questions. For Mei and Li, the day was a sad one because they knew they would never see their school friends again, yet they could not tell them good-bye.

That evening at just a little before eight o'clock, Ting and the children were relieved to hear the familiar signal—one knock followed by three rapid ones.

"Okay, I have the papers," Chang Wei said as he closed the door behind him. "Mr. Fong has risked his own life to obtain them. Let us hope they open all the doors we must pass through in the coming days."

After a simple supper of rice and dried fish cakes, Chang Wei walked one last time through the house. For five generations, the Chang family had lived within its walls. Mei and Li's generation would be the last.

"Is everything packed?" Wei asked Ting. "The pictures? Grandfather's watch?"

"Everything is ready." Ting sighed as she looked around the house that held many of her most precious memories.

"Then let us go." Chang Wei blew out the candle on the table and turned to open the door. "Now quietly, very quietly, children. Stay close to the buildings, out of the street. At the edge of town, we will take the canal path to the rice fields. We should be safe once we get there."

Through the darkened village streets, along the canal path, and finally across the rice field Chang Wei and his family moved silently, never looking back. When they came to the road that led to Mr. Wong's, they kept to the trees along the side of the road.

"Are we doing a good job at being sneaky, Papa?" Li whispered.

"A very good job, my bright one," Chang Wei whispered back. "A very good job."

An hour later they arrived at what they thought was Mr. Wong's house. Ting asked apprehensively, "Are you sure this is the place? It's so dark. It looks completely abandoned."

"Wait here with the children," Wei said quietly. "I've been told to tap on the window shutter by the back porch four times. If Mr. Wong is here and the plan is working, he will let us in."

Wei moved quietly to the back of the old farm house. *This could be a trap*, he thought. *What if Mr. Wong is working for Mao?* He stepped lightly onto the porch and tapped on the shutter. The back door opened slowly, and he heard a gentle and reassuring voice from the darkness.

"Mr. Chang? Is that you?"

"Yes," Wei replied. "Are you Mr. Wong?"

"Yes, but please come inside quickly."

Wei signaled his family, who quickly and quietly emerged from their hiding place and entered the old farmhouse.

"Welcome," Mr. Wong said. "You must be tired and hungry. My wife has prepared some tea and dumplings. Please sit down. We don't have much time, so while you are eating I will get the wagon ready. We will depart in fifteen minutes."

Mei asked, "Is this when we get to ride in the hay wagon, Papa?"

"Yes," replied her father with a laugh.

"But you won't be sitting on top of the hay—you'll be underneath it! Now hurry and finish your tea and dumplings."

The wagon ride was uncomfortable for the Changs, as the weight of the hay and the dust made breathing difficult. But they remained silent and uncomplaining as Mr. Wong drove the wagon through the darkened countryside toward Shan Teng. Just before midnight, at the edge of the village, the wagon came to a stop.

"This is far as I dare take you," Mr. Wong said as he pushed aside the hay. "The village is occupied by revolutionary soldiers. There's an abandoned barn over there," he said, pointing away from the road. "Wait inside. Someone will come soon with food

and instructions for the next part of your journey. Now do hurry. And may you arrive at your destination safely."

"Thank you, Mr. Wong," Chang Wei whispered as everyone climbed down from the wagon. "We can never thank you enough for your help."

Without further words, Mr. Wong turned his wagon toward home.

Inside the abandoned barn, Mei began to shiver. "I'm scared, Papa," she cried. "And I'm cold."

"Me, too," Li said.

Wei took off his jacket and wrapped it around both children. "Soon someone will come with food. Now sit and rest and don't worry. Everything will be fine."

After about an hour, the faint sound of footsteps could be heard outside the barn door. Then all was quiet.

Chang Wei motioned for everyone to remain absolutely silent. Then the sound of footsteps was heard again, this time moving away from the barn. After several minutes, Wei stepped cautiously to the barn door and eased it open. On the ground just outside the door was a package, which he quickly picked up and carried back into the barn.

"What is it, Wei?" Ting asked.

"It's food and a map. Whoever brought them did so at great risk. Now eat quickly while I study the map and instructions. The next part of our journey will be the most difficult."

Indeed, the journey was difficult. The weary family trudged up a low pass in the mountains. As they neared the top of the pass, Li began to cry. "Papa, I cannot walk anymore. I just can't."

Without a word, Chang Wei gave Li's small pack to Ting and lifted his son onto his shoulders. "Do not worry, my bright one," he said. "Papa will carry you. And you, Mei? How are you doing, my beautiful one?"

"I am well, Papa," she said bravely, although she too felt she could not walk much farther.

Silently and with few stops for rest, the Chang family crossed over the pass and down the other side of the mountains toward the sea. Soon, as the family moved down the path toward the beach, they could see the dawn beginning to break on the eastern horizon. Just before the last trees of the forest gave way to the open beach, they stopped.

"There! Over there in the little cove," Wei said. "Do you see it? It's the fishing boat."

As they approached the boat, an old fisherman climbed up from the lower deck, surprising the family. "Mr. Chang, we've been waiting for you," he said cheerfully. "Welcome aboard the *Jinhai* (JIN-HI), China's most luxurious ocean liner. I am your host—Captain Quan (KWON)." The old man bowed with a mock flourish. "Breakfast will be served in the Fish Hold Restaurant on the lower deck in five minutes. After breakfast, you will be shown to your Engine Room Cabin where your bunks are ready. Unless, of course, you are neither hungry nor tired."

The captain's sense of humor broke the tension for everyone, and Chang Wei laughed with relief. "Captain Quan, we accept your invitation to dine and cruise aboard the *Jinhai*. And we thank you for your gracious hospitality."

Below deck, the stuffy little cabin reeked with the smell of fish and diesel motor fuel, but no one complained. With great enthusiasm they quickly ate a fisherman's breakfast of dried squid, steaming rice, and hot tea.

"It's about four hours across the channel to Lang Tin Harbor," Captain Quan explained as they ate. "I suggest you try to sleep on the way. Once we get to the harbor, you will all need to be alert and careful. Many people are attempting to flee China these days, and the revolutionary soldiers are watching the port."

"But we have our papers and passports," Chang Wei said, trying to hide his concern from his family.

Captain Quan replied, "The soldiers are checking everyone, looking for people known to have made statements against Mao."

Ting looked at her husband anxiously, for he had been outspoken in his opposition to the revolution.

"Well, we have our papers," Wei assured Captain Quan. "I'm sure everything will be fine. Now, as you said, we should get some sleep. Thank you again, Captain, for your hospitality and for helping our family. You know we can never repay you."

"No need," said the captain. "I am an old man. What can they do to a simple fisherman like me? And unlike you, I have no children to protect. Now off to sleep, all of you."

The channel was anything but calm as fierce winds churned angry black waves over the bow of the *Jinhai*. Yet Mei, Li, Ting, and Wei were so exhausted from their journey that they slept soundly. They awoke only after the sound of the winds and the grinding of the engine had ceased, signaling their arrival at Lang Tin harbor.

"When we get to shore," Captain Quan said, "you will see a long line of people waiting to board the freighter. Have your papers ready. I'm sure everything will go well. At least, that is our plan and our hope."

"Thank you, Captain Quan. Thank you very much," Chang Wei said earnestly.

Wei and his family disembarked and joined the long line of people hoping to board the freighter. Soldiers mingled among the people, speaking harshly and demanding to see papers.

"Stop!" An armed soldier had appeared from behind a large crate. He was pointing a rifle at Wei and his family. "In the name of the People's Liberation Army, stop!"

Shaking involuntarily, Mei grabbed her father's hand. Ting held tightly to Li.

"Are you Chang Wei?" the soldier demanded.

Wei stood stiffly and was silent.

"I asked you: Are you Chang Wei?"

"I am," Wei said, trying to appear calm. "I have our papers and passports. You will see everything is in order."

"You are under arrest, Chang Wei. And your family as well. Now walk ahead of me to the shipping office," the soldier ordered, gesturing with his rifle.

"But we are due to board the freighter," Chang Wei insisted.

"The shipping office, Mr. Chang," the soldier commanded.

Drawing his frightened family close, Wei led them toward the office. The office was empty. The soldier closed the door behind them and locked it.

"Sit down," he said. "Let me see your papers."

After examining their papers, the soldier said, "Do you understand the charges against you?"

"I've never been charged with anything," Wei answered. "But if you're asking me if I support the revolution, well, my answer is no."

"That, Mr. Chang, is why orders have been issued for your arrest. Your opposition to the Communist Party is well known, and word of your disappearance has spread. These are serious charges against you—charges that could result in your death."

"I am not afraid to die for my beliefs," Wei said calmly.

"Nor am I. That is why I have brought you here."

"I do not understand."

"Mr. Chang, forgive me for not introducing myself," the soldier said, beginning to smile. "My name is Fong Gui (GWEE). You know my father. He is the mayor of your village."

Chang Wei was stunned. How could the son of Mayor Fong, who had obtained all the papers and passports for the Chang family, be involved with the Communists? he thought. "Yes, I know your father," Wei acknowledged. "I have known him for many years.

He is a good and honorable man. What I cannot understand is how . . ."

"How his son could join the revolutionary army?"

"Exactly."

"There is no time to explain now. Just know that I am here to make sure you and your family board the freighter safely. If you had remained in line out there, you would most certainly have been arrested."

Fong Gui then led the frightened family through the back door of the shipping office into a large warehouse filled with crates and baggage waiting to be loaded into the freighter's cargo hold. He said, "Friends of mine will hide you in the cargo hold where you must remain until the freighter is out to sea. They will then come and show you to a small cabin where you will be safe. It's no cruise ship, to be sure, but it will take you to America."

"I still don't understand," Chang Wei said. "Why are you doing this? Why would a member of the revolutionary army help us escape?"

Fong Gui smiled broadly. "I am not a soldier. Please forgive me for frightening you. I had to act the part until I knew for sure that you were the family I was looking for. Now I must go. May God bless your journey and your new life in America. But before we part, I have a small gift for all of you—something to read on your long voyage."

Chang Wei accepted a package wrapped in plain paper. "But what is this gift?" he asked.

"It is a Bible, Mr. Chang. Now I must say good-bye."

"Good bye, Fong Gui," Wei said. "And . . . thank you, my friend. Thank you for saving our lives."

"There's no need to thank me or my family."

"Your family?"

"Of course," Fong Gui said with a mischievous smile. "The man who hid you in his hay wagon—he is my uncle. And the woman who brought the map and food to the barn—she is my cousin Ai."

"And do you also know Captain Quan?" Ting asked.

"Of course!" Gui laughed. "He is my grandfather."

Then Fong Gui turned and disappeared among the crates and baggage.

A Chinese man distributing Bibles.

THINK ABOUT IT

» In China, a person's surname, or family name, is said first. Why do you think the Chinese follow this custom? Who is honored when the surname is said first?

» Why must the Chang family leave China, their homeland?

» Why do you think Fong Gui gives the family a Bible to take on their voyage?

» Can you remember all the people who serve the Chang family in the story? Why would so many members of the Fong family help people who are not Christians escape from China?

» What kind of future do you think awaits the Chang family in America? Why?

SHIPPING OUT!

It's likely that very few of the products your family buys and uses are made in your home country. Massive ships called freighters, or cargo ships, transport oil, grain, electronics, and automobiles all around the world. Often this is the only way goods from one country can reach other countries. Without freighters, you wouldn't be able to go to your local grocery store and buy bananas from Chile, parmesan cheese from Italy, or coffee from Hawaii.

Freighters vary in size, but the largest of these ships can transport up to 500,000 tons of oil. Of course, the bigger the ship, the fewer places it can go. Some cargo ships are too big to navigate man-made shortcuts like the Panama Canal, so they are forced to sail all the way around the southern tips of Africa and South America to reach their destinations. Most cargo ships have a set route of ports they visit, like neighborhood buses. But some small freighters, called tramps, are more like taxis, hauling special loads of cargo wherever they need to go. Freighters can dock only at ports that are equipped with special cranes and machines to load and unload their bulky cargo.

If you're feeling adventurous and want to spend some time at sea, you could book a trip as a passenger on a freighter. This takes much longer than traveling by plane—a round trip between California and Australia takes over a month! There's not a lot to do on a cargo ship, so bring a good book as you'll have to be prepared to entertain yourself. But you would meet people from many countries and have a wonderful view of the sea from your cabin's porthole. Just be prepared to climb a lot of stairs during your trip, because cargo ships don't have elevators!

Photo: Lukas Riebling.

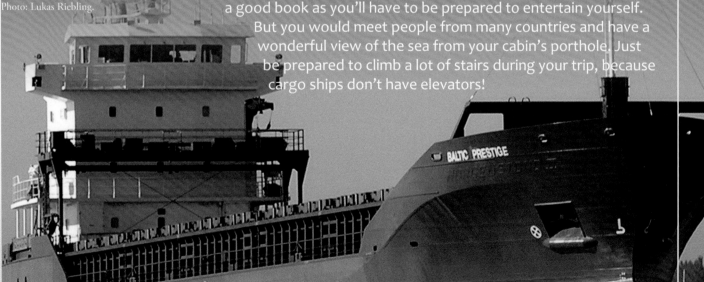

WORDS YOU NEED TO KNOW

- » **Social:** Needing and enjoying the companionship of other people
- » **Triune:** A word meaning God exists as three Persons—the Father, the Son, and the Holy Spirit—who live in perfect harmony as the one true God
- » **Interdependence:** A relationship in which two or more people help one another and depend on each other for help
- » **Servanthood:** Building a relationship of harmony with others as we serve them in love
- » **Trusting God:** Having complete confidence that He will always do everything He promises

HIDE IT IN YOUR HEART

Serve one another in love. (Galatians 5:13)

Trust in the LORD and do good. Then you will live safely in the land and prosper. Take delight in the LORD, and he will give you your heart's desires. (Psalm 37:3–4, NLT)

WE WERE MADE FOR EACH OTHER

God made people to be **social**, meaning we need and enjoy the companionship of other people. Indeed, contemporary health studies clearly show that our relationships matter. Time and again researchers have concluded that strong connections to friends and family are absolutely vital to a person's emotional and physical well-being. In fact, for many who live alone, a lack of regular human contact can be as harmful to their health and longevity as the regular use of tobacco or alcohol.

Let's face it: We are happier and healthier when we are surrounded by people who know us, take an interest in us, and actively participate in our lives. An abundance of these kinds of relationships gives us a sense of security—they make us feel safe, knowing there's always someone to turn to in times of difficulty. They also influence the way we see ourselves—it's easier to feel good about yourself when others feel good about you.

True, we don't always get along with the people in our lives, whether it's the neighbor next door or the brother or sister in the next room. Even the simplest of human relationships can be complicated because they involve imperfect people who don't always know or choose the best way to express their thoughts and needs and feelings. And yet these same relationships, when properly cared for, can bring amazing growth, joy, and contentment to everyone involved.

The fact is that we are better together than we are apart. A family, a neighborhood, a church, or a country is more than just a collection of what each person brings to the group. Together, we enrich each other's lives through our individual interests, gifts, and talents. And only when we live and work and play together can we become the kinds of healthy, balanced, purpose-filled people God created us to be.

Why did God make us this way? Why can't we all just go our own way, do our own thing, and ignore the rest of humanity? If we are truly to understand why people need one another, we must first look back at something important we've already learned about God. As we discovered in this series, God has never lived alone. Despite the fact that He created everything and everyone and without Him nothing was made that has been made (John 1:3), God has always lived in relationship. How is this possible? Because He exists as one God in three Persons—God the Father, God the Son, and God the Holy Spirit. We call this the Trinity.

A word we use to describe God's nature is **triune** (TRY-YOON). This word combines the prefix tri-, meaning "three," with a Latin word meaning "one." The word *triune* means God exists as three Persons who live in complete harmony as the one true God. Each member of the Trinity—Father, Son, and Holy Spirit—is fully God, with all His attributes. All live eternally in perfect unity. Although each of these Persons has special responsibilities, not one of them does anything without the full cooperation and support of the other two.

An anonymous painting from an altarpiece showing the Trinity.

You see, God has always lived and *will* always live in harmonious relationship. Relationship is part of His very nature. So when He decided to create human beings in His own image, He also made us to live in relationship. We were meant to enjoy among ourselves the kind of harmony, fellowship, loyalty, and unity that the Trinity has always known.

We see this from the very beginning of the world. When God created the land and plants, the sun and moon and stars, and all the animals, He said they were good. Then He said, "Let us make man in our image, in our likeness, and let them rule over the fish of the sea and the birds of the air, over the livestock, over all the earth, and over all the creatures that move along the ground" (Genesis 1:26).

But after He created Adam, God said something was not good. He didn't mean that Adam was not good; He meant that it was not good for Adam to be alone:

> The LORD God said, "It is not good for the man to be alone. I will make a helper suitable for him." (Genesis 2:18)

First, God brought all the animals and the birds to Adam so that he could name them. So he gave names to all the animals, but no suitable helper was found for him among the animals (Genesis 2:20). Did God make a mistake when He created a man first before He created a woman? Was He surprised that none of the animals was a sufficient companion for the man? Of course not. God already knew that He was going to create Eve to be Adam's helper and wife. But He also wanted us to know that people made in His image were never meant to live in isolation.

The Creation of Adam and Eve in Paradise from an old Bible.

So God caused Adam to fall into a deep sleep; and while Adam was sleeping, God took one of Adam's ribs and made a woman from it. And only when God finished creating both Adam and Eve did He say it was "very good" (Genesis 1:31).

You see, people were made to live and work and play together, to experience relationships, because we were made in the image of a triune God. Therefore, the more we learn about what it's like to live in relationship, the better we will understand God's nature.

MAKE A NOTE OF IT

Popular books, movies, and television series have been made about children befriending dogs, horses, dolphins, lions, seals, and even a 650-pound bear! What kind of animal would you like to have for a friend? Why do you think Adam's ideal helper could not be found among the animals?

THE BUDDY SYSTEM

Have you ever heard the saying that "two heads are better than one"? That's the idea behind the buddy system, in which two people function together as one, encouraging each other, helping each other, and keeping each other out of trouble. Perhaps you've participated in the Boy Scouts or Girl Scouts, where participants are taught never to go hiking or swimming without a partner. Maybe you're part of a large family that uses the buddy system, where an older child is assigned to help care for a younger brother or sister.

Think the buddy system is just for kids? Think again. One of the first lessons scuba divers learn is never to go into the water without a dive buddy to help in case of an emergency. Every firefighter knows never to enter a burning building without another firefighter, and they don't come out until they come out together. A good fighter pilot never leaves his wingman. And in the army, soldiers are taught never to go into battle or enter unfamiliar territory without their buddy, even when they're off duty. Why? For several good reasons:

> » Two people working together can accomplish significantly more than one.
> » There is safety in numbers—a person alone is more vulnerable to an accident or attack.
> » An extra set of eyes can provide a clearer perspective in a difficult situation.
> » One can help prevent the other from making a bad decision.
> » One can provide medical attention or go for help if the other is injured.

The buddy system is a biblical principle we see implemented throughout the Scriptures. When God told Moses to go to Pharaoh and demand that he free the children of Israel, God sent Aaron to go with him (Exodus 4:14–15). When Jesus sent His disciples to go ahead of Him into the towns and villages, He sent them out in pairs, "two by two" (Luke 10:1). The apostle Paul was accompanied on his missionary journeys by various companions including Barnabas, Timothy, and Titus.

As children of God, we could all use a "spiritual buddy," someone we can count on in times of need. It's easy to get yourself into trouble when you try to go it alone when dealing with unpleasant emotions, a difficult decision, temptation, or a sin you've committed. One of the reasons the army uses the buddy system is so that soldiers will lift up and inspire one another to act with honor, integrity, and courage. Likewise, leaning on a brother or sister in the Lord in tough times—or lending a shoulder to someone in need—can help you both to "be all that you can be" in Christ.

WHAT DO YOU HAVE TO OFFER?

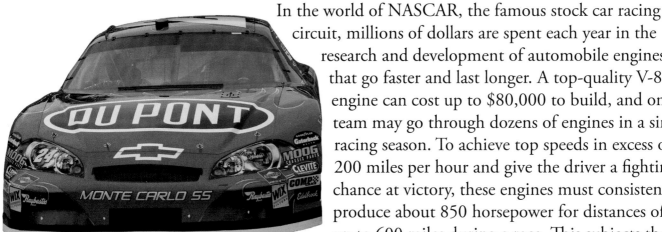

Photo by Bo Nash.

In the world of NASCAR, the famous stock car racing circuit, millions of dollars are spent each year in the research and development of automobile engines that go faster and last longer. A top-quality V-8 engine can cost up to $80,000 to build, and one team may go through dozens of engines in a single racing season. To achieve top speeds in excess of 200 miles per hour and give the driver a fighting chance at victory, these engines must consistently produce about 850 horsepower for distances of up to 600 miles during a race. This subjects the various parts of an engine to intense heat—about 2,000 degrees Fahrenheit—and enormous pressure—about 1,500 pounds per square inch, or more than a hundred times the normal air pressure we feel around us every day.

True, engine parts in a race car are bigger, stronger, and thicker than those in your family car. However, every piston, valve, and sparkplug must work together in perfect synchronization, or the engine is vulnerable to breakdown. If just one tiny valve spring breaks during a race, if just one of the eight cylinders fails to do its job properly, the engine will begin sounding "sick." Soon the engine will "blow up," spewing oil all over the track and rendering the car useless for the rest of the day.

Like the parts of an engine, God made us to depend on each other. This is called **interdependence**. An interdependent relationship is one in which two or more people help one another and depend on one another for help. Within a family, a church, a nation—in fact, any social or business organization—every member brings a unique set of talents, skills, and experiences to the mixture that enrich the group and make up for what may be missing among the other members. This is true even if the group is just two or three in number. Ecclesiastes 4:9–13 tells us:

> *Two are better than one, because they have a good return for their work: If one falls down, his friend can help him up. But pity the man who falls and has no one to help him up. . . . A cord of three strands is not quickly broken.*

In order for the group or organization to function at its best, every member must contribute to the best of his or her ability while working toward a goal agreed upon with the other members. If the members cannot agree or do not work together efficiently, or if one of the members is not doing his or her part, the group is vulnerable to breakdown just like a car with a sick engine.

Despite the fact that we were made to depend on one another, it's not unusual to sometimes feel like you're not holding up your end of the bargain. When things aren't going your way, when you're having a bad day and you're feeling sorry for yourself, when all your friends are busy and you're left alone, you might begin to wonder if you have anything of value to offer the world. After all, if you were prettier, smarter, funnier, and more fun to be around, people would be beating down your door to spend time with you, right? Wrong. But when you sit around focusing on yourself and your problems, it's easy to wallow in feelings of worthlessness and uselessness.

However, these feelings are nothing more than lies from your enemy, the devil, who wants to keep you from recognizing your true worth in the grand scheme of things. Remember, as you learned earlier in this series, your emotions are notoriously unreliable and you can't always trust them to tell you the truth. So whenever you find yourself becoming overwhelmed by your feelings, turn to the one place you can always find the truth, the Bible, and read what God says about you.

Consider the following: If you have chosen to follow Jesus Christ, you have been adopted as a child of the Most High God (John 1:12–13), with all the privileges and purpose that come with the position. Therefore, you have unrestricted access to the throne room of Almighty God (Hebrews 4:14–16). You can go boldly before Him and ask anything in His Son's name according to His will, and it will be done for you (John 16:23). Every day you encounter several people with needs that you can bring before your heavenly Father in prayer. Are you ready to move heaven and earth with your prayers?

As a child of God, you have been filled with the Holy Spirit. God literally lives inside you, working in you and through you, giving you the desire and the power to do what pleases Him (Philippians 2:13). The Holy Spirit not only helps you understand and remember God's Word (John 14:26), but He also equips you to tell others about God and show them His love through acts of kindness and goodness (Galatians 5:22–23).

These are not just *random* acts of kindness. *You are on a mission from God.*

You have been made new in Christ Jesus to do good works He planned for you long, long ago (Ephesians 2:10). You have been specially chosen by Him for this mission, and He has already equipped you with the tools and skills you need to see it through to completion. From the time you were born, God has provided you with a special set of gifts—your talents, your personality, your experiences—which no one else possesses. And God has been placing you in specific situations and introducing you to specific people who need your help.

YOU ARE HERE TO MAKE A DIFFERENCE

The apostle Paul wrote, "When you do things, do not let selfishness or pride be your guide. Instead, be humble and give more honor to others than to yourselves. Do not be interested only in your own life, but be interested in the lives of others" (Philippians 2:3–4, NCV). God created you to glorify Him by showing love to others through your words and actions, just as Jesus did. According to 1 Peter 2:21 (NLT), Jesus is your example, "and you must follow in his steps." This means that you must set aside your rights as a son or daughter of the Most High King and make yourself a servant to others:

> *In your lives you must think and act like Christ Jesus. Christ himself was like God in everything. But he did not think that being equal with God was something to be used for his own benefit. But he gave up his place with God and made himself nothing. He was born as a man and became like a servant.*
> (Philippians 2:5–7, NCV)

Speaking of Himself, Jesus said, "The Son of Man did not come to be served. He came to serve others" (Matthew 20:28, NCV). Indeed, He was the perfect example of servanthood. Jesus loved the people of this world more than He loved His own life, and He "died a criminal's death on a cross" to pay the penalty for our sins (Philippians 2:8, NLT).

Now, you may never be called to give your life to save another's, but you are called to die to selfishness and "do good to all people" whenever you have the opportunity (Galatians 6:10). In this way people will see the Father's love in action, and perhaps they will be drawn to God's grace and come to know the joy and peace and life

Crucifixion of Christ by Botticelli.

that you have. That's what **servanthood** is all about: building relationships of harmony with others by showing them God's love.

The truth is, God did not call you "out of darkness into his wonderful light" (1 Peter 2:9) just so you could rest secure in the knowledge that you will someday spend eternity with Him. He did not give you the Holy Spirit just so you would have peace, patience, and self-control. He did not give you special talents and abilities just so you could earn a living when you're an adult.

Don't misunderstand—these are good things, to be sure. But if you choose to keep God's gifts to yourself, then you will never complete your mission. If you hide yourself away from the world, content to live out your days quietly and uneventfully until the Master returns, then you will fail to become what God always intended you to be: a blessing to the world.

You are here to make a difference.

You are here to change lives.

You are here to change your community.

You are here to change the world.

"Change the world? But I'm just a kid," you might say. "What can I do?"

That's what this book is about.

WHAT SHOULD I DO?

The Agony in the Garden by El Greco.

It's easy to let our fear of the unknown keep us from loving others or doing good or sharing the gospel. We may be afraid that people will laugh at us, mock us, or even become angry because of what we believe. Or we may worry that someone will hurt us by taking advantage of our love. But Jesus showed us in the Garden of Gethsemane that we can endure such hurts with grace and obedience, always trusting God to deliver us.

In the hour before He was delivered into the hands of those who would torture and crucify Him, Jesus prayed to the Father and asked if there was any other way to accomplish His purposes. Jesus knew what the coming day held for Him, and His soul was "crushed with grief to the point of death" (Mark 14:34, NLT). The emotional distress was so great, so agonizing, that His "sweat fell to the ground like great drops of blood" (Luke 22:44, NLT). There was nothing easy about going to the cross; the pain would be incomprehensible.

Three times Jesus prayed that this "cup of suffering" would be taken from Him

(Matthew 26:39–44, NLT). Yet He trusted God's plan and knew that the Father would raise Him up when the work had been accomplished. So Jesus said, "I want your will to be done, not mine," and He endured the cross without complaint.

Trusting God means having complete confidence that He will always do everything He promises. Even your favorite people will sometimes let you down, but you can always count on God. He will always be there for you:

"The LORD himself goes before you and will be with you; he will never leave you nor forsake you. Do not be afraid; do not be discouraged." (Deuteronomy 31:8)

Trust in the LORD with all your heart and lean not on your own understanding; in all your ways acknowledge him, and he will make your paths straight. (Proverbs 3:5–6)

Trust in the LORD and do good. Then you will live safely in the land and prosper. Take delight in the LORD, and he will give you your heart's desires. (Psalm 37:3–4 NLT)

God promises that He will be glorified by your obedience to serve others rather than be served (Matthew 5:16). He promises that when you speak His words they will succeed in doing what He intends them to do (Isaiah 55:11). And He promises that if you have faith as small as a tiny mustard seed, you will move mountains in His name (Matthew 17:20).

MAKE A NOTE OF IT

Whether it's joining a club, playing on a sports team, starting a new job, or getting married, people often feel both excitement and fear about becoming part of a group. Write about or draw a picture of a group you want to be part of someday. What kind of positive and negative feelings might you have about joining this group? Do you ever worry about not being allowed to belong to a group or being rejected by a group? Why?

A PRAYER

Dear God, thank you for the relationships in my life. Thank you for all my family and friends. Please give me the heart of a servant so that I may give you glory by showing your love to the people around me. Help me to follow your example and consider others before myself. Help me not to be afraid to love people but to trust that you are always with me. I ask these things in Jesus' name. Amen.

ENCOUNTERS WITH JESUS

THE WEDDING FEAST

In 1897, an American minister named Charles Sheldon published a novel titled *In His Steps*. The main character of the story is Rev. Henry Maxwell, pastor of the First Church of Raymond, who is deeply moved by his encounter with a destitute vagabond. The following Sunday, Maxwell challenges his congregation to not do anything for an entire year without first asking themselves, "What would Jesus do?" Nearly a hundred years after its first publication, Sheldon's novel had a resurgence when WWJD bracelets became a popular item among young people. Today *In His Steps* ranks as one of the fifty best-selling books of all time.

The question "What would Jesus do?" is not just a slogan or meaningless platitude. It's a question you and I should be asking ourselves every day. During His time on earth, Jesus took everything to God in prayer, studied the Scriptures, and allowed Himself to be led by the Holy Spirit. He is our example and we must follow in His steps (1 Peter 2:21). As God's image-bearers made new in Christ, we are to "reflect the Lord's glory," becoming more like Him every day (2 Corinthians 3:18). Therefore we should do the things Jesus did, touching lives the way He did with compassion, mercy, gentleness, patience, and kindness. As Christ suffered unjustly without complaint for doing what was right, so we must respond with love to those who hate us and say false and unkind things about us (Matthew 5:44). And we are called to minister to this world by the power of the same Spirit that raised our Lord from the dead (Acts 1:8; Romans 8:11).

If we are to know what Jesus would do, we must first know what Jesus did by exploring the Scriptures. Throughout the Gospels of Matthew, Mark, Luke, and John, we see Jesus responding to the needs of men and women from all walks of life—children and adults, wealthy and poor, widows and prostitutes, soldiers and lepers, Jews and Gentiles. Sometimes Jesus sought out the persons in need or even called them by name. Sometimes these people interrupted Him during His travels, during meals, even while He was teaching!

Near the end of each lesson in this book, you will meet one or more persons who encountered Jesus during His time on this earth. You will see how He showed God's love to them in their time of need and how each person responded differently. As you will see, not everyone accepted what Jesus had to offer. Yet the lives of most were changed forever by their meeting with the Man from Galilee.

First, let's meet a young bride-to-be who is about to encounter Immanuel—God with us—in her hour of need.

Cana in the early 1900s.

Miriam rested her chin in her hands, elbows propped on the low wall surrounding the flat roof of her family's home, and breathed in the cool morning air. From up here she could look south toward the town of Nazareth, larger than her own small village of Cana, or southwest toward Galilee's busy capital of Sepphoris, gleaming like a faraway jewel. This was Miriam's favorite way to start the day.

Her younger sister Rachel came up behind her, wrapped an arm affectionately around her waist, and rested her chin on Miriam's shoulder. "So," she said dramatically, "today we lose you forever to Shimon. Maybe Mama will let me be the grown-up daughter of the house now that you will be taking care of your new husband and his family."

Miriam squeezed her sister's hand. No matter how much she might joke, Miriam knew Rachel was sad to see her leave. "You know I'll be over here as often as I can. Besides, with Shimon's mother gone, I'll be the sole mistress of his house and will need lots of advice. And since Mama can't leave her bed right now, she can't exactly come to me."

Rachel sighed, her breath visible in the moist cool air. Their mother had been ill for months, so the two girls had taken over most of the household chores. When Miriam left, seventeen-year-old Rachel would have to carry the full burden of cooking, cleaning, and caring for their four younger siblings.

"I wonder when Father will get an offer for my hand," Rachel mused. "You weren't much older than I am now when Shimon and his father asked for you."

Miriam smiled a bit at the mention of her bridegroom. Although both families had lived in the same town for years, Miriam had spent very little time with Shimon. He was five years older than she and always seemed to be busy doing a man's work. And when his mother had died in childbirth three years earlier, he and his father had taken up the tasks normally left to the women of the house. "Don't worry, Rachel, your turn will come," she said.

Typical home similar to what would have been found in Cana.

Twelve months ago, Shimon and his father had approached Miriam's father to ask for her hand in marriage. Within a few weeks, she had been betrothed to Shimon, legally bound to him but not living as his wife until he had built a house for them and she had prepared goods to fill it. A whole year of preparation had led to this day, one every Jewish woman dreamed about as a girl and looked back on as a woman.

"Miriam, are you sad to leave?" Rachel asked.

Miriam snuggled closer to her sister. "Of course I'm sad to move away from you, even if it's just to the other side of the village. But I am excited to start a life with Shimon. I know he will always work hard to provide for me, and he is kind to everyone around him. After all, Papa trusts him enough to give him his first-born daughter!" Miriam paused in thought. "But it's more than that. I can really make a difference there. His younger brothers and sisters all miss their mother terribly, and I can help ease the pain of their loss."

Rachel smiled. "I'm sure it doesn't hurt that he's tall and handsome."

Miriam blushed. "He is handsome, isn't he?"

Groaning, Rachel pulled her toward the steps. "Let's go back in the house before you get lost in your dreams!"

Already, bundles of clothing and household articles lay about the courtyard, ready to be moved to Shimon's house. And the last of the food the family was preparing for the wedding feast would be ready well before dusk. Just about the only thing missing were several skins of special wine Miriam's father had ordered from Jerusalem, delayed by heavy spring rains and flooded rivers. The etiquette of Jewish weddings took the sacred duty of hospitality to new heights, and running short on wine was an offense few guests would overlook.

Looking about her, Miriam shook her head, trying to banish the fears that threatened to overwhelm her. She knew Shimon would be coming to claim her sometime after sunset, but she didn't know exactly when, so everything had to be ready for his arrival. The list running through her head seemed longer every time she stopped to think about it.

Out-of-town relatives would arrive throughout the day. Among the first to appear that morning was her Aunt Mary from nearby Nazareth. Running to greet her at the gate, Miriam threw her arms about her favorite aunt. "Oh, I'm so glad to see you! There are so many last minute details to take care of, and Mama's fretting that she can't leave her bed to help."

Mary returned her niece's hug, then held her out at arm's length. "Blessings on your marriage, dear one. May you be like Rachel and Leah, bringing fruitfulness and honor to your husband's house. Now, let me get a good look at you." She pretended to look Miriam up and down carefully. "Yes. I think you look all grown up. Maybe taller too."

"Well, if being grown up means handling too much responsibility, then I think you're right!" Miriam said through a worried smile.

Mary laughed. "First, let me wash the dust off and I will go see your Mama. We'll see if I can help ease her mind a bit."

Miriam took a clay jar and filled it from the clean water stored in large stone pots next to the entrance. Then she knelt in front of her aunt and poured the water over her dusty feet, wiping away the last traces of dirt with a cloth. "Much better, my dear," Mary said, slipping her clean sandals back on. "Now I'll go sit with your mother for a few minutes, then I'll meet you back at the kitchen and together we'll take care of everything."

Miriam joined Rachel near the round brick oven where she was removing freshly baked loaves of barley bread and setting them into baskets to cool. Rachel wiped beads of sweat from her forehead. "Good thing we only need to make half the bread for the feast," she said. "Otherwise, we might both miss the wedding."

Miriam poured clean water over her hands, then started kneading the next batch of dough. "I haven't seen this much food since last year's Passover when we hosted Papa's cousins on their way to Jerusalem." Separating the dough into equal pieces, Miriam shaped it into loaves and scored lines along the tops so the bread would tear easily after it was baked.

She handed the loaves to Rachel, who put them carefully inside the hot oven to bake. Miriam wiped the flour from her hands and began setting out food for the midday meal—

warm bread, pickled olives, dates, and raisins. With Rachel's help, she moved the food up to the roof, where the baskets and bowls were set out on a colorful rug in the shade of a canopy.

On her way to the roof, hands full, Miriam stopped and watched another group of guests being greeted by her father. Among them was her cousin Jesus, Mary's son. She hadn't seen him in a long time, but to Miriam's eyes he looked almost gaunt, as if he had just endured a great trial. Yet his eyes seemed to shine with an inner brilliance. Miriam also recognized one of the men who were with him, Shimon's friend Nathaniel who had grown up in Cana.

Miriam was strangely drawn to Jesus. There was something unusual about the way he looked at a person, almost as if he knew everything—good and bad—that you had ever done or said and accepted you anyway. She watched him interacting with his friends and noticed that they treated him with the respect due a great rabbi, rather than a simple carpenter with calloused hands. Jesus looked up and caught her watching them. Miriam only had time to give him a welcoming smile

before Rachel passed her with another basket headed for the roof. "Come on, silly, or everyone will think you have fluff for brains!" she teased.

Miriam deposited her armload on the roof and took a last look around, making sure everything was in order, before walking back down to the courtyard and giving her father a nod. He smiled back, then ushered their guests up to the roof for the midday meal. Miriam met Rachel and Mary back in the kitchen. They would wait until the men had eaten their fill before taking food themselves.

"My, the day certainly turned out warm, didn't it?" Mary remarked.

Miriam nodded. Clear skies and sunshine had burned away all traces of the cool dawn she had enjoyed earlier. She hoped that the good weather would allow the wine caravan to arrive before the feast.

The rest of the day passed in a blur of hurrying feet, busy hands, and bundles and baskets going to and fro.

As the sun started to set, Mary shooed Miriam and Rachel into their mother's room. "You need to stop being the mistress of the house now and go be a bride," Mary said with a smile. "This is a moment you will treasure all your life."

Tears springing to her eyes, Miriam gave her aunt a hug.

Shut away from the pleasant chaos, Miriam enjoyed a cooling bath. Then she sat on her mother's pallet while her mother worked her long dark hair into an intricate braid, dotted with the first almond flowers of the season.

By the light of the first lamp of the evening, her youngest sisters rubbed scented oil into her clean skin, filling the room with a light fragrance. Rachel helped her dress in the carefully embroidered robes Miriam had been stitching for months and wrapped a soft blue sash around her waist. When she was ready, Miriam, Rachel, and their mother sat in anxious anticipation, waiting for the shout that signaled Shimon's approach.

At long last, the cry spread through the house that the bridegroom was nearly here. Miriam kissed her mother good-bye, then fastened on her veil with trembling fingers and emerged into the courtyard. Surrounded by friends and relatives, she waited at the gate for Shimon to come claim his bride. Miriam looked around at the faces of the people who meant the most to her, trying to memorize the moment: The look of beaming pride her father gave her. Rachel's fingers clasped tightly in her own. Her aunt Mary, surrounded by her children. And Jesus' wise, serene face.

When Shimon arrived, he looked magnificent, wearing robes suited for royalty. Holding out his hand to Miriam, Shimon led her onto the road that pointed to her new life. Everyone gave a triumphant shout and followed in a merry, chaotic party. It seemed like the whole village of Cana, torches in hand, had turned out for their wedding celebration! Miriam had never felt more special or more alive. Propelled along by the enthusiasm of the crowd, she fairly floated along the streets.

Peasant wedding in Palestine, early 1900s.

By the time they reached Shimon's home, the first stars were shining brightly. Miriam followed him through the courtyard into the room he had built for them. In the presence of her father and his, the rabbi officially married Shimon and Miriam, placing crowns of greenery on their heads. Then the men left them alone to enjoy their first private moments as husband and wife, while they saw to it that the hungry and thirsty guests outside were served the best food and wine they could afford.

An hour or so later, Shimon led Miriam to the place of honor reserved for them under a special canopy on the roof. From her perch overlooking the festivities, Miriam looked around in amazement. The courtyard had been transformed, with colorful rugs stretched from wall to wall, laden with bowls of food, baskets of broken bread to serve as utensils, and clay cups and jugs of wine.

The guests were gathered in small groups around the food, sharing jokes and stories and shouting blessings for the bride and groom. Everyone appeared to be enjoying the fellowship. Miriam took a deep breath, inhaling the smells of fresh bread and olive oil mingled with the aroma of meat roasting over a fire. Miriam's father had pledged to provide the wine, while Shimon's father had purchased several sheep to feed the guests. The thought of juicy roasted meat instead of the usual evening meal of boiled fish made Miriam's mouth water.

Reaching for the cup she would share with Shimon, Miriam took a sip of wine and coughed in surprise. This was not the fine wine her father had ordered. This was inexpensive, everyday wine, highly diluted. Her breath caught in her throat. If all they had to serve was the plain wine that should have been reserved for the very end of the feast, then the skins of wine from Jerusalem must not have been delivered.

She managed to catch Rachel's attention and beckoned her closer. "Didn't the wine arrive from Jerusalem?" she whispered frantically.

Rachel shook her head. "And the regular wine is almost gone too."

Miriam's concern turned to panic. Running out of wine was disastrous—her neighbors would never let her live this down. She rubbed her forehead, trying to think faster than the headache that was starting to roar in her ears. She was married to Shimon now—sole mistress of his father's household—so she didn't have a mother-in-law to turn to. And her own mother was at home in bed.

Miriam gripped Rachel's arm and pulled her close. "Go tell Aunt Mary. Maybe she knows of a guest that brought some wine as a gift." Rachel nodded quickly and hurried down the stairs without appearing to hurry, trying to keep up the illusion that everything was fine.

Miriam watched as Rachel pulled Mary aside and explained. Mary's smile disappeared, and she looked up at Miriam for confirmation. Miriam nodded. Forehead wrinkling, Mary said something to Rachel before leaving the courtyard. Miriam waited in agony as Rachel slowly made her way back up to the roof, bringing a basket.

"What did she say?" Miriam asked as Rachel appeared under the canopy.

Rachel added more bread to the supply at Miriam's elbow. "She said that no one brought any wine as a gift, but not to worry. She had another idea." Chewing on her lip, Rachel cleared a few empty bowls and left.

Unable to sit quietly, Miriam rose and walked to the far edge of the roof. She felt her reputation crumbling and with it the honor of her husband's family. A wife was supposed to honor her husband, not ruin his good name hours into the marriage. It didn't matter that the wine being delayed was a circumstance beyond her control—she blamed herself for not ordering it earlier or providing for a backup just in case. She sneaked a look at Shimon, who was currently listening to a story being told by his uncle who had been appointed steward of the feast. Neither of them seemed alarmed or aware of any problem.

Heart pounding, Miriam closed her eyes and murmured a prayer of desperation to the God of Abraham, Isaac, and Jacob. "Creator of the universe, the One who provides, please hear my plea. Grant your servant your favor and do not let this circumstance harm the honor of my new husband or of my father."

Unable to find the words to strengthen her plea, Miriam opened her eyes. Below her, near the entrance to the courtyard, stood Mary with Jesus and his friends. The hired servants stood nearby. Mary had her hand on Jesus' arm, seemingly caught between question and answer. Jesus responded carefully, his tone gentle but firm as he removed his mother's hand. Mary stood silent for a moment, watching his face, then gave the servants a quiet command before stepping back into the chaos of the feast.

Both the servants and Jesus' companions seemed perplexed, looking to this man to tell them what to do. After a moment's pause, Jesus gave the servants an order that sent them scurrying for jars. Miriam watched as they slowly refilled several nearby water pots—huge stone vessels that could hold enough for several baths—with clean water from the well, right to the brim. She was confused. They had plenty of water; what they needed was wine!

Marriage at Cana by Veronese.

When they were finished, the servants waited expectantly. At Jesus' command, one of the servants dipped his jug into the water, filled it, then took it away. Miriam watched in horror as the servant climbed the stairs and headed for the steward of the feast, who was responsible for tasting the wine. Hand over her mouth, Miriam held her breath as the steward took a long gulp from the cup the servant had poured for him.

The steward's eyebrows rose in surprise and he turned to Shimon. "This wine is superb! Most men serve their best wine first and save the cheaper wine until the guests have had too much to drink. But you have saved the best for last!" Shimon just smiled. The steward laughed and held out his cup to be refilled. "Servant, make sure that everyone's cups are refilled immediately!"

To Miriam's eyes, the servant looked pale, scared even. But he said nothing and hurried to comply.

Shimon beckoned Miriam to come and sit next to him. He leaned and whispered in her ear, "Your father's special wine must have arrived just in time."

Miriam sat stunned as the enormity of what had just happened washed over her. It had clearly been water that the servants poured into the stone vessels. She reached for Shimon's newly refilled cup and took a tentative sip. The best wine she had ever tasted flowed over her tongue.

With tears in her eyes, she realized that her prayer had been answered, and in a much greater way than she could ever have imagined. The wine in those huge stone jars was enough to supply half a dozen weddings! Cup in hand, she stood and searched the crowd for Jesus, but he and his friends were nowhere to be seen. Then she spotted her Aunt Mary laughing and talking with friends. For a brief moment, Mary looked up to where Miriam was standing and gave her a knowing smile before returning to the conversation.

As she slowly sat down again, Miriam knew that this day truly would be impossible to forget.

TAKE A CLOSER LOOK

- This story is a fictionalized account of an actual event from the life of Jesus. We have imagined the wedding day from the unique perspective of one of the participants while providing cultural details to help you better understand what is happening in the story. Now read the biblical account of the wedding at Cana in John 2:1–11 and compare it to the story you've just read.

- Why was Miriam so distressed that the wedding party was running low on wine? What might people have said if the wine had run out so early in the festivities?

- According to the apostle John, this was the first of the miraculous signs Jesus performed. So why did Mary come to Jesus with this problem? What do you think she expected Him to do? Why?

- Although the time for Jesus to reveal Himself to the world as the Son of God had "not yet come," He chose to turn the water into wine. Why do you think Jesus made this decision?

- How did Jesus serve this young bride? What need did He meet? Whom else did He serve through this miracle?

HOW CAN I MAKE A
DIFFERENCE?

> MY CHILDREN, WE SHOULD LOVE PEOPLE NOT ONLY WITH
> WORDS AND TALK, BUT BY OUR ACTIONS AND TRUE CARING.

1 JOHN 3:18 (NCV)

THE BIG IDEA

A tale as old as time, the beloved fairy tale "Beauty and the Beast" dates back to the days before Ancient Greece. The story first appeared in print in a 1740 French storybook, and variations of the tale have been told around the world. Perhaps the best-known version is the 1991 Disney movie, the first animated film to be nominated for the Academy Award for Best Picture.

In this musical telling of the story, Belle's father gets lost in a storm and takes shelter in an enchanted castle. There he is discovered by the monstrous Beast who rules the castle, and the old man is locked away for trespassing. When Belle finds her father, she agrees to take his place and remain with the Beast as his prisoner. What she doesn't know is that this is an enchanted castle and the Beast is really a handsome prince who was cursed because of his selfish heart. If he can learn to love and have someone love him, too, then the curse will be broken.

Of course, Belle and the Beast have nothing in common. Belle is a beautiful young woman who loves books and is devoted to her father, an eccentric inventor. The Beast is a hideous monster, bitter over his fate and a gruff master to his servants, who remain loyal despite the fact that they, too, live under a curse because of him. At first neither beauty nor beast will give an inch to understand the other—that is, until the Beast risks his life to save Belle from a pack of hungry wolves. The Beast is injured in the battle, and the first stirrings of communication are seen as Belle lovingly tends to his wounds. Every important development in the story involves an act of love or compassion that builds a bridge between people or an act of selfishness that drives a wedge between them. In the end, the Beast sacrifices his own needs and desires for the good of another: He gives up his one chance for redemption and sets Belle free to care for her sickly father, even though it means he might be trapped as a monster forever. The Beast has finally learned to love.

If you are going to make a difference in this world, you must first learn to love. Yes, learn to love. That's because love does not come naturally to people who live in a fallen world. Since sin first entered the garden, it has been human nature for people to put themselves first. We choose to do what is in our own best interest without thinking much about how our actions will affect others, and we measure our happiness in terms of what we own, where we live, and who we know.

However, God did not place us on this earth to collect the most toys or

Illustration by Alice Ratterree.

to fulfill our own wishes and desires. He did not command us to hide ourselves within the safety of our homes and churches. He put us here to love Him and to love others. You may one day achieve worldwide fame and amass great riches, but if you fail to love people you will have failed at life. You may become the smartest person in the world, understanding all the mysteries of the universe, but if you do not love, you are nothing (1 Corinthians 13:2).

Your life as a young Christian is about learning to love. Indeed, Jesus called love the "greatest commandment" (Matthew 22:38). Why? Because God is love, and He wants you to become more like He is. God loves you deeply and unconditionally, and He showed it by sending His only Son to die on a cross for you. Now He wants you to love others as He loved you.

Sadly, much of the world has no idea what real love is. Songwriters and moviemakers earn millions of dollars selling us a cheap imitation of love based on physical attraction and emotional hunger. They tell us that love is something you can fall in and out of, as though it were a kind of cosmic accident. After all, you can't control how you feel, right? But that's not real love. Although love can generate intense feelings, love is much more than an emotion. Love is a choice, an action, a way of behaving. Real **love** is placing the needs of someone else before your own.

Love is the opposite of selfishness, and that's why you must learn to love. Love isn't easy. It takes lots of practice, so let's get started.

WHAT YOU WILL DO

» You will begin to take up your cross daily and follow Jesus' example.

» You will discover what love in action looks like.

» You will learn to find joy in being God's hands and feet on earth.

» You will define true greatness as God sees it.

» You will define compassion and be encouraged to demonstrate it in your relationships with others in response to God's compassionate gift of salvation to you.

SAN FRANCISCO'S CHINATOWN

Chinatown in San Francisco is the oldest and largest Asian community in the United States. During the late 1800s, many Chinese men came to America to find jobs. Most worked in the California gold mines or helped build the Transcontinental Railroad. But the American government soon set strict limits on how many Chinese immigrants could enter the country, and many were not allowed to bring their families along.

The Dragon Gate, photo by Toffel.

Most Chinese immigrants traveling to this country by boat first stopped in San Francisco Bay. Because they were not yet American citizens, they had to wait at Angel Island—the West Coast equivalent of Ellis Island in New York—until they received permission to enter the United States. Even then, the San Francisco city government and local property owners set aside just one neighborhood where Chinese immigrants were allowed to live within the city, an area that became known as Chinatown.

With many people living in such a small space—a little more than one square mile—Chinatown became a vibrant ethnic community. When the neighborhood was destroyed in the 1906 San Francisco earthquake, local officials rebuilt the area to look more Asian in order to attract tourists. Centered around Portsmouth Square, Chinatown is still one of the most densely populated neighborhoods in the United States and is where more than two-thirds of the Chinese population of San Francisco choose to live.

Today, Chinatown is a major tourist destination, drawing more visitors annually than the Golden Gate Bridge. Popular attractions include the Dragon Gate on Grant Avenue, the Golden Gate Cookie Factory, the Chinese Cultural Center, and more than 300 restaurants. Plan your visit at the right time and you may even get to see lion and dragon dancers parading down the street during the Autumn Moon Festival or Chinese New Year.

Photo by Murdocke.

UNCLE PING'S SURPRISE

The ocean voyage was not as exciting as the children had anticipated. There really was nothing to do but walk around the ship's decks, at all times being careful to stay out of the way of the freighter's crew and equipment. The food was simple but filling, and the family's tiny cabin seemed to grow smaller and smaller with each passing day.

"Today's the big day," their father announced early one morning. "Today's the day we're to arrive at San Francisco!"

"Oh, Papa," Mei cried. "I can't wait. Let's go up on deck right now."

After breakfast, Chang Wei led his family to the upper deck where many of the freighter's crew and passengers were crowding the stern to catch their first glimpse of America.

"Good morning, Captain," Wei said in greeting. "We are most grateful for your kindness to us all these weeks at sea. Are we still scheduled to arrive today?"

The captain smiled. "If you look to starboard, I think you'll answer your own question."

Wei led his family to starboard, or the right-hand side of the ship. In the distance, rising out of a light fog, they saw a rugged coastline.

"Is that America?" Mei asked with eager anticipation.

"Yep," the captain replied. "That's the California coastline. You're a very long way from China now," he added with a cheerful chuckle.

The Chang family stood silently, each of them squinting to better see their new homeland.

"It won't be long now," Wei said. "Not long at all."

Just before noon, the freighter slipped into port and docked. As the other passengers began to disembark, Wei spoke firmly to Mei and Li. "Stay close to me. Hold tight to your parcels. Uncle Ping will soon meet us and tell us where to go."

Suddenly the excitement of their arrival gave way to panic as the family stepped off the gang plank and was jostled among the crowds pushing their way about the dock. Wei looked anxiously about him at the chaos, trying to figure out where they should go. But he found himself confronted with signs in a language he could not understand.

"Where is Ping?" Ting asked, surprised that he wasn't on the dock to greet them.

"I don't know," Wei said, trying to hide his confusion from his family. "Just stay close together."

"Papa, I can't read any of the signs," Mei cried. "I'm afraid."

Wei held his daughter's hand tightly, while Ting held on to Li.

"Keep moving," a voice called above the din. "All arriving passengers will enter through the door marked 'Immigration.' Have your passports and papers ready."

Angel Island and the Golden Gate Bridge. Photo by druchoy

Some people clearly understood and began moving to the left, but Chang Wei stood still as if frozen. Why hadn't he thought before about the language problem? None of his family knew a word of English. He became desperate to find Ping, who would help them navigate this strange new world. But Ping was nowhere to be found, and Wei's heart sank. Then he gathered himself and shouted to his family over the commotion, "Just follow the people! But stay together!"

Once inside a large hall, the arriving immigrants were being directed to sit on long, hard benches. Across the way, men and women wearing official-looking uniforms sat at desks. Others were interviewing groups of people who were seated around tables.

"What do we do?" Ting asked as she fought her own fears.

"I don't know," Wei answered. "Perhaps someone will call our name."

After an hour of waiting, watching, and worrying, Wei heard his name called in Chinese. "Chang Wei, please come to desk number five. Chang Wei, please come to desk number five." Wei began searching for a desk designated as number five, but the long lines of people made it impossible to see any markings. In desperation, Wei jumped up on one of the benches and waved his arms to get the attention of the immigration officials. Then jabbing his finger into his chest over and over again, he shouted, "Chang Wei! Chang Wei!"

A few people seated near the family began to snicker, and Ting's face and neck turned red with embarrassment. "Please, Wei, come down from there."

"I am not moving until someone helps us," Wei said with a determined look on his face.

The Chinese monument on Angel Island. The inscription reads, "Leaving their homes and villages, they crossed the ocean only to endure confinement in these barracks. Conquering frontiers and barriers, they pioneered a new life by the Golden Gate." Photo by Jsalsman.

Then a kind-faced woman in a uniform walked over to them. She smiled and said in perfect Chinese, "Mr. Chang, please follow me. I will take you to desk number five."

"Thank you," Wei said, smiling with relief. He stepped down from the bench and, with his family, followed her across the crowded hall. There, an official looked over their travel papers and passports. After stamping each one in all the appropriate places, he looked up and said courteously in Chinese, "Welcome to America, Chang Wei. Welcome, Chang Ting, Chang Mei, and Chang Li. If you are expecting people to meet you, you will likely find them waiting just outside those large doors to the left."

With a gracious bow, Wei thanked the official. He then led his family through the exit doors, which opened into another hall filled with expectant people waiting for friends and relatives arriving from China.

After a few moments of scanning faces, Wei said excitedly and with no small relief, "There's Ping!"

"Welcome to your new home, dear brother," Ping exclaimed as he pushed through the crowd and embraced Wei. "Welcome to your new home."

"Oh, Ping!" Wei cried unashamedly. "How good to see you! How good to see family in a strange new country!"

There were hugs and tears of joy all around. There were tears of weariness after the long ocean crossing and tears of relief for their safe arrival. And behind all the tears of joy and relief there was fear—fear of the unknown. Not one of the Changs knew what it would take to adjust to a place that looked and sounded so different in every respect from their village in China.

"Where are Auntie Luli and your children?" Ting asked as they loaded their belongings into Ping's car.

Ping laughed. "My car is much too small for both families and your luggage. You'll see them later today."

As Ping drove through the busy San Francisco streets, Mei exclaimed, "Look, Papa! Look at the tall buildings. And all the people! San Francisco is so big."

"Yes, it is all very different. But I'm sure we'll learn our way around in no time."

"There's our church," Ping announced as he drove up a steep hill. "It's that building with the tall steeple and a cross on top of it."

"Church?" Wei asked.

"Yes," Ping replied. "We are Christians now."

Wei frowned. "But the Chang family has always followed the religion of our ancestors."

Ping smiled. "Everyone in my family received Jesus Christ as Lord and Savior last year. I've been meaning to write to tell you, but with the revolution in China and the preparations for your arrival, well, I never got around to mentioning it. Please forgive me."

Wei nodded but didn't say a word. *What is happening?* he thought. *Everything is changing. China has fallen to the communists. America is now my home, but it may never feel like home. Even my own brother has changed. What will happen to my family in this strange new land?*

Sensing that his news had made Wei uncomfortable, Ping asked enthusiastically, "So who's hungry?"

"I am," Mei said cheerfully.

"Me, too!" Li replied.

"I guess we all are," Ting admitted.

"Well, then, I think I'll treat you to something truly American for your first meal in your new country," Ping said, smiling broadly. "No rice or fish cakes today!"

"What is it?" Li asked.

"Hamburgers!" Ping announced with a laugh. "Can you say *hamburger*?"

Li attempted to speak his first English word. "Hambulgul."

"That's pretty good for your first try at English," Uncle Ping said encouragingly.

"What's a 'hambulgul'?" Mei asked.

"It's a surprise," Uncle Ping said as he pulled into the parking lot of a small diner.

Once inside, Ping ordered for everyone. "Let's see," he said in English to the waitress, "we would like five hamburgers, five orders of French fries, and five colas. And for dessert we'll have five ice cream cones. Chocolate, I think."

"Where are the chopsticks?" Li asked, curiously examining a rolled-up napkin.

"Oh, you won't need chopsticks for this meal." Ping chuckled. "We'll just pick everything up and eat with our fingers. You'll see."

As the Chang family hungrily devoured their American meal, they began to relax for the first time since disembarking from the freighter.

"I *like* America," Li announced. "And I love 'hambulguls'!"

As they drove away from the diner, Uncle Ping said, "Now, let's go have a look at your new apartment. I searched a long time for just the right one. It's in the same part of the city where Luli and I and the children live. We thought our family in America should live close to each other."

"Is it in Chinatown?" Wei asked. "We hear that many Chinese immigrants live in Chinatown."

Photo: Sarah Labieniec & Ryan Meis.

"Well, no," Ping replied.

"But we were hoping to live in Chinatown so we can communicate in our own language. We want to be able to buy what we need in Chinese markets. And Mei and Li can attend Chinese schools in Chinatown."

"Well, that's all true," Ping said, stopping at a red light. "But Luli and I discussed it, and we think it would be better for you to live in our neighborhood. It's a mixed neighborhood, with people who have lived here a long time and others who have moved here recently from many countries, not just China. We think you'll learn to speak and write English sooner if you live in a neighborhood where many people already speak the language."

"But that will be hard for us," Wei said, surprised and disappointed at Ping's plans for his family.

"I understand. At first it was hard for Luli and me when we moved here ten years ago. Many times I wanted to go back to China. But we've met many good people who have helped us learn English and many great things about this country. And our kids learned English even faster than we did. I know you'll like the neighborhood once you get used to it."

Chang Wei was too weary to argue with Ping. He was thankful that their dangerous journey was behind them and that Ping had found them a place to live.

"And a job?" Wei asked after a while. "Were you able to find a job for me?"

"Yes," Ping said enthusiastically, "just two days ago I found one. It's in a bank."

"A bank," Ting said. "Why that's perfect! My husband is a good businessman. He understands how to work with money."

"Well, yes, I suppose I do," Chang Wei replied, not wanting to boast about his abilities.

"Oh, he won't be working with the money," Ping said. "At least not right away. He's going to be a janitor. You know— sweeping and cleaning."

"A janitor?" Ting exclaimed in alarm. "But Wei is a professional man! In China, he would never stoop so low as to be a janitor. That is work for servants."

"My dear Ting," Ping replied patiently. "There aren't many jobs for immigrants in the city, especially for those who don't speak English. When I first arrived here, I was without any work for many months."

"Yes, but now you have your own clothing store. You're a successful businessman," she insisted.

"But it's taken many years to build my business. And unfortunately, I don't have work for you or Wei at this time." Sensing Ting's dismay, Ping changed the subject. "I know all of you must be very tired. When you've had a chance to settle in to your apartment, we'll talk more about the arrangements I've made for you."

Ping turned the car down a narrow street of older apartment buildings all in a row up a steep hill. Chang Wei stared at the canyon of brick and stone and thought longingly of the mountains and rice fields surrounding his village back in China. "Where are the trees? And the sky?" he asked wistfully. "How do people live in such a place?"

"There's not a lot of open space in the middle of a large city," Ping replied. "But I think you'll like your new apartment. And here we are!"

Almost too tired to think clearly, Wei's family unloaded their few belongings and followed Uncle Ping up three flights of stairs to apartment 3B.

"Here's the key," Ping said. "Everything is ready for you."

As Wei opened the door to the darkened apartment, he thought to himself, *Why did we leave China? Why did we leave our home near the mountains? Maybe the revolution would have passed by our village and left us in peace.*

Suddenly, lights came on in the apartment, and Chang Wei's family was greeted with a loud chorus of "Surprise! Surprise! Welcome to America!" Before they could set their belongings down, they were caught up in a sea of hugs from people they had never seen before.

"Come in, come in," Auntie Luli said warmly as she appeared from the kitchen. "You aren't going to live in the hallway, are you? Please do come inside and see your new home. Our friends have prepared some wonderful food for you!"

"I— I don't know what to say," Ting stammered as she hugged Luli and burst into tears.

"You don't need to say anything," Luli assured her as she took Ting's bag and set it on the floor. "We're just so happy that some of our own family will be with us here in America. Let me introduce you to some of our friends . . ."

"Look, Papa," exclaimed Mei. "Look at the flags on the wall. One of them is Chinese, and one is American."

"We don't want you ever to forget China," Ping said with a tinge of homesickness in his voice. "But we certainly want you to feel you belong here in your new country."

Chang Wei missed China—its people, its culture, and members of his family who still lived there. Yet in spite of his sadness, he tried to convince himself he had done the right thing in bringing his family to America.

"Thank you, Ping. Thank you, Luli," he said. "And thank all of you for making us feel welcome here. I am sure we will grow to love our new country even as we keep memories of the old country close to our hearts."

After much laughter, conversation, and a delicious buffet of Chinese and American dishes served and eaten with chopsticks, Ping announced, "It's getting late. Our new friends must rest. But before we go, I want to ask God to bless my brother's family in their new life."

"Dear Father in heaven," Ping prayed. "Thank you for bringing Wei, Ting, Mei, and Li safely to America. Please watch over them here. Help them as they learn the language and culture of their new country. Bless this home and make it safe by night and day. In Jesus' name, Amen."

After everyone had left for their own homes and Mei and Li were tucked into their beds, Wei sat down at the small kitchen table with Ting. They sat quietly for a long time, sipping cups of hot tea. Finally Wei spoke.

"You know, Ting," he said, "so much has happened since we left our home and began our journey to America. Sometimes I feel I will awake from a dream. Are we really in America? Will we ever see our family and friends in China again? And what about my brother's family? What has happened to them? How can they be Christians now? Does everything have to change? Can nothing stay the same?"

"I do not know," Ting said sadly.

"And how will we ever learn a new language? How will we learn the ways of a new culture? I already miss your delicious fish cakes."

"I will cook fish cakes soon, my precious Wei," Ting promised. "Perhaps I will make some for Ping's family, too. I feel terrible about complaining to him about your job as a janitor. I just think you deserve something better."

"Perhaps," Wei said. "But it is a job. And we should be grateful to Ping for finding it for me. Possibly in time I will find something . . . something more honorable." After taking another sip of tea, he said sleepily, "You know, Ting, there is something else I keep thinking about."

"What is it, Wei?"

"During our three weeks on the freighter I had time to think about our escape. Do you ever wonder why all those people who were strangers to us took such risks to help us? Why should they put their own families at peril to help us leave the country?"

"Yes, I have wondered about this," she admitted. "Surely they understood the dangers. And we could not give them anything in return. And what about Ping's friends who brought us food today? We are strangers to them, but they treated us as friends and tried to make us feel welcome in a strange place."

Ting washed the tea cups in the kitchen sink, while Wei began to unpack his small suitcase. There, in the bottom under his clothes, he discovered the small package the young man disguised as a soldier had given him the day they boarded the freighter.

"Why, I completely forgot about this," Wei said.

"Forgot what?"

"The package Fong Gui gave us in the warehouse at Lang Tin harbor."

Carefully, Wei removed the wrapping paper to reveal the promised Bible. He opened the cover and said, "There's a message here, written to us."

"What does it say?" Ting asked.

"It says, 'May God bless your family in your new nation.'"

"Is that all?" Ting asked as she dried a teacup.

"No, there's something else. It says, 'This is how we know what love is: Jesus Christ laid down his life for us. And we ought to lay down our lives for our brothers.'"

"That's a strange saying. I wonder what it means."

"It is strange. It makes me wish I knew Gui better and could ask him about what this writing means and why his relatives were

so kind to us. It's very odd, don't you think, that we were given a Bible by a stranger as we left China, and the very day we arrive in our new country, we learn that my brother and his family are now Christian? Do these things mean something, or are they just coincidences?"

Wei wearily laid the Bible on the table and took Ting's hands in his.

"You know, my precious wife, before we left China I believed we were moving to a new country just to escape the violence of the revolution. But America is turning out to be more complicated than I ever imagined. I hope we are prepared to meet new challenges as they come. And I hope we can become good Americans without having to give up being good Chinese. But for now we must rest. Who knows what other surprises await us tomorrow?"

THINK ABOUT IT

» How do you think the members of the Chang family felt when they saw the American coastline in the distance? When does the family's excitement and joy turn into anxiety and fear? Why?

» What does the Chang family seem to think Uncle Ping will be able to do for them?

» How do Wei and Ting respond to news of Wei's new job at the bank? Why?

» How do you think you would feel if your family moved to a new nation and you had to adapt to a different language and culture?

» What other kinds of adjustments do you think Wei's family will have to make in the days ahead? What adjustments do you think will be hardest for them to make?

WORDS YOU NEED TO KNOW

» **Love:** Choosing to place the needs of someone else above my own

» **Self-centered:** Making decisions based only on my own desires, needs, and interests

» **Taking up my cross:** Letting my selfishness die so that I can know the joy of following Christ

» **Hospitality:** Generously meeting the needs of a guest

» **Sacrifice:** Giving myself, my time, my possessions, or my pride to help someone else

HAMBURGERS TO GO

The hamburger is one of America's favorite foods and is a staple of family picnics and social gatherings. But did you know the hamburger's origins can be traced to eighteenth-century Europe?

The term hamburger comes from Hamburg, Germany's second-largest city and the port from where many set sail for America. When German immigrants arrived in this country, they brought their recipes with them. One of those recipes was for Hamburg steak, a hard slab of salted minced beef, slightly smoked and mixed with onions and breadcrumbs. No one knows for certain who first put the hamburger patty on a bun, but popular legend has it that the bread-covered sandwich was first served at the 1904 World's Fair in St. Louis where customers were delighted to be able to eat with their hands while strolling around the fair. This idea was later popularized by the new fast-food restaurants like White Castle in the 1920s and McDonald's in the 1940s.

Today, it is hard to imagine America without hamburgers. The backyard barbeque and drive-through window just wouldn't be the same without them. Today, hamburger toppings run the gamut from one or two simple condiments to "the works"—lettuce, tomato, onion, cheese, pickles, mayo, mustard, and ketchup. Some people even experiment with the basic ingredients, substituting ground buffalo, turkey, ostrich, or even soy for beef, or adding gourmet toppings like blue cheese or sautéed mushrooms.

Let's try an easy gourmet hamburger recipe with bacon and barbeque sauce to spice it up a little. Ask your mom or dad help you with the cooking!

Easy BBQ Bacon Burger
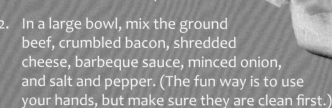

1 ½ lbs. ground beef
8 slices of bacon
6 oz. shredded cheddar cheese
⅓ cup barbeque sauce
2 T. dried minced onions
Salt and pepper to taste
6 hamburger buns

1. Cook the bacon until crispy and place on a paper-towel-covered plate to cool. Then crumble the bacon into bite-size pieces.

2. In a large bowl, mix the ground beef, crumbled bacon, shredded cheese, barbeque sauce, minced onion, and salt and pepper. (The fun way is to use your hands, but make sure they are clean first.)

3. Shape the hamburger mixture into 6 patties and cook in a frying pan or on a grill until done. Toast the hamburger buns, too, if you want.

4. Serve on buns with your favorite toppings.

HIDE IT IN YOUR HEART

Then he said to them all: "If anyone would come after me, he must deny himself and take up his cross daily and follow me." (Luke 9:23)

This is how we know what real love is: Jesus gave his life for us. So we should give our lives for our brothers and sisters. (1 John 3:16, NCV)

TAKE UP YOUR CROSS DAILY

As you know by now, if you have accepted God's free gift of salvation and you have chosen to follow Jesus Christ, you are called by His name. The word *Christian* means "follower of Christ." But what does it mean to "follow" Jesus? Simply put, to follow a leader means going where he (or she) leads, obeying his (or her) commands, and imitating his (or her) example of behavior. Throughout the New Testament, we are commanded to do all these things as followers of our Lord. If we are to make a difference in this world, then we must do the good works God has prepared for us (Ephesians 2:10), we must obey His command to "serve one another in love" (Galatians 5:13), and we must "be imitators of God . . . and live a life of love, just as Christ loved us and gave himself up for us as a fragrant offering and sacrifice to God" (Ephesians 5:1–2).

Jesus was very specific about what it takes to follow Him:

*"If any of you wants to be my follower, you must turn from your selfish ways, **take up your cross daily**, and follow me." (Luke 9:23, NLT)*

The New International Version says, "If anyone would come after me, he must deny himself." In other words, we must forget the way we used to live—the way we used to behave, the things we used to talk about, and the way we used to entertain ourselves. We must change direction and walk in a whole new way. You see, the Christian faith is not a fashion accessory you can just add to your existing lifestyle. It's not like a belt or a hat or a pair of shoes you put on to make people say, "Wow! Where can I get one of those?" It's not a T-shirt that says *My Boss Is a Jewish Carpenter*. You cannot "put on" Jesus (Galatians 3:26–27, NKJV) and then

continue to live the same selfish way you lived before, doing the same sinful things you did before.

When you were an infant, you were completely **self-centered**. As far as you were concerned, the whole world revolved around you, your wants, and your needs. If your needs were not met in a timely manner, you pitched a fit as a way of demanding action. Sadly, many people never seem to grow up, to mature beyond this self-centered phase. However, as one who has chosen to follow Jesus, you must give up this kind of selfish thinking and walk and talk and live in a brand-new way—His way.

But what did Jesus mean when He said you must "take up your cross daily"? Let's begin with what He did not mean. Many people, including many Christians, think that taking up their cross means carrying a heavy burden in their lives—such as pain, sickness, or money problems. They may even believe the burden was given to them by God. They wallow in self-pity and say "spiritual" things like "Oh, it's just my cross to bear." But Isaiah 53:4–5 tells us that Christ carried our sickness and our sorrows and by His wounds we are healed! And Jesus said, "Come to me, all you who are weary and burdened, and I will give you rest. Take my yoke upon you and learn from me, for I am gentle and humble in heart, and you will find rest for your souls. For my yoke is easy and my burden is light" (Matthew 11:28–30).

In order to understand what Jesus meant by "take up your cross," we need to understand what the cross represented to His first-century listeners. For two thousand years Christians have cherished the cross as a symbol of forgiveness, grace, and the ultimate act of love. But when Jesus walked the earth the cross meant one thing only: a painful, humiliating death reserved for the very worst criminals. Because the Romans forced convicted criminals to carry their own crosses to the place of crucifixion, bearing your cross meant carrying your own execution device while being ridiculed by a crowd of onlookers.

When Jesus spoke of taking up your cross, He was not talking about living with a burden or experiencing difficulty in life. He was speaking of death, pure and simple. Jesus was talking about the need to die to your old, selfish ways—to surrender totally and be born again into a new life that you live completely, unashamedly, and unreservedly for Him. The apostle Paul wrote, "I have been crucified with Christ and I no longer live, but Christ lives in me" (Galatians 2:20).

A true follower of Christ does not simply attend church every week, put a few dollars in the offering plate, and bake cookies for the occasional potluck dinner. Followers of Christ are called to put to death their own ideas, plans, dreams, and desires and exchange them for His. Indeed, we are to lay down our selfishness and pick up our cross every morning so that we may follow Jesus wholeheartedly throughout the day, every day.

Are you ready to fulfill God's plan for your life, no matter the consequences? Are you willing to tell people about Jesus if it means someone will make fun of you? Are you willing to obey Jesus if it means missing out on the hottest new TV show, movie, concert, or book? Are you willing to follow Jesus' example if it means losing a friend? Are you willing to go where Jesus leads if it means losing your life?

MAKE A NOTE OF IT

Write out Acts 10:38, which reads, "You know about Jesus from Nazareth, that God gave him the Holy Spirit and power. You know how Jesus went everywhere doing good and healing those who were ruled by the devil, because God was with him" (NCV). Imagine what the world would be like if every Christian followed Christ's example and did these same things, loving people as Jesus loved them. Write about or draw five things that might be different from how they are now.

> *Any time you have an opportunity to make a difference in this world and you don't, then you are wasting your time on Earth.*
> **Roberto Clemente**
> 1934–1972

TRADE IN YOUR TITLE FOR A TOWEL

A hush fell over the city of Jerusalem as the people settled in for the traditional Passover Feast. Knowing that His time on this earth was quickly coming to a close, Jesus had gathered his twelve closest followers in a furnished upper room to share one last supper with them. Now, it was the custom in those days to welcome guests by providing a servant and water to wash their feet. However, this was a borrowed room and there was no such servant, nor did any of

the disciples appear willing to wash the feet of the others. Every one of them must have seen the basin and towel when they entered the room and simply walked past it without a second thought. But Jesus got up from the meal, took off His cloak, and wrapped the towel around His waist. Then He poured water into a basin and began to wash His disciples' feet.

Just a few days earlier Jesus had entered the city to shouts of "Hosanna in the highest!" and "Blessed is He who comes in the name of the Lord!" The people had hailed Him as King, spreading their cloaks and palm branches on the road before Him. But on this

Christ Washing Peter's Feet by Ford Madox Brown.

night Jesus knelt before His disciples to perform the lowly task of washing the dust from their feet. When He had finished washing and drying their feet, He put on his cloak and returned to the table. "Do you understand what I have done for you?" He asked the disciples. "You call me 'Teacher' and 'Lord,' and you are right, because that's what I am. And since I, your Lord and Teacher, have washed your feet, you ought to wash each other's feet. I have given you an example to follow. Do as I have done to you" (John 13:13–15, NLT).

In Jesus' time, walking was the most common way to travel, whether you were going across town or to another village. Few roads were paved, there were no sidewalks, and most people in Palestine wore only the most basic sandals to protect the soles of their feet. They didn't have sneakers or boots as we know them, so their feet would have been significantly dirtier than you and I are used to when we sit down for dinner. The washing of feet was an act of **hospitality**, though it was a filthy job reserved mainly for servants and slaves. Certainly kings did not stoop to washing the feet of their subjects.

Yet Jesus' washing of the disciples' feet did not make Him any less of a man or any less of a king. The Bible says He knew exactly who He was, what He had been given, and where He was going:

Jesus knew that the Father had put all things under his power, and that he had come from God and was returning to God; so he got up from the meal, took off his outer clothing, and wrapped a towel around his waist. (John 13:3–4)

Jesus did not embarrass Himself or bring shame to His Father or jeopardize His status by washing His followers' feet. Rather, He demonstrated how to live a life full of meaning by putting others first *despite* His status. He set an example for us by setting aside His position as King to provide for the needs of others.

As a child of God and follower of Christ, you are royalty. John 1:12–13 says you have been born again into the family of the King of kings, the Most High God. Indeed, you are a co-heir of glory with the one and only begotten Son of God (Romans 8:17). You need to understand who you are in Christ, what you have been given, and where you are going to spend eternity. But if you want to make a difference in this world, if you are to faithfully follow Christ's lead and serve others, you, too, must be willing to lay aside the rights and privileges of your position and get your hands dirty.

Of course, times have changed and so have our customs. We wear shoes and socks and travel in cars, so it's usually not necessary to have our feet washed when we arrive at our destination. However, the principle of serving others in love still applies. In love, we are to

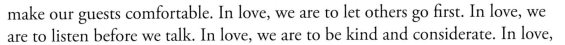

make our guests comfortable. In love, we are to let others go first. In love, we are to listen before we talk. In love, we are to be kind and considerate. In love, we are to provide for those who are in need of food and clothing and shelter. In love, we are to vacuum carpets, stack chairs, and scrub toilets at church. No job is too small, no labor is too menial.

James 4:17 says, "Anyone, then, who knows the good he ought to do and doesn't do it, sins." Is there a job you are capable of doing at home that you tend to avoid because it's dirty or difficult? Will doing this job lighten the load for another family member? Could doing this job at church or a homeless shelter minister to the staff or residents? Think about it. "Now that you know these things," Jesus said, "God will bless you for doing them." (John 13:17, NLT)

MAKE A NOTE OF IT

Work with a parent to organize a foot-washing ceremony for your family. You will need a large basin or bowl, a plastic pitcher full of warm water, and a bath towel. (No soap required.) Have each family member write his or her name on a slip of paper and place it in a box, then ask each person to draw one name randomly from the box. The person whose name you draw will be the person whose feet you will wash. Begin the service by reading aloud John 13:1–11. Take turns until everyone's feet have been washed. Remember to do this as Jesus did—humbly, lovingly, and gently. Then read aloud John 13:12–17. Now answer these questions in your journal: How did it feel to place yourself in the position of a servant? What was it like to have someone else, perhaps even a parent, wash your feet? What would you think if a king began washing your feet?

BE THE HANDS AND FEET OF JESUS

Paul called the church "the body of Christ" (1 Corinthians 12:27). Now that Jesus has ascended to heaven and is seated at the right hand of the Father, you and I are to serve as His hands and feet here on earth. Teresa of Ávila, a sixteenth-century Carmelite nun, wrote, "Yours are the eyes through which Christ's compassion for the world is to look out; yours are the feet with which He is to go about doing good; and yours are the hands with which He is to bless us now."

Our cities and nations are filled with hurting and forgotten people who have little hope or vision for their lives. But when confronted with such problems as widespread hunger and poverty, many Christians have plenty of excuses to offer:

The problem is too big for our church to handle.
There are just too many people who need help.
We don't have the resources to make a real difference.
Doesn't the government have a program for this?
I don't know where to begin.
I'm just one person.

But these are all poor excuses. "I tell you the truth, anyone who has faith in me will do what I have been doing. He will do even greater things than these, because I am going to the Father" (John 14:12). When it comes to doing God's will, no job is too big. You plus God constitute an overwhelming majority. You plus God are bigger than any problem confronting your city, your nation, or the world. With God you have access to infinite resources, infinite power, and infinite love. With God *all* things are possible (Matthew 19:26). The question is not "Can it be done?" The real question is this: Will you do it?

Jesus established the church to be a beacon of hope and love and carry the light of truth to a dark, selfish world. We are to be Jesus' feet, going out into our neighborhoods and to all corners of the world to share the good news that God loves *all* men, women, and children and wants to have a relationship with them. We are to be Jesus' hands, serving, comforting, and bringing healing and grace to those who are hurting. Whether it's taking a meal to a family whose mother is too sick to cook, distributing blankets to the homeless, or answering the call to be a missionary to Botswana, you can know the joy of being an answer to someone's prayer and a physical expression of God's love to people in need.

Not sure where to begin? Start by taking inventory of what you have to work with. As we have seen, God has given you a unique set of talents, abilities, experiences, and resources that He intends you to use for His glory. Make a list of your skills and interests, then consider how you might use them to help someone else. Consider Austin, a nine-year-old boy who loved basketball. He also loved Jesus and wanted to do something that would make a difference in the world. After seeing a short video about children orphaned by the AIDS crisis in Africa, Austin came up with the idea of raising money for the orphans by gathering pledges and shooting a free throw for every child around the world whose parents would die from AIDS in a single day. This was a simple enough idea that didn't require a lot of resources to get started—just time, a basketball, and a hoop. But the idea grew. As of this writing, Austin is sixteen and the ministry he started, Hoops of Hope, has raised more than $1.5 million to build schools, dormitories, and medical clinics in Zambia, Swaziland, and India.

So begin by taking inventory of your talents, abilities, experiences, and resources, and then keep your eyes open for opportunities to serve. Proverbs 22:9 (NKJV) says, "He who has a generous eye will be blessed, for he gives of his bread to the poor." Develop a generous eye. Look and listen for ways to love your heavenly Father by showing His unconditional love to the people around you. In this way you will give the world a glimpse of what God intended all creation to be, and you will provide others an accurate picture of Christ, who is our hope and the Savior of all who receive Him.

MOTHER TERESA

Photo: Evert Odekerken.

A humanitarian is a person devoted to helping people in need, especially those who are sick, poor, or handicapped. Mother Teresa, a small Albanian nun, was among the best-known humanitarians of the twentieth century. She chose to spend her life among the poor in India, setting up hospices to care for the dying, homes for people with diseases like leprosy and tuberculosis, and orphanages and schools to care for children without homes and families.

Mother Teresa was born Agnes Gonxha Bojaxhiu in 1910 in what is now Skopje, Macedonia. As a girl she was fascinated by stories of missionaries in far-off lands, and when she turned eighteen she left home to become a nun. After learning English at an abbey in Ireland, she traveled to Calcutta, India, where she took the name Teresa and taught children at a convent school. Although she enjoyed teaching, she became increasingly disturbed by the poverty surrounding her. One day she felt called by God to leave the school and go live among the poor. So she left everything behind, trading in her nun's habit for a white and blue sari, a style of Indian dress she wore for the rest of her life.

After a couple of difficult years, Mother Teresa established the Missionaries of Charity, an order of nuns who would care for "the hungry, the naked, the homeless, the crippled, the blind, the lepers, all those people who feel unwanted, unloved, uncared for." The order eventually spread to other countries, and today operates more than 600 missions, schools, and shelters in more than 120 countries.

Mother Teresa received numerous awards in recognition of her service, including the Nobel Peace Prize, which is given to people who have made important contributions to peace and the well-being of the human race. Yet despite her fame, she continued to work among the poor, saying, "Love has no meaning if it isn't shared. Love has to be put into action."

> *Without love, deeds, even the most brilliant, count as nothing.*
> **Thérèse of Lisieux**
> 1873–1897

DARE TO BE GREAT IN GOD'S EYES

Jesus and His followers were on the road to Capernaum when a disagreement broke out among the disciples. When they arrived at their destination, the Lord asked what they had been arguing about. No doubt the twelve had been walking some distance behind their Master so that He wouldn't overhear, and no one was now willing to speak up to confess his arrogance. But Jesus knew they had been arguing about which of them was greatest. So He said to them, "If any among you wants to be first, he must become the very last and the servant of all."

This story is found in the ninth chapter of Mark and is one of the more humbling Gospel stories told about the disciples. But the message didn't quite sink in the first time. In the very next chapter, the brothers James and John come to Jesus with a special request. "When you sit on your glorious throne," they say, "we want to sit in places of honor next to you, one on your right and the other on your left." Naturally, when the others hear about this, they become indignant. So Jesus calls them all together and tells them:

> *"Whoever wants to become great among you must be your servant, and whoever wants to be first must be slave of all. For even the Son of Man did not come to be served, but to serve, and to give his life as a ransom for many."*
> (Mark 10:43–45)

Popular culture leaves little doubt about how the modern world defines greatness. The media is quick to turn its spotlight on an individual who demonstrates a conspicuous combination of power, wealth, ambition, talent, knowledge, benevolence, and/or beauty. Politicians, pundits, and talk show hosts remind us of their importance by telling us how to think and feel about the critical issues of our time. The entertainment industry stages numerous award shows each year to declare "winners" and remind us of the cultural influence they wield as a group. Business executives throw lavish affairs to trumpet their acquisitions and multimillion-dollar bonuses, while celebrities and billionaire philanthropists hold press conferences to announce their donations to worthy causes.

Jesus made it clear, however, that such attributes and activities hold no sway with God. He doesn't care how much money you have, how many prizes you've won, how fashionable you are, or even how much you know. He doesn't care how many people watch you on TV or how many presidents and princes keep your number on speed dial. Even your gifts to the poor mean little in God's kingdom if you feel the need to be recognized for your charitable work (Matthew 6:2).

There's nothing wrong with wanting to be great. No young man grows up hoping his life will amount to nothing, and no young woman prays that she will never make a significant impact on the world. According to God, however, everything the world teaches us about success and greatness is upside down. The world says you get to be number one (first place) by looking out for number one (yourself). But Jesus taught—and showed by example—that to be great in God's eyes, you must humble yourself and put *others* first. You must first *be* a servant if you ever hope to hear God say, "Well done, good and faithful servant!" (Matthew 25:21).

WHAT SHOULD I DO?

The apostle John wrote, "We know what real love is because Jesus gave up his life for us. So we also ought to give up our lives for our brothers and sisters. . . . Dear children, let's not merely say that we love each other; let us show the truth by our actions" (1 John 3:16–18, NLT).

Police officers, firefighters, rescue workers, and soldiers regularly risk their lives to serve the needs of others. They are prepared to sacrifice their lives to save the lives of their friends, coworkers, and perfect strangers. Jesus said, "Greater love has no one than this, that he lay down his life for his friends" (John 15:13). Although you may never be called to serve someone by dying physically, there are other ways to "lay down your life." Love requires sacrifice, and sacrifice always costs something.

Hebrews 13:16 says, "Do not forget to do good and to share with others, for with such sacrifices God is pleased." **Sacrifice** means giving something of yourself, whether it's your time, your possessions, or just a little of your dignity. Sacrifice can mean picking up trash off the street to make your neighborhood a more pleasant place. It can mean giving your little sister first choice when leftovers are for dinner. Or it can mean using your vacation money for a missions trip to build houses for the poor in Haiti.

Sacrifice is required if you are to think and act like Jesus in all things:

He gave up his place with God and made himself nothing. He was born to be a man, and became like a servant. And when he was living as a man, he humbled himself and was fully obedient to God. He obeyed even when that caused his death—death on a cross. So God raised Christ to the highest place. God made the name of Christ greater than every other name. (Philippians 2:7–9, ICB)

The Way to Calvary by Domenichino.

A PRAYER

Dear God, thank you for loving me so much that you sent your Son to die on a cross for me. Teach me to love others the way you love me! Help me to lay down my selfishness and take up my cross daily so that I can live every day for you with my whole heart. Let me be your hands and feet and share your love by helping those who need it. In Jesus' name I pray. Amen.

Be the change you want to see in the world.
Mahatma Gandhi
1869–1948

ENCOUNTERS WITH JESUS

WHO'S GOING TO FEED ALL THESE PEOPLE?

Judah awoke at the touch of his father's hand on his shoulder. Quietly, he dressed in the sparse dawn light, not wanting to wake his brothers and sisters. Sitting by the fire, Judah and his father ate a simple breakfast of freshly baked flatbread and washed it down with goat's milk.

"Will you be back before dark?" Judah's mother asked as she wrapped more of the flatbread for their lunch, adding dried salted sardines for flavor.

Judah's father shook his head. "I don't know. Depends on how big our catch is this morning."

Judah's mother added a few more pieces of flatbread to the bundle. "With you growing the way you are, there's no telling how hungry you'll get," she said, running a hand through Judah's tousled hair.

"Mama," he protested, squirming out from under her hand. He was twelve now, soon to be a man, and men weren't supposed to let their mothers rumple their hair, were they?

His mother just laughed and handed him the bundle. "Keep this dry. It's probably all you'll eat today."

Judah followed his father from the small house, through the tangled streets of Capernaum, to the busy Galilean harbor where their employer, Zebedee, was already on board his boat and checking his nets. Although Judah had fished with his father for as long as he could remember, this was the first season he was old enough to hire himself out as a day laborer.

"Shalom!" the older man called heartily. Judah liked Zebedee because he was loud and boisterous and laughed from somewhere deep in his stomach, the sound rumbling up like thunder.

Returning his greeting with a wave, Judah's father went to pick out a casting net from the orderly row laid out on the dock. He was a burly man, and he chose one of the largest nets Zebedee owned, a big circle made of flax thread with little lead weights attached all around the perimeter. Judah wasn't strong enough yet to handle such a gigantic net—after all, it weighed almost as much as he did! Instead, he chose a net of medium size and weight, just right for a growing young man.

Leaving their outer clothes and their lunch in Zebedee's designated area, Judah and his father walked along the northern shore, carrying their nets and large baskets for their catch. Today they would be casting their nets in a protected little cove where the lapping waves often carried schools of fish near shore. There Judah and his father waded into the lake and began casting their nets.

Fishermen on the Sea of Galilee.

With practiced ease, Judah coiled the net in his left hand. Spinning quickly, he threw the net at the water, watching it flatten out in the air like one of his mother's flatbreads and hit the surface with a splash. Judah waited a moment, letting the weights sink to the bottom, and then began reeling the net back in. A rope attached to his wrist cinched the net closed, trapping any fish inside.

Judah and his father worked briskly, slowly filling their large baskets to the brim with sardines. Judah's father could catch many fish in one throw, but Judah could throw and empty his smaller net faster.

"Bet I can fill my baskets before you can!" Judah challenged, smiling.

His father laughed and roared back, "I'd like to see you try!"

About midday, Judah and his father wrapped the wet nets around their bodies to keep them from tangling, then hoisted the heavy baskets of fish on poles balanced across their shoulders. The fishermen needed to count and sell their catch right away. Some of the fish would be cooked and eaten locally, and some would be shipped south to Magdala to be dried and salted then sold throughout Palestine.

When Judah and his father arrived back at Zebedee's boat, they found a group of men on deck. Among them were Zebedee's sons James and John. Judah also recognized the brothers Peter and Andrew, who he knew lived in Capernaum although he hadn't seen them lately.

Zebedee said to Judah's father, "James and John are back, and they're with the rabbi. Can you sail them over to Bethsaida this afternoon?"

"Right away," Judah's father answered.

"There is no hurry," Andrew said. "We are only going to a quiet place outside of town to get some rest."

After Judah and his father turned in their catch, Judah ran to get their outer garments and lunch while his father put away their nets and baskets.

The boat was the length of eleven of Judah's father's long strides and three wide, with one flax sail. Judah tucked their lunch up under a wooden seat where it would stay dry and took his place at one of the oars. The wind wasn't blowing in the right direction this afternoon, so they would have to row, two on each side.

Judah's father took the oar behind him, while Peter and Andrew settled into the other side and John took the tiller. The rest of the men stood or sat wherever they could. As they pulled away from shore, Judah could see a crowd gathering on the beach, pointing and shouting. One man even tried to swim after them, but he tired quickly and gave up. When they were about halfway across the lake, the wind picked up. Judah and Andrew stowed the oars and jumped up to raise the sail to catch the breeze, and the wind began pushing them northeast across the lake to Bethsaida, just a few miles away.

Judah's father then took the tiller, and John sat down with the others to listen to their teacher. His name was Jesus, and despite his ordinary appearance, he fascinated Judah who stood as close to the teacher as he dared. The others called Jesus "rabbi," or teacher, yet he didn't talk like the rabbis in the synagogue, who spoke as if their own importance lent gravity to their words. Jesus spoke as though the words *themselves* were important and full of power. Even Judah's father, who was usually interested only in practical things, seemed enthralled by the teacher.

As the sun reached its highest point in the sky, Jesus paused a moment, and in the sudden silence, Judah's stomach rumbled loudly.

"Better feed that boy before he wastes away," Peter said.

The men all laughed, and then everyone began pulling out their lunches. Judah ate contentedly, imagining the lake to be the open sea and his mother's bread and fish to be delicacies from a far-off land.

When they arrived at Bethsaida, Judah helped lower the sail, then worked one of the oars to guide them to a safe anchorage. As the men started to disembark, Judah caught his father's attention and silently pleaded to go along with them.

His father frowned slightly and was opening his mouth to refuse when Andrew spoke up. "Would it be all right if Judah comes with us? We could use someone to carry the water skin."

Judah's father looked between the two of them before reluctantly nodding. "You'll need this," he said, handing Judah the rest of their food, along with his outer robe. "Just be on your best behavior," he warned.

"Oh, I'll look after him," Andrew said.

Beaming from ear to ear, Judah climbed out of the boat and followed Andrew. Slinging the water skin over his shoulder, Judah trailed Jesus and his disciples through the streets of Bethsaida. It looked like they were heading for the northern edge of the town, to the green spaces beyond the ford of the Jordan River.

Bethsaida around 1900.

As they walked, a group of young men raced up to them. Judah recognized one of them from the dock in Capernaum. "They must have run along the coast road to get here before us," Andrew muttered under his breath.

Near the ford, the land flattened out into a broad plain where a few hundred people already waited for them. Most of them were travelers making their way to Jerusalem for the Passover, which was only days away. Others had heard of Jesus' arrival and were helping sick and injured people coming from Bethsaida and the surrounding villages. When the crowd saw Jesus, they talked excitedly among themselves and craned their necks to see him.

Peter sighed loudly. "I thought we came here to get away from the crowds," he said.

Judah glanced at Jesus. But instead of anger or annoyance, the teacher's face revealed only compassion.

Walking among the people, Jesus stopped whenever he saw someone in need. To his surprise, Judah saw a lame man get up and start walking. People with fevers were suddenly healthy again, and sight was restored to two blind people. Judah wasn't sure what to make of all this. Was this Jesus a prophet?

Unhurried, Jesus moved among the people until he reached a high point on the plain. There he sat down on a broad, sun-warmed rock and began to teach. By now the crowd had grown to several thousands. Judah thought that those young men running along the coast must have told everyone they met that Jesus was coming here!

The chaos of the crowds stilled as Jesus began to speak. Judah knew he had never before met anyone like him. He spoke with authority, yet as one very much concerned about the welfare of ordinary people.

Finally, Jesus paused, and Andrew motioned for Judah to hand him the water skin. With a start, Judah realized that the sun now hung low over the lake. His father would be wondering what had happened to them.

In the quiet, Judah could hear some of the disciples murmuring among themselves. Then John moved close to Jesus. "Lord, this is a remote place, and it's already very late," he said. "Perhaps we should send the people away so that they can eat and find places to sleep for the night."

Jesus was silent for a moment. Then he turned to another disciple, a man from Bethsaida called Philip. "Where can we buy bread to feed these people?" Jesus asked. Philip looked startled, glancing around at the other disciples. They all looked out over the hillside, mentally tallying the thousands of people gathered there.

Philip swallowed. "Even if we spent eight months' pay, we couldn't provide enough for each person to have more than a mouthful of bread."

Looking at the disciples, Jesus asked, "How much food do you have here?" The disciples looked around at each other again. They had already eaten everything they brought from Capernaum.

Suddenly, Judah remembered the leftovers his father had given him. Untying the bundle from his belt, he tugged on Andrew's sleeve. With a smile, Andrew pushed him gently forward to the place where Jesus was sitting. "This young man has some bread and fish, Teacher."

Timidly, Judah handed Jesus the cloth that held only two sardines and five small loaves of his mother's barley flatbread. Jesus smiled and thanked him, and Judah knew he had nothing to fear.

Then Jesus said to the disciples, "Have the people sit down in groups of fifty and a hundred on the grass." The men looked puzzled, but they quickly moved among the crowd and organized the people.

Holding a piece of flatbread in his hands, Jesus looked up to the heavens and spoke a traditional prayer of thanksgiving, just as if he were the host and had invited all these people to his home for supper. "Blessed are you, O Lord our God, who brings forth bread from the earth." Then he tore the bread in half.

Jesus then began handing out flatbread and sardines to the people gathered around him, and he instructed his disciples to do the same. No matter how much food was handed out,

there was always enough for the next person.

Judah could not believe what he was seeing. He tried counting the pieces of bread and fish being handed out, but he soon lost track because there were so many. How was Jesus doing this?

Slowly the disciples distributed food to all the people sitting on the spring hillside. Andrew made sure that Judah was served, too. Carefully, Judah bit into his piece of flatbread. Yes, it tasted like his mother's bread, the cheap barley flour that left coarse bits on his tongue as he chewed. And the sardines tasted just like the ones he and his father had shared at lunch.

When they had all had enough to eat, Jesus told his disciples to gather up the scraps, just as they would at a sacred feast where nothing was to go to waste. By the time all the broken rounds of flatbread and extra sardines had been collected, each of the twelve disciples had filled a small basket. Judah could not imagine how there could be so much left over when so many people had eaten their fill!

Judah couldn't wait to tell his father what he had missed by staying with the boat—how Jesus had healed people and then fed so many with Judah's small lunch. He wondered what his mother would say when he told her that her bread had fed thousands that day!

TAKE A CLOSER LOOK

- Read the biblical accounts of these events in Mark 6:30–39 and John 6:1–15 and compare them to the story you've just read.
- Why do you think crowds seemed to gather wherever Jesus went?
- Jesus knew the disciples could not provide enough food for five thousand people, so why do you think He told the disciples to give them something to eat?
- What do you think the disciples were thinking when Jesus told them to feed the people?
- Whom did Jesus serve that day? How did He serve them?
- What do you think these events meant to the boy who brought the loaves and fishes?

THE HOUSE OF TRUTH: THE NINTH PILLAR

Throughout the What We Believe series, you have been building a House of Truth to help you remember what God says in the Bible about Himself, who you are, and how God expects you to live. This is a special house, not one built with lumber, bricks, and other ordinary building materials. The plan for building your House of Truth is the Bible. Each part of this worldview model represents an essential truth from God's Word. Just as we build strong houses with good materials on strong foundations, so we must build our lives with the truths God gives us in the Bible. These truths will be displayed on the rock and in the foundation, walls, and roof of the House of Truth.

In the first book, *Who Is God? (And Can I Really Know Him?)*, you learned that if you are wise, you will build your life on the Rock that is God and His Word. You also learned that wise people build a foundation of wisdom for their lives by knowing and loving God and obeying His commands. You then built on your foundation with four important biblical truths:

1. God always tells me what is right and true.
2. God is the only true and almighty God.
3. God is God the Father, God the Son, and God the Holy Spirit.
4. God is the Creator.

In that book you also constructed the first wall of your house, the Fellowship Wall, with four essential truths about your relationship with God:

5. God created me to be His child and to give Him glory.
6. God created me to need Him for everything.
7. Sin causes separation and disharmony between me and God.
8. Jesus died to restore fellowship and harmony between me and God.

In the second book, *Who Am I? (And What Am I Doing Here?)*, you learned what it means to be made in the image of Almighty God. In that book you built the second wall in your House of Truth, the Image-Bearing Wall—a wall that represents your relationship with yourself as you grow in your faith and become more like the One who made you. This wall was constructed from these important biblical truths:

9. God created me in His image.
10. God has crowned me with glory and honor.
11. Sin causes disharmony within me.
12. Jesus died to restore harmony within me.

THE SERVANTHOOD WALL: YOUR RELATIONSHIP WITH OTHERS

As you work through this book, together we will build the third wall in your house—the Servanthood Wall. This wall represents your relationship with others. The Servanthood Wall will consist of the next four pillars in your house. In these first two lessons, you erected the first pillar in your Servanthood Wall:

BIBLICAL TRUTH 13:

God created His image-bearers to love and serve one another.

Biblical Truth 13
God created me to love and serve His people

SERVANTHOOD WALL
My relationship with others as I serve them in love

Biblical Truth 3
God is God the Father, Son, and Holy Spirit

FOUNDATION OF WISDOM
Knowing, loving, and obeying God my Rock

THE ROCK
God and His Word

WHO IS MY NEIGHBOR?

I TELL YOU THE TRUTH, ANYTHING YOU DID FOR EVEN
THE LEAST OF MY PEOPLE HERE, YOU ALSO DID FOR ME.

MATTHEW 25:40 (NCV)

THE BIG IDEA

Imagine for a moment a young African-American man walking home from a Bible study at a friend's house. He is wearing headphones and listening to music by his favorite Christian band, and he doesn't notice the car barreling down the street as he crosses at an intersection. The woman driving the car is intoxicated and never sees the stop sign or the pedestrian. The young man is thrown into the air by the impact, landing in a gutter where he lies bleeding and unconscious. But the drunk driver does not slow or stop.

A few minutes later, the minister from the young man's church stops at the same stop sign. He is running late for an awards banquet where he is to be honored for his charitable work. The minister sees the boy lying in the gutter but doesn't recognize him. He assumes the young man is either drunk or high on drugs and just needs to "sleep it off." The minister drives on and keeps his appointment.

Soon after, the choir director from the minister's church drives by on her way to the same banquet. She spots the young man in the gutter and sees that he is bleeding. She is a retired nurse, so she stops the car, gets out, and starts to go help the man. Then she thinks, *What if this man was robbed and beaten by a gang and the gang is still nearby? Or what if this man is only pretending to be hurt to lure me closer?* She thinks better of it, climbs back into her car, says a quick prayer, and drives away.

Then an older man, a Muslim, drives by and sees the injured man lying in the gutter. He stops his car and rushes to the young man's side. He sees that the young man is clutching a Bible and wearing a cross. He also sees that the man is bleeding from a head wound. The older man knows not to move a person with this type of injury, so he calls 9-1-1. Then he waits with the young man, speaking words of comfort to him. When the time comes, he follows the ambulance to the hospital and then offers to pay for the young man's treatment if he has no insurance.

Does this story sound familiar? Perhaps you have read a similar story told by Jesus. On this occasion a man skilled in Jewish law stands up to "test" Jesus (Luke 10:25). We don't know the lawyer's motive for doing this. Maybe he was trying to expose Jesus as an uneducated carpenter trying to pass Himself off as a teacher. The lawyer asks Jesus, "What must I do to inherit eternal life?"

Jesus knows He is being tested and answers with a question of His own: "What is written in the Law? How do you read it?"

The lawyer answers well, quoting Deuteronomy 6:5 and Leviticus 19:18, "'Love the Lord your God with all your heart and with all your soul and with all your strength and with all your mind,'" he says, "and, 'Love your neighbor as yourself.'"

"You have answered correctly," Jesus replies. "Do this and you will live."

However, the lawyer is an important man, and although he tithes and gives alms to the poor in accordance with the Law, he knows he has rarely put the needs of his fellow man ahead of his own. So he tries to justify his actions with a bit of legal maneuvering. "And who is my neighbor?" he asks, challenging Jesus to define His terminology.

The Good Samaritan by Van Gogh.

Instead of quoting from the Law or the dictionary, Jesus responds with a parable in which a man was attacked by robbers while traveling alone on a dangerous stretch of road between Jerusalem and Jericho. The thieves took the man's clothes, beat him, and left him for dead. First a priest and then a Levite passed by—they saw the man but did not stop to help him. Then a traveler from Samaria came upon the injured man. Now, you must remember that Jesus' listeners were Jews, and Jews did not associate with Samaritans (John 4:9). The Jews and Samaritans hated each other. Yet in this story, the Samaritan took pity on the injured man and attended to his wounds. He then took the man to an inn and paid for him to be cared for and fed.

Jesus finishes His story and then asks the lawyer, "Which of these three do you think was a neighbor to the man who fell into the hands of robbers?"

The lawyer replies, "The one who had mercy on him."

Jesus tells him, "Go and do likewise."

Jesus' story teaches us that our neighbors are not just those who live on the same block or in the same city. Our **neighbors** are not just those who share our faith or vote the same way we do. Our neighbors are not defined by the language they speak or the color of their skin or even the beliefs that make up their worldview. The parable of the good Samaritan teaches us that we must see all people as our neighbors, especially those who are in need of our help.

The Samaritan saw a person in need and took compassion on him. He could have easily continued on his way as the other two men did and saved himself the time, money, and inconvenience. All too often we are faced with a similar choice. We see a homeless woman whose shopping cart has tipped over, spilling her few precious possessions onto the sidewalk, and we ask ourselves, *If I stop to help this person, what will happen to me?* Instead, we should be asking, *If I do not stop to help this person, what will happen to her?*

In order to be good neighbors, we must take action. We must not only see the needs of others, we must act to meet those needs. This may involve nothing more than opening a door for someone whose hands are full. Maybe it's offering a kind word to someone who's having a difficult day. Maybe a lonely widow just needs some company. Whatever the need, we must show by our actions that we care about our neighbors. In this "me first" world, others will definitely notice when we take time to help and encourage them.

WHAT YOU WILL DO

» You will explore different ways of being a good neighbor.

» You will expand your definition of *neighbor* beyond those who live near you.

» You will learn to find delight in serving others.

» You will define friendliness and be encouraged to be a genuine friend to others.

PEOPLE IN MOTION

Since the time men and women began to spread out across the earth, people have needed to get around. Traveling on foot is fine if you don't have far to go or you have plenty of time to get there. But what if you need to go across town or buy groceries and you don't own a car?

Public transportation is a passenger service available for use by the general public. The earliest forms of public transportation were stagecoaches and ferries, which relied on humans or animals to move people from place to place. But new forms of power quickly made travel faster, easier, and cheaper. The invention of the steam engine meant that people could be carried faster than any horse could run, and soon trains became a part of everyday life. When the automobile was invented, this technology was quickly applied to transportation and buses became a common sight around town.

Due to the unique geography of some cities, other methods of public travel have been developed. Trolleys and cable cars used tracks set into the street or cables strung high above traffic. Gondolas lifted people along cables to mountain tops and floated them along canals.

As cities continued to add more businesses and more people, local governments began to look to underground tunnels and trains as a way to save space. In America, we call this the subway; in other countries, it is called the underground or the metro. Today, most major cities have some kind of subway system. Some, including Munich, Shanghai, Paris, Madrid, and Moscow, even offer high-speed trains that transport passengers as fast as 150 miles per hour!

Public transportation offers many benefits. Travel by bus or subway is generally safer and costs less than driving and reduces traffic and pollution in crowded urban areas. These types of transportation also provide mobility to people who can't or don't want to own a car. The success of many of the world's largest cities is due in part to reliable public transportation systems.

AN UNHAPPY DAY

As Chang Wei's family sat down to their breakfast of fried rice, everyone was unusually quiet. After several minutes of awkward silence, Wei decided he needed to encourage his wife and children. He smiled, clapped his hands together, and said, "Today we are all going to have an adventure! All of us are going to have new experiences. Mei and Li, you are beginning classes in a new school. Ting, you're going on your first shopping trip in America. And I—well, I begin my new job at the bank."

"Will there be anyone at the bank who can speak Chinese if you need help?" Ting asked.

"Yes, Ping said there are several people who can help me." Turning to the children, he said, "And your uncle assured me there are teachers at your school who can speak Chinese, and they'll be able to help you."

Mei seemed to be filled with apprehension about going to school, but Li was excited about the possibility of meeting new friends. "Don't worry, Mei," he said, trying to reassure his sister. "I'll be there. You can always talk to me."

"Mei," her father said, "I want you to look after Li to the best of your ability. Do you understand?"

Mei nodded that she understood, excused herself from the table, and went to the bathroom to brush her teeth.

As Wei helped his children organize their jackets and school supplies, Ting stood thoughtfully looking at the three most important people in her life. "I will miss all of you today," she said. "Auntie Luli's going to show me how to get to the neighborhood market.

She wrote out a list of words for me in English that I can show the grocer."

"We'll have much to share with each other this evening," Wei said cheerfully as he hugged Ting and opened the door. "Now let's hurry, children. We will catch a bus at the corner that will take us to your school, and then I'll catch another bus to the bank."

Mei and Li clung closely to their father as they neared the crowded bus stop where people were jostling each other for a good place in line for the approaching bus.

"Hurry now," the bus driver ordered. "Put your money in the fare box and move to the back. We've got a schedule to keep."

Not understanding what he was saying, Chang Wei watched nervously as the passengers in front of him dropped coins into the box and then pushed their way to the back of the bus. As he fumbled in his pocket to find the coins Ping had sorted out for their fare, someone shouted from behind, "Hurry up, mister! We ain't got all day."

Chang Wei didn't understand the words, but he understood perfectly the impatient tone of voice.

Wei dropped the coins in the box and then handed the driver a note Ping had written, asking the bus driver to let Chang Wei know when they were to get off at the school. The driver smiled and nodded, assuring Wei that he understood and would help him.

Mei and Li tried to keep their footing as they were sandwiched together among the crowd of riders who completely blocked the view from the bus windows.

"Don't turn loose of Papa's hand," Mei instructed her brother.

Just when Mei thought she could no longer bear the crush of people around her, the driver motioned to Chang Wei. "This stop," he said, pointing out the front window to a large stone building on the corner.

Chang Wei nodded courteously and helped the children push forward toward the door. As it opened, Mei and Li felt a welcome rush of cool fall air in their faces, and each of them breathed deeply.

"That was awful," Mei said. "I thought I was going to suffocate."

Her father smiled but said nothing as he led the children up the steps of the school and into a very wide and nearly deserted hallway lined with doorways.

Not knowing where to go or what to do first, he thankfully remembered the instructions Ping had written out for them. He found the piece of paper in his pocket and handed it to an older woman who had just appeared in the hallway from one of the classrooms.

"Right this way," she said. "I'm Mrs. Belmont, the principal. I will help you enroll your children in their classes. And we have someone on staff here who speaks Chinese who can help us with the details. I'll call for her."

Chang Wei, Mei, and Li silently followed the woman into her office. Soon after, a Chinese-American woman courteously helped Wei complete all the necessary paperwork. "I'll take the children to their classes now," she said. "And who will be picking them up after school?"

"Their Uncle Ping," Wei answered in Chinese. "And thank you very much for your help."

Chang Wei hugged his children goodbye, then turned and walked down the hallway. Suddenly, Li began to cry.

"Now, now, everything will be okay," the Chinese lady assured the children as she led them to their classrooms. "You'll make lots of new friends today. And before long, you'll be speaking English as well as the other children."

Leaving Mei and Li at their new school was one of the most difficult things Chang Wei had ever done. He felt remorse for having taken them from their ancestral home and bringing them to this new world of strange language and foreign customs. He could easily imagine their fear and sense of helplessness because he felt much the same. *How will I ever learn to be an American?*

Wei pushed open the heavy front doors of the bank and stepped into the marble-floored lobby. Again, not knowing where to go or what to do first, he handed another note Ping had written to a woman standing in a line.

"I don't work here," she said, a bit flustered. "I'm a customer."

Embarrassed by his mistake, Wei nodded apologetically. Then he slowly approached an official-looking man sitting at a desk in the lobby. Wei handed him the note.

"Ah, the new janitor. Mister," the man said, not knowing that Wei spoke no English, "our janitors are supposed to come in the back door through the alley." Wei showed no sign of comprehension, so the man got up and led Wei out the front door, around the block, down a narrow alley, and to a windowless steel door marked First National Bank.

"From now on, use this door," he said curtly. Then he turned and walked away.

Standing in the dimly lit hallway, Wei took a deep breath before looking for someone else to help him. The unpleasant smells of furniture polish, bathroom cleansers, and musty wet mops nearly overwhelmed him, but he continued walking.

"What do you want, mister?" a large, bald-headed man asked as he came out of a small office into the hallway. "Oh, are you the new Chinaman who's coming to work here?"

Again, not understanding the man's English, Wei reached into his pocket and handed him the note Ping had prepared.

After reading it, he said, "All right, I'll show you what to do. But first there's been a change in your hours. You won't start work until after the bank closes. From now on, get here by five o'clock in the afternoon. You'll work until midnight or until your duties are finished."

Wei stared blankly at the man, again not understanding.

"Oh, that's right," the man said smugly. "I forgot. You don't speak English. Why don't they teach you people the language before you get off the boat?" He sighed heavily. "Wait here until I find another Chinaman."

Wei watched helplessly as the man disappeared down the hall. Worse than the feeling of helplessness was the humiliation he felt for being an unprepared and unwelcome alien in this place. Soon, however, a young Chinese man approached Wei.

"Mr. Chang," he said with a smile, "I am Chou Ling. I've been sent to show you what to do. Follow me and we'll get started."

Chang Wei was so happy to hear his native language, he smiled and said, "Thank you for your kindness to me. I don't know if I will ever learn this language or how you do things in this country. By the way, who was the man I met here in the hallway—the heavy-set man?"

"Oh, you must mean Mr. Blackstone," Chou Ling answered. "He's the boss—well, he's in charge of the janitors. We just call him Boss Man. Just do your job and he'll leave you alone. But don't expect any compliments or friendly greetings. And if you don't do a good job, be warned: He has a bad temper. Now follow me and I'll show you your cleaning responsibilities and the correct way to do them."

Ling led Wei through the maze of hallways and offices on each floor of the bank, carefully pointing out the areas Wei would be responsible for cleaning.

"This office is very important," he said as he knocked respectfully on a large wooden door on the third floor. "Mr. Long, the president of the bank, works here. Before we go in, try to say his name—Mr. Long. Mr. Long."

"Mis-tah Long," Wei pronounced slowly. "Mistah Long."

"Good," Chou Ling said, encouraging Wei with a smile as he knocked again on the office door.

"Come in," said a gruff voice on the other side of the door.

Courteously, Chou Ling opened the door, and Chang Wei followed him inside.

"Mr. Long," Chou Ling announced politely, "this is Mr. Chang Wei. He's our newest janitor, just arrived from China. He'll be responsible for cleaning several offices, including yours."

"Very well. Show him what I expect each night," Mr. Long said, continuing to work at his desk without looking up or greeting Chang Wei.

Chou Ling carefully explained the details of how to clean Mr. Long's office and then led Wei quietly back into the hall by a side door.

"Use this door only," he explained. "Don't ever use the front door when Mr. Long is here. Sometimes he'll have important customers in his office and, as you saw, he doesn't like to be interrupted."

"I understand," Wei acknowledged, sensing that janitors, especially Chinese janitors, were not considered important by bank presidents.

After showing Wei through all the halls, offices, and lavatories he would be responsible for cleaning each night, Chou Ling led him into a small room furnished with a table and chairs in the middle. "This is the break room for the janitors. Some of the men and women are Chinese, others are different nationalities. But I think you'll like most of them. The evening crew usually eats dinner at nine o'clock. Now have a seat. I need to explain a few unofficial things to you about working here."

As Wei sat down, he saw that Chou Ling's expression had become more serious.

"Most of the employees here at the bank are friendly. But there are some who don't like people from China and other countries. Most of the workers will call you Mr. Chang or Wei, but some may call you 'Chinaman.' Try to ignore them and just do your job."

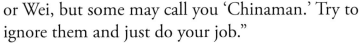

"But I thought America welcomed immigrants," Wei said with some surprise.

"Most people do, but there are some who hold prejudices about foreigners, especially those who don't speak English. Just do your job well, be on time, and things should go pretty well for you. Oh, and don't forget to clean Mr. Long's office meticulously. He's been known to blow his top if things aren't just to his liking. You'll begin this afternoon at five o'clock, so I suggest you go home now and rest."

Wei nodded his agreement and thanked Chou Ling for his help. Then he hurried to catch a bus home, knowing he would need to return in only a few hours for his first night on the job.

"Why are you home so soon?" Ting asked in surprise when Wei arrived at their apartment. "How was your first day of work?"

"I haven't even begun yet," Wei explained wearily. He was exhausted from the stress of learning bus routes, taking the children to school, and learning his work responsibilities.

"What happened? Is everything okay?"

"Well, my first surprise is that I won't be working during the day. I begin my shift at five o'clock in the afternoon and finish around midnight or later. This is going to mean a drastic change to our family's routine. Mei and Li will have to take the bus to school by themselves, and I must leave for work before they get home. I will hardly ever see them." He paused, then cried, "Oh, Ting, what have I done to our family by coming to America?"

Ting gave her husband a hug and tried to comfort him with a smile, although she, too, had encountered some unpleasant surprises during her day. "We will be okay eventually. We'll figure things out little by little. You should have seen me at that huge American supermarket. I did manage to buy several groceries all by myself, and everyone was very helpful. Well . . . almost everyone."

"What do you mean?" Wei asked.

"Well, I didn't have enough money to pay for everything I had put in my cart," Ting said, recalling her moment of helplessness. "I was confused trying to decide what I should put back, and the clerk lost patience with me. I don't know exactly what she said, but I knew she was angry that I didn't speak English and couldn't understand her. Finally, she took the bag of rice I wanted and put it back on the shelf. Then she gave me my change and waved for the next customer in line. I felt so embarrassed, and I know some of the people behind me were laughing."

"Perhaps the clerk, too, was having a difficult day," Wei reasoned.

Just then the door opened and Uncle Ping entered the apartment behind Mei and Li.

"I'm never ever going back to that school!" Mei cried angrily.

"Me neither!" Li shouted as he threw his school bag on the floor. "I hate that school. I hate all the kids in it."

Uncle Ping stared quietly at the floor.

"What happened?" Wei asked as he knelt down to comfort Mei and Li.

"Some boys made fun of Li and me," Mei said. "They squinted their eyes and called us names. We didn't know what they were saying, but another girl who speaks Chinese told us they were calling me 'China Girl' and laughing. Oh, Papa, I want to go back home to Kam Tin."

"Me, too," Li said as he began to cry.

"Ping, how could this have happened?" Ting asked. "Will you go to the school and talk to the director and the teachers? This is not right!"

"Yes, I will go to school with both of you tomorrow," Ping promised Mei and Li, saddened by what he was hearing. "I know there are some people who don't like Chinese immigrants. They can be cruel, and I should have warned you about them beforehand."

"Speaking of warnings," Wei said to his brother, "maybe you should have warned me about my job at the bank. Apparently, janitors in America do not enter through the front door. Then I found out I'm to work the night shift. What kind of job did you find for me, Ping?"

Sensing Wei's growing disappointment at many of the things that were happening to his family in their new country, Ping answered carefully, "Wei, I'm sorry you're having so many problems. But most of all, I'm sorry you're meeting people who are not being kind and helpful. Yet I am certain you will meet many more people who will welcome you and help you here in America. Don't forget the surprise party and the warm welcome you received the day you arrived."

Wei nodded, knowing Ping was right. But for now, the difficulties of adapting to a new culture and meeting disagreeable people seemed too great a burden to bear. "Thanks, Ping. Thank you for everything. I don't know what we would do without your help. Now, I have to catch the bus and get back to the bank. I start work in an hour."

"I'll take the children to school every day for a while until they get settled in," Ping said. "I'm sure in a week or so they'll be able to ride the bus on their own." Then he hugged Mei and Li, said good-bye, and left.

As Ting prepared a meal for Wei to take to work, no one said anything. Finally, Mei broke the silence. "I hate America," she said. "I want to go back home."

Li echoed his big sister's sentiments. "I want to go back home, too."

"This is now your home," Chang Wei said firmly. "Now, both of you go to your room. I don't want to hear another word about it, ever again. Do you understand?"

Mei and Li saw an anger in their father that they had never seen before. They stared at him in silence. He seemed like a stranger to them.

"I said go to your room—now!"

As Mei and Li walked slowly to the bedroom they shared, Ting turned to her husband. "I've never seen you so angry. I don't like it," she said, trying not to let her own anger and fear show. "You know you made the right decision in coming to America. Why, our village is probably now controlled by the revolutionary army. Who knows if we would even be alive had we stayed?"

Ting's words were like cold water in Wei's face. For a moment, he felt like shouting back. But instead he slumped into a chair and covered his face with his hands.

"Everything's gone wrong since we arrived here," he said in self pity. "I, too, am beginning to wish we hadn't come. Perhaps Mei is the only one in the family with enough courage to say out loud what each of us is really feeling."

"But you just told Mei and Li that America is home now, remember?" Ting said.

"But if I am to be honest, it really isn't home. I have doubts it ever will be," Wei said dejectedly.

"If that's what you really believe," Ting said, no longer trying to mask her frustration, "I will start packing tonight. But you'll have to get all the papers and passports arranged for us to go back. And just in case you've forgotten exactly why we came here, look at this." Ting thrust a Chinese-American newspaper into Wei's hands. "I bought this at the market. The war in China is getting worse every day. Mao is destroying his enemies. Is this what you want to take your family back to?"

Ting's words were delivered with such passion that Wei was deeply confused.

"Why are you talking to me this way?" he asked. "I've never heard you talk this way before."

"And I've never heard you talk the way you just talked to the children," Ting replied, trying to hold back her tears.

Chang Wei wanted to argue the point, but something inside warned him to stop. "I must leave for work soon," he said.

Without further words, Ting wrapped Wei's dinner, put it in a paper bag, and handed it to him. Wei headed for the door but stopped when he got there.

"I am sorry," he said. "I'm sorry for everything I said. I just don't know how the children will adjust. I don't know how you and I will adjust."

With tears in her eyes, Ting gave him a hug. "I love you, Wei," she said. "It's going to be okay. But please, before you leave, tell the children good night. Tell them, too, that we are all going to stay in America and that everything will be okay."

Wei kissed Ting gently and called for the children.

"Mei and Li," he said, fighting back his tears. "Please come out here. Papa has something important to say."

THINK ABOUT IT

» What kinds of people do Mei and Li encounter on the bus and at school? Who is kind to them? Who is unkind?
» Who is kind to Chang Wei on his first day at the bank? Who is unkind?
» What unhappy surprises does the mother, Ting, experience while shopping?
» How does this unhappy day affect the harmony in the Chang family? Why?
» What does Chang Wei finally do to help restore harmony in his family?

MISTER ROGERS' NEIGHBORHOOD

Fred Rogers was a Presbyterian minister who didn't like the way television treated children. Instead of talking down to them or bombarding them with color and noise, Mister Rogers wanted to speak to children honestly about important issues in a way that made them feel comfortable. So he developed a program called *Mister Rogers' Neighborhood*, inviting children of all ages into his home to sing songs and chat with his neighbors.

Photo © The Fred Rogers Company, used with permission.

Mister Rogers started out each episode by singing a song called "Won't You Be My Neighbor?" while changing out of his suit jacket and dress shoes into a sweater and sneakers. He spoke directly to his young viewers, taking them on tours of places like a factory or a bank or a bakery, constructing crafts, playing music, and interacting with his friends. He also told stories using hand-puppet characters who lived in a fantasy land called the Neighborhood of Make-Believe. With simple charm, Mister Rogers taught kids many lessons about growing up, from how to tie their shoes to how to handle scary things like war and death.

One of the most important things Mister Rogers wanted children to learn was that everyone is special and important. Because of this, he said, we should treat each person we meet with respect and courtesy, as we would a special neighbor. Mister Rogers also wanted to help children learn to cooperate with each other, be patient and attentive, and work through their feelings without losing control.

During his lifetime, Fred Rogers won many awards including the Presidential Medal of Freedom, the highest award given to U.S. civilians. Although Mister Rogers died in 2003, many stations around the country still run *Mister Rogers' Neighborhood* each day. Today, one of his sweaters hangs in the Smithsonian Institution, a testament to his influence on American culture and children of all ages.

WORDS YOU NEED TO KNOW

- » **Neighbor:** Every fellow human being
- » **Compassion:** Acts of tenderness and love we give to those who are hurting
- » **Friendliness:** Kind actions and gentle words that show and tell others how special they are

HIDE IT IN YOUR HEART

"Love your neighbor as yourself." (Leviticus 19:18)

A friend loves at all times. (Proverbs 17:17)

GOD'S GOOD NEIGHBOR POLICY

An insurance policy is an agreement in which a company promises to pay you money if you get sick or are injured, or to pay you money equal to the value of your property if it is damaged, lost, or stolen. Your parents probably make regular payments to at least one insurance company to protect your family from financial ruin in case of bad things that *might* happen in the future.

About four thousand years ago, the Babylonians developed an early form of insurance practiced by merchants who bought and sold goods among the port cities on the Mediterranean Sea. When a merchant received a loan to fund a venture, he would often pay the lender an additional sum of money in exchange for a guarantee that the lender would cancel the loan if the shipment were stolen or lost at sea. In this way, the merchant's business would be protected from ruin in case of a devastating loss.

During the nineteenth and twentieth centuries, insurance companies grew into huge corporations by offering affordable policies on people's homes, automobiles, valuables, health, and even their lives. In 1971, a then little-known songwriter named Barry Manilow was hired to compose a "jingle" to advertise the services of one of these companies. The song was catchy, and the commercials proved popular because they made people feel good about buying insurance. The lyrics went something like this:

Whenever you're driving
and wherever you're bound . . .
You'll feel better knowing
Anytime, anywhere,
That like a good neighbor
State Farm is there!

Since then, State Farm has grown to become the world's largest property and casualty insurance firm, and the company still uses the "Like a Good Neighbor" theme in many of its commercials.

Why would an insurance company want to compare itself to a good neighbor? Because a good neighbor is someone you can count on to be there for you. You might think of a corporation as cold and unfeeling, but a good neighbor is friendly and supportive. A corporation is concerned primarily with making money, but a good neighbor will give you the shirt off his back in times of need.

God wants His children to be good neighbors to the people around them, but being a good neighbor is about more than inviting the family next door to a backyard barbeque. Leviticus 19:18 says, "Love your neighbor as yourself." As we have seen, loving someone means placing the needs of that person before your own. Sometimes this will be inconvenient for you. The couple down the street might need an emergency babysitter when you were planning to go to the movies. The little boy next door might ask for help fixing a bicycle tire when you're on the phone with a friend. The family across the street might need a place to stay at two in the morning because a tree fell on their roof.

However, you shouldn't wait to be asked for help to show God's love to others. Here are just a few ways you can be a good neighbor starting right now:

» Look for opportunities to serve. Does your elderly neighbor's lawn need mowing? Has the wind or an animal tipped over a neighbor's trash can? If so, lend a helping hand.
» Share a smile with everyone you see.
» Spread cheer by speaking words of encouragement to others (Proverbs 12:25).
» Get to know your neighbors. The better you know your neighbors, the more ways you will see to help them.
» Treat others the way you want to be treated (Luke 6:31).

You can begin by trying to do at least one good deed every day, but don't call attention to the things you do for others. And do not expect to be thanked or paid for your kindness. God will know when you help a neighbor out of the goodness of your heart, and He will reward you (Matthew 6:4).

Kindness has converted more sinners than zeal, eloquence, or learning.
Henrietta Mears
1890–1963

DELIGHT IN SERVING YOUR NEIGHBOR

We've talked a lot already about how God wants us to serve others. But an act of service is sometimes just that—an act. Some Christians participate in mission trips or ministry outreaches just to impress their friends or hang out with the youth group. Others do it to feel good about themselves. Some serve because they feel guilty, while others do it to earn favor with God. But all these people are missing the point. Servanthood is not just something we're supposed to *do*; it's something we are meant to *be*.

Ruth and Boaz by von Carolsfeld.

True servanthood is an attitude of the heart, and you can always recognize a true servant by the joy and delight he or she takes in serving others. Ruth joyfully served her mother-in-law, Naomi. Joseph delighted in serving first Potiphar and, later, Pharaoh and did so to the very best of his ability. Paul poured himself out on behalf of the churches he served and was overwhelmed with joy when they followed his example (Philippians 2:1–4).

Loving your neighbors should never be considered drudgery. You see, serving others is not something you *have to do* in order to be saved—your ticket to heaven has already been punched because Jesus paid for your sins in full. Serving people is something you *get to do* because He has saved you. The people of this world need what you have, and because God has brought you into His family, you now have the wonderful opportunity to share through your words and deeds the good news of His amazing love and His free gift of salvation!

If you ever find yourself having "one of those days" when things aren't going your way and you get caught up in thinking about yourself—*your* problems, *your* wants, *your* needs, the things *you* don't have—then it's time to shift your focus. Stop thinking about yourself and start thinking about what you can do to help someone else. When you choose to give up self-centered thinking and instead focus on helping others, the joy of the Lord will fill your heart and be your strength.

God says, "My servants will shout for joy because of the goodness of their hearts" (Isaiah 65:14, NCV). Allow the Holy Spirit to stir up joy within your heart and give you the boldness to share your joy with others. True joy is a sign of God's presence, and when you serve others joyfully, people will sing the praises of the God who sent you (Matthew 5:16).

This doesn't mean you should put on a smile and *pretend* to be happy when you serve others. People are quick to recognize a phony. True joy means constantly delighting in God regardless of your circumstances. Indeed, when you selflessly serve others with acts of genuine love, the Lord will rejoice over you and you will share in His joy as a reward! (Matthew 25:21).

"I Was Hungry, and You Gave Me Food"

You learned from Jesus' parable of the good Samaritan that not all your neighbors live in your neighborhood. Your neighbors include people you like and people you don't like. Your neighbors include people who live in a different town, a different state, or a different country. Your neighbors include people who speak a different language, people whose skin is a different color, and people who practice a different religion. That's because we are commanded to love all people, no matter who they are or where they live, simply because God loves them and made them in His image.

Loving our neighbors also means serving people from all walks of life, including strangers, widows, the poor, the sick, and even prisoners. Today, as in Jesus' time, such people are often neglected. But if we are to be the Lord's hands and feet in this world, we must share His love for "the least of these" (Matthew 25:40). Jesus angered many "religious" people and defied the expectations of others by caring for the lost, the forgotten, and the downtrodden. He touched lepers (Matthew 8:3). He welcomed the company of women (Luke 8:1–5) and children (Luke 18:16). He dined with criminals (Luke 19:1–10), and He preached to heretics (John 4:4–14). He took compassion on the poor (Luke 6:20–21), and

He defended the powerless (John 8:1–11).

When you see a person who is in need, remember what God has done for you. God showed his great love for you by sending Christ to die for you while you were still a sinner (Romans 5:8). He took compassion on you and sacrificed His Son as the payment for your guilt so that you could be called His child and have a home with Him. **Compassion** is an act of tenderness and love given to someone who is hurting or in need. Compassion isn't always our first reaction when we see someone in need. We might feel sorry for the person, but there's a big difference between pity and compassion. God commands us to take action and follow His example by giving love and mercy to those who are poor, hungry, sick, far from home, or in prison:

Whoever is generous to the poor lends to the LORD, and he will repay him for his deed. (Proverbs 19:17, ESV)

"When you give a banquet, invite the poor, the crippled, the lame, the blind, and you will be blessed. Although they cannot repay you, you will be repaid at the resurrection of the righteous." (Luke 14:13–14)

The stranger who dwells among you shall be to you as one born among you, and you shall love him as yourself. (Leviticus 19:34, NKJV)

Remember those in prison as if you were their fellow prisoners, and those who are mistreated as if you yourselves were suffering. (Hebrews 13:3)

James wrote, "Suppose a brother or sister is without clothes and daily food. If one of you says to him, 'Go, I wish you well; keep warm and well fed,' but does nothing about his physical needs, what good is it?" (James 2:15–16). The apostle John wrote, "If someone has enough money to live well and sees a brother or sister in need but shows no compassion—how can God's love be in that person? Dear children, let's not merely say that we love each other; let us show the truth by our actions" (1 John 3:17–18, NLT).

Jesus declared that one day every one of us will stand before His throne, and we will have to answer for how we treated our neighbors. Our King will then say to those who have loved their neighbors, "Come, my Father has given you his blessing. Receive the kingdom God has prepared for you since the world was made. I was hungry, and you gave me food. I was thirsty, and you gave me something to drink. I was alone and away from home, and you invited me into your house. I was without clothes, and you gave me something to wear. I was sick, and you cared for me. I was in prison, and you visited me." Then the people will ask, "Lord, when did we see you hungry and give you food, or thirsty and give you something to drink? When did we see you alone and away from home and invite you into our house? When did we see you without clothes and give you something to wear? When did we see you sick or in prison and care for you?" Jesus will answer, "I tell you the truth, anything you did for even the least of my people here, you also did for me" (Matthew 25:35–40, NCV).

The eighth-century monk and historian known as the Venerable Bede wrote, "He alone loves the Creator perfectly who manifests a pure love for his neighbor." Will you serve Jesus today by serving your neighbors? God may never call you to sell everything you have and give it all to the poor, but He does want you to get started helping people. Of course, when we open our eyes to all the heartbreak and pain and suffering in a world that has been ravaged by sin, it's easy to become overwhelmed by the many needs and throw our hands up in despair. But God promises that you *can* make a difference. He is at work in the world, and He wants to work through you. What an awesome privilege!

WARNING!

We live in a fallen world where there are people who might want to hurt or take advantage of a young person, even one who is trying to do good for others. Such people are looking for children and teens who are alone, not walking in pairs or groups. Remember the buddy system! Even the grown-up disciples were sent out two by two to share the Good News (Luke 10:1). It's always wise to bring a parent or a friend when you're ministering to others. If you go with a friend, be sure to tell your parents where you are going and what you are doing.

DAVID AND JONATHAN

One of the Bible's most vivid examples of friendship is the relationship between David and Jonathan. Jonathan was the son of King Saul and a fine warrior in his own right (1 Samuel 14:1–13). Yet he understood that the shepherd David was blessed by God to become a great leader. So Jonathan gave up his rightful ambitions and made it his mission to support and protect his friend, even though it meant Jonathan would never be king.

Early in their friendship David and Jonathan made a vow of loyalty, promising to care for one another as much as they cared for their own lives. As a sign of their friendship, Jonathan took off the robe and tunic he was wearing and gave them to David, along with his sword, his bow, and his belt (1 Samuel 18:1–4). Several times King Saul tried to kill David, and several times Jonathan stopped him. By setting aside his rights as a prince and supporting God's chosen one wholeheartedly, Jonathan demonstrated a friendship that was true and pure.

The friendship between David and Jonathan is illustrated in a beautiful painting from the early 1500s by Italian artist Giovanni Cima de Conegliano. In the painting David holds the head of the giant Goliath and carries a sword, his slingshot hanging from his belt. Next to him, Jonathan carries a javelin, perhaps the one his father would later use to try to strike David (1 Samuel 19:9–10). David looks straight ahead, focused on his destiny, while Jonathan watches David rather than the road ahead, showing that his loyalty to David is more important to him than princely ambition.

LOVE YOUR FRIENDS—AND YOUR ENEMIES

There's an old saying that goes, "A friend in need is a friend indeed." True friendship is a rare jewel that, once you find it, is to be greatly prized. Such friendships are uncommon because true friendship requires unconditional love and self-sacrifice, and each must be willing to serve the other whatever the need. Selfishness has no place in such a relationship. Yet Proverbs 18:24 tells us, "There is a friend who sticks closer than a brother." One such friendship was that of David and Jonathan.

Jonathan was a prince, the oldest son of King Saul, and probably would have succeeded his father on the throne of Israel if Saul had not repeatedly disobeyed God. Jonathan loved the Lord and His people and trusted God to go with him into battle (1 Samuel 14:6). David, on the other hand, was a shepherd boy and the youngest of his father's sons. He, too, loved the Lord and His people, and when the Philistine giant Goliath terrorized the armies of Saul, David trusted God to go with him into battle (1 Samuel 17:37).

David and Jonathan became the closest of friends. Indeed, the Bible says that Jonathan loved David as he loved himself (1 Samuel 20:17) and that they were "one in spirit" (1 Samuel 18:1). And although David had been anointed to replace Jonathan as the future king of Israel, there was no rivalry or jealousy between them. They accepted the Lord's will and trusted His wisdom. Still, the bonds of their friendship would be tested on more than one occasion, but the two friends remained steadfastly committed to one another.

David and Saul by Josephson.

Several years after David had been crowned king and Jonathan was killed in battle, David sought out one of Saul's former servants. David asked him, "Is there anyone still left of the house of Saul to whom I can show kindness for Jonathan's sake?" (2 Samuel 9:1). The servant told him of Mephibosheth, Jonathan's son who was lame in both feet. David summoned Mephibosheth to Jerusalem.

Mephibosheth, who also had a son, must have been terrified as he bowed before the king. After all, his grandfather had tried often to kill David, and David must surely count Saul's descendants among his enemies. The best he could hope for was exile. But David said to the young man, "Don't be afraid, for I will surely show you kindness for the sake of your father Jonathan. I will restore to you all the land that belonged to your grandfather Saul, and you will always eat at my table" (2 Samuel 9:7). Mephibosheth had been crippled in a childhood accident (2 Samuel 4:4) and could not work the land, so David assigned servants to farm the land for him, thus providing for his family. From that day David cared for Mephibosheth as his own son.

The unconditional love David showed to Mephibosheth is a beautiful expression of love and mercy and a sign of his friendship with Jonathan. It's also a wonderful illustration of the love that God has for you and me. There was no law that required David to take care of Mephibosheth, but when David learned of the man's condition, he was moved to compassion and reached out to the son of Jonathan. Mephibosheth had done nothing to earn this act of grace, and he could do nothing to repay the king for his kindness. Nevertheless, David raised him up from his lowly condition, welcomed him into the kingdom, and embraced him as his own child.

Likewise, you and I were once enemies of God (Romans 5:10). As descendants of Adam, who was given dominion over the earth but then was exiled from Eden for his disobedience, we are members of a fallen family. Born into sin and helpless to overcome our predicament, we were alienated from the King and lived in fear of His wrath. But God loved Adam, and He loves us, too. And in His infinite mercy and grace, He sought us out and called us to Him. Now a place has been prepared for us in the King's house (John 14:2), and we have the privilege of being called children of God (John 1:12–13). We enjoy loving fellowship with God because He first loved us (1 John 4:19).

So if God loved you and reached out to you when you were still His enemy, how then should you treat those who hurt you or ridicule your beliefs? What about the enemies of your country, those who hate you and curse you because of where you were born? Jesus said it plainly: "Love your enemies, do good to those who hate you, bless those who curse you, pray for those who mistreat you" (Luke 6:27–28).

Betrayal of Christ by van Dyck.

Love your enemies? Do good to those who hate you? Serving friends and strangers may not always be easy, but the idea of loving and serving your enemies can seem downright unpleasant. Once again, we must look to Jesus for our example to follow. On the night before His death, He not only humbly washed the feet of His friends, but He also washed the feet of Judas, the man He knew was about to betray Him to the authorities (John 13:2–5). And even in Jesus' final hours, He prayed for those who were crucifying Him (Luke 23:34). He could have called down twelve legions of angels to vanquish His enemies (Matthew 26:53). Instead, He asked His Father to forgive them.

Yes, even Jesus had enemies, and despite how good and kind we may be, we too will have enemies. Jesus warned us, "You will be hated all over the world because you are my followers" (Matthew 24:9, NLT). But the apostle Paul makes it clear that no matter what people say about us or do to us, we must love them as God loves them:

Never pay back evil with more evil. . . . Do all that you can to live in peace with everyone. (Romans 12:17–18, NLT)

Jesus said, "Blessed are the peacemakers, for they will be called sons of God" (Matthew 5:9). As Christians, we should always be willing to take the first step toward peace through acts of love. There are some who will not want peace, but as far as it depends on us, we should strive for harmony with our neighbors.

Revenge is never an option. The Bible tells us, "Do not be overcome by evil, but overcome evil with good" (Romans 12:21). Proverbs 16:7 (NCV) says, "When people live so that they please the Lord, even their enemies will make peace with them." Think of that: The key to victory over our enemies is not being bigger and stronger. It's not superior strategy, greater numbers, or the element of surprise. Instead, the way to overcome our enemies is by doing good and living in a way that pleases the Lord.

Your task is to love all people, including those who treat you badly. If you love your enemies and serve them, your actions might transform their attitudes. But even if they never change their minds about you, remember that if you don't forgive those who offend you then you cannot expect God to forgive you when you sin (Matthew 6:14–15).

MAKE A NOTE OF IT

Are there certain individuals or groups of people you dislike or feel uncomfortable around? People from a certain country? People of a particular race or religion? Teens who wear strange clothes and weird haircuts? The neighborhood bully? Be honest. Now make it a goal to pray for everyone on your list every day for a month. How might praying for these people change the way you think about them?

> *We can find no greater inspiration to love even our enemies as brothers and sisters . . . than grateful remembrance of Christ's wonderful patience.*
> **Aelred of Rievaulx**
> 1109–1167

WHAT SHOULD I DO?

Do you consider yourself a "friendly" person? **Friendliness** consists of kind actions and gentle words that show others how special they are. Are you friendly only to those people you think of as your friends? The Bible tells us that friendliness is more than a feeling; it's a character trait that shows people what is in our hearts. As followers of Christ, we are to be friendly to our enemies (Romans 12:20) and to people who come from other lands (Exodus 22:21; Hebrews 13:2), as well as to

the poor, the physically handicapped, and those who have been rejected by society (Luke 14:12–14).

Too often people are friendly only to those whose friendship is desirable or useful. Some seek friendship with wealthy people who will buy them nice gifts and get them into all the best parties. Others seek friendship with influential people who can help them get better jobs or increase their own influence. Some will hang out only with physically attractive people, while others limit their social interaction to those who share their particular interests and attitudes. These kinds of relationships last only as long as it's convenient for both parties. Because there's no real loyalty or commitment involved, such fair-weather friendships are often quickly ended when difficult circumstances arise.

A true friend, on the other hand, loves at all times (Proverbs 17:17). Being a friend is a commitment to serve and to be loyal to others just as Jesus Christ is committed and loyal to us. Biblical friendliness is not self-seeking but is shared in a spirit of self-sacrifice, humility, and grace toward others. And because we were all created by the same God in His image (Malachi 2:10), we are to think of all people as important and treat them as we want to be treated (Matthew 7:12).

To be a good friend, you must honor your neighbors (Romans 12:10), be hospitable and share with those in need (Romans 12:13), be patient with those whose faith is weak (Romans 15:1), and do all you can to encourage and build up others in every way (Romans 15:2). By loving others in this way and sharing your faith through words and deeds, you can bring many into the unity of believers whom Jesus calls His friends (John 15:12–17).

MAKE A NOTE OF IT

Write about or draw pictures of at least three ways in which Jesus has shown Himself to be your friend.

A PRAYER

Dear God, thank you for loving me even when I sinned against you. I want to be a good neighbor. Help me to love my neighbors all over the world and serve them the way Jesus served people. Help me to forgive those who hurt me or hate me. And work in my heart to help me to be friendly to everyone I meet. I pray this in Jesus' name. Amen.

Friendship is born at that moment when one person says to another, "What! You too? I thought I was the only one."
C. S. Lewis
1898–1963

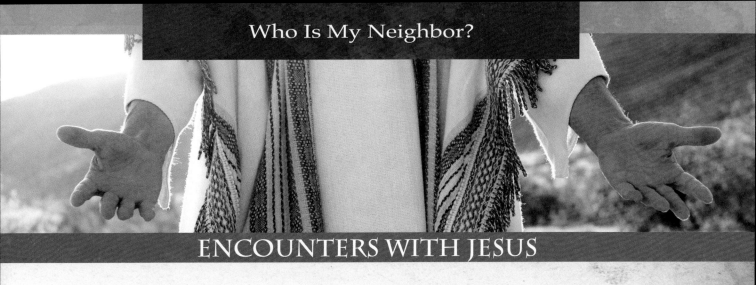

ENCOUNTERS WITH JESUS

SCRAPS FROM THE TABLE

Antonia said nothing but listened closely. The women at the market had been going on and on about the miracle worker from Galilee, but no one seemed to know exactly what he looked like or where he could be found. Some said that he traveled on foot and dressed like a common worker. Others said he was a king and that hundreds followed him wherever he went.

"My cousin talked to a man whose wife had been sick for months," one of the women said. "This Jesus just touched her, and she was completely healed!"

Another woman spoke up eagerly. "My brother was there when Jesus fed a huge crowd from a few pieces of barley bread and some sardines!"

But it was one old woman's story that really captured Antonia's attention. "My grandson followed this Jesus for a whole week, listening to him teach and watching what he did. And he said that the man even drove demons out of people."

Antonia's daughter Cassandra was controlled by an unclean spirit. Antonia had thought for the longest time that her daughter was just throwing temper tantrums. But as Cassandra grew, the fits had come more often and lasted longer each time. Lately, Antonia could find little of her daughter anymore among the ravings of the demon within her. The sight of her daughter's anguish broke Antonia's heart.

Now hope rose within her at this news of a healer who could cast out demons. She slipped away from the others and hurried through the market, asking everyone who looked like a traveler if they knew of Jesus and where he was to be found. At last a man told her he had just come from Damascus and had seen Jesus and his followers walking the western road toward Tyre.

Tyre at the turn of the last century.

As she ran home, Antonia was already planning. The city of Tyre drew many visitors to the Roman province of Phoenicia in Syria. Antonia's

Canaanite ancestors had settled in these coastlands centuries ago when the Jews drove them out of Palestine. Antonia decided she would go to Tyre herself, find this Jesus, and plead with him to cast the demon out of her daughter.

Breathlessly, she told her husband, Marcus, what she had learned. "And they said that this Jesus was on his way to Tyre! If only I could talk with him and tell him of the way Cassandra suffers, surely he would have compassion for her."

Marcus furrowed his brow. "You have already traveled to Rome to pray in the temples there. You've consulted doctors, priests, and magicians, but their charms and potions only made her worse! How is this man any different?"

Antonia fell to her knees and pleaded with her husband. "Because people speak of many being set free from demons. I asked everyone in the market who had even heard this

man's name, and they all spoke of his power." She twisted her hands in her lap. "If Jesus cannot heal our daughter, I know she will soon die. The demon will cause her to throw herself into the fire or drown herself in the sea. I don't know what else to do." Tears rolled down her cheeks, welling up from the anguish deep in her soul.

Marcus stepped behind her and put his hands on her shoulders. "Very well. You may go to Tyre to find this Jewish healer. I will send a servant to accompany you."

Antonia leapt to her feet. "Oh, thank you! Thank you!"

Marcus almost smiled at her enthusiasm, but he then turned grim. "But if this does not work, I fear I will have to send Cassandra away before she harms you or one of our neighbors."

"I know he can help us," she said.

Antonia rubbed at the headache that was spreading across her forehead. Her eyes were gritty, and dust had collected like a second skin on her arms and feet. But a little dirt would not stop her from finding the man she sought.

Already she had stopped countless times along the road to ask if anyone had seen Jesus. Every time, she had received the same answer: no. She didn't care that she was making a spectacle of herself—a married woman traveling without her husband and speaking boldly to strangers. She cared only about finding the man who could heal her daughter.

When she and the servant arrived in Tyre, she went first to the local inn to inquire after Jesus, but no one knew of his arrival. She then went to the marketplace and talked with every seller of goods. Just when Antonia was ready to move on, a merchant told her about a Jewish man who was hosting a large group of men at his home for the Passover feast.

"I think it was unexpected, the men arriving, because Abraham came to buy extra food and wine. There were at least a dozen of them. I think they're all friends or business associates or something."

Antonia gripped the man's hand eagerly. "Please tell me the way to his house. I must speak with Jesus immediately."

The merchant pointed behind her. "I don't have to—there are a few of Abraham's guests right there."

She turned quickly. Three commonly dressed men were leaving the market. "Thank you!" she gasped, then hastily followed them.

Antonia hurried down the crowded street, forgetting everything, even the servant trailing behind her. She must see Jesus today, for she had lost much time already and was trying not to imagine what could be happening to Cassandra while she was gone.

Antonia followed the three men closely, not bothering to disguise her intentions. Occasionally, the men would look back at her as if to ask why she was following them, but they did not speak to her. Antonia was not offended. She was, after all, a woman and a foreigner. She knew that Jews weren't allowed to associate with foreigners, especially during their sacred holidays—they were to keep themselves pure so that their god would accept their sacrifices and prayers.

She herself had gone through many hardships on account of the gods, prostrating herself before cold marble statues and offering countless gifts and sacrifices, trying to earn the favor of a god powerful enough to heal Cassandra. But all her efforts had been in vain, and Cassandra weakened more every day under the demon's influence. The miracle worker from Galilee was her last hope.

Arriving at what Antonia assumed to be Abraham's door, the men knocked and were admitted. Afraid they would disappear into the house for good, she desperately tried to slip in after them.

"Please, I must speak with the man called Jesus, the one they call the Son of David."

The servant at the door grabbed her arm and wrestled her back across the threshold. "No!"

Antonia shrieked, terrified at the thought of failing when Jesus was so near. "I must speak with him!"

"You cannot bother the rabbi here. He seeks seclusion and has been granted refuge in my master's house." The servant pushed her out into the street and shut the door before she could respond.

Antonia leaned against the wooden door, trying to calm her rising panic. Jesus was here! She had finally found the man who could cure her daughter, but they would not let her see him. In desperation, Antonia did the only thing she could think of: She began to wail loudly, as if someone had died. Passersby looked at her strangely, but Antonia persisted. If she returned home without a miracle, these mourning wails would eventually be for Cassandra.

Within moments the servant opened the door again. "Stop that!" he ordered. "You will not win anyone's favor like this!"

"I must speak with Jesus!" she cried. "I must speak with the King of the Jews!"

The servant appeared shocked and looked up and down the street for Roman soldiers. This kind of attention could get his master and his guests arrested for stirring up rebellion against Rome. Quickly, he shut the door again.

Antonia continued her cries, beating her fists against the door. "I must speak with him! Let me speak with Jesus!"

Soon the door reopened, but this time it was the master of the house who answered, the servant standing nervously behind him. "Woman, what are you doing?" Abraham asked. "I cannot admit a Gentile into my house, especially during the Passover."

Antonia knelt at his feet, her tears dropping into the dust. "Please, sir, my daughter is grievously afflicted by a demon. I beg your permission to ask Jesus to release her from it."

Whether it was her humble tears or

Courtyard of an ancient home in Palestine.

the passage of a Roman courier in the street behind her, Abraham sighed and relented. "You may come into the courtyard, but I cannot allow you any further into my home. If you agree to behave like a sane person, I will ask the rabbi if he will come speak with you. You cannot touch him, though, or you will make him unclean."

Antonia wiped the tears and dust from her face with a corner of her sleeve. "I will do anything you ask, sir, if only I may speak with Jesus."

Abraham's servant ushered her into the center of the courtyard, then hovered in the background, watching to make certain she didn't do anything foolish. After a moment, Abraham returned, bringing with him a group of men. Among them were the three she had followed to the house.

"That is the woman we were telling you about, Lord," said one of them, a fisherman by the look of his strong arms and tanned skin.

Antonia fastened her gaze on the one called Jesus as he stepped toward her. She felt instantly that this was a man of true power—not like the priests and doctors she had consulted before.

Carefully, reverently, she prostrated herself before Jesus, keeping well out of his reach, knowing she had already violated many cultural boundaries. Now that she had gained an audience with Jesus, she didn't want to risk losing his favor by breaking any more rules.

"Please, Son of David, I beg you to deliver my daughter from the power of the demon that controls her." She dared to glance up at his face, hoping for a sign of compassion.

But Jesus answered not a word.

She held her breath, thinking perhaps it was some trait of a great rabbi to make petitioners wait.

In the awkward silence, one of the men said to Jesus, "Teacher, please send her away, for she is bothersome. We came here seeking peace and solitude, but she is drawing attention to us."

Eyes never leaving Antonia's face, Jesus said to her, "I have been sent only to the lost sheep of Israel."

"Sir, please help me," she said, no longer crying. "I have no other hope."

Jesus said, "It is not right to take away the children's bread and give it to their dogs."

Antonia was startled for a second. For a moment, she wanted to scream. Her every thought, her every breath had been concentrated on freeing her precious child. Why wouldn't this man help her when it was within his power to do so? But her fear and anger melted away as she looked into the eyes of the man before her. His compassion for the suffering of her daughter was clear.

With a burst of clarity, like lightning to her heart, the thought came to her that it was not his will that prevented him from granting her request; it was her own stubbornness and lack of faith.

Tears streaming from her eyes, Antonia laid her face in the dust and let go of all her hopes, dreams, and desires. There was no reason in earth or heaven that this holy man should heed her request. She knew she was unworthy to even be in his presence. Only the mercy in his eyes gave her hope and boldness.

"Yes, Lord," she said. "But even dogs are allowed to eat the crumbs that fall from the table during the meal."

Jesus said, "Woman, you have great faith! Go in peace, for your daughter is healed." The warmth and tenderness in his voice filled Antonia's heart with an amazing peace, chasing away all the fear and worry that had weighed her down for so many years.

A drawing of Jesus healing by Rembrandt.

As she lifted her face to Him, she knew without a doubt that Cassandra was now free—as certainly as if she were standing by her daughter's bedside at that very moment, watching her sleep peacefully, untroubled by nightmares for the first time in years. Antonia also knew her own life would never be the same because she had seen the power of the living God.

TAKE A CLOSER LOOK

- Read the biblical accounts of these events in Mark 7:25–30 and Matthew 15:21–28 and compare them to the story you've just read.

- What made Antonia believe that Jesus could heal her daughter? How would you tell someone about God's love and His power to heal?

- Antonia wouldn't take no for an answer. Why did the master of the house finally let her in?

- Read Luke 11:5–9. What do you suppose Jesus thought of Antonia's determination?

- Jesus told the woman, "I was sent only to the lost sheep of Israel. It is not right to take the children's bread and toss it to their dogs." Was He insulting her? What do you think He meant by using this metaphor?

- Jesus said the woman had "great faith." How did she demonstrate her faith?

- Have you read the book of Leviticus lately? The Jewish people had to follow a great many rules and rituals to cleanse themselves and live as God's chosen people. As followers of Christ, how are we made clean in the sight of God?

- How did Jesus serve Antonia? What do you think His actions meant to her? How does this story help us understand who our neighbors are?

WHY DID GOD MAKE FAMILIES?

> THEREFORE WHAT GOD HAS JOINED TOGETHER, LET MAN NOT SEPARATE.

MARK 10:9

THE BIG IDEA

As we have seen, God made us to live in relationship with Him, to depend on Him, but He also made us to depend on one another. The Bible says that God made Eve to be, among other things, Adam's "helper" (Genesis 2:18), but what was she meant to help him do? After all, what kind of work was there to do in the Garden of Eden? Wasn't it perfect already?

Many people think work is a punishment we received when Adam and Eve sinned against God and were evicted from the garden. But work has always been a part of God's perfect plan, even before the Fall. God works, and so do people made in His image. Jesus worked as a carpenter, building furniture and plows, until He was thirty because that's what His Father in heaven (and His father on earth) showed Him to do. Work is a very good thing, and hard work is rewarded in many ways, including the satisfaction of a job well done. Indeed, the apostle Paul taught the believers at Thessalonica that they should "aspire" to work with their hands (1 Thessalonians 4:11, NKJV). After all, the Bible says, "The sleep of a laborer is sweet" (Ecclesiastes 5:12).

And so when God made Adam and Eve, He didn't tell them to just kick back, relax, and enjoy the scenery in the garden. Instead, He gave them a list of very important jobs to do:

God blessed them and said to them, "Be fruitful and increase in number; fill the earth and subdue it. Rule over the fish in the sea and the birds in the sky and over every living creature that moves on the ground." (Genesis 1:28)

And you think *you* had a long chore list when you got up this morning!

Think about the size of the earth and the enormity of what God was telling Adam and Eve to do. Fill the earth? Subdue it? Rule over every living creature? How would they accomplish these things? Clearly, they would need some help. So God blessed Adam and Eve and said to them, "Be fruitful and increase in number; fill the earth." The traditional King James Version reads, "Be fruitful and multiply." One modern translation simply says, "Have a lot of children!" (CEV).

Having children is not something any one person can do alone. A man and a woman are required in order for children to be conceived. And so God created marriage, in which a man and woman are joined together as husband and wife to form the beginnings of a family. Of course, even a family cannot fill the entire earth. When God commanded Adam and Eve to fill the earth, He was telling them to populate the earth through *many* generations of families. And as the number of people on the earth increased, together they would be able to obey God's command to take care of the earth.

So when exactly does a married couple become a family? Sometimes we think a family is not really a family until a husband and wife have children. But in fact, a husband and a wife are already a family. This family grows larger when the man and woman give birth to children or adopt them. An "extended" family also includes such people as grandparents, aunts, uncles, and cousins.

Today, people have different beliefs about what makes a family. Some think a family is any group of people who want to live together. But the Bible teaches that God creates a new family by bringing one man and one woman together in marriage as husband and wife. And it's within the family that we learn to serve our neighbors in love. After all, the people who share a home with you are the closest neighbors you'll ever have.

God wants the husband and wife to love, honor, and care for each other as long as they both live. Children are to serve and honor their parents with respect and obedience, and parents serve their children by lovingly nurturing them, teaching them, and providing for their needs. Children in the family are to serve one another by putting the needs of their brothers and sisters ahead of their own.

But people aren't perfect, and families sometimes have problems. A husband and wife might choose to divorce, or a parent may die. Sad situations such as these change a family, but they do not change God's love for us or His perfect plan for our lives. God still wants parents to raise their children in love and teach them about Him, and He still wants children to honor and obey their parents in the Lord (Ephesians 6:1–4).

WHAT YOU WILL DO
» You will understand God's plan for marriage and recognize the covenant between husband and wife as the foundation of the family.
» You will identify the basic responsibilities of parents in a family.
» You will identify the basic responsibilities of children in a family.

FRANCIS OF ASSISI

Francis of Assisi was born in 1181 to wealthy parents in an Italian village. He served as a soldier and worked as a merchant, living the carefree, high-spirited life of a wealthy young man. But in his early twenties, Francis had a vision that changed his focus.

Leaving behind his wealth, Francis exchanged his finery for beggar's clothes and became a wandering preacher. He wanted nothing more than to follow Jesus' teachings and "walk in His footsteps," without possessions or material wealth to distract him from God. Within a year Francis had eleven followers. They spent their days preaching and ministering to ordinary people in the countryside, always cheerful and full of songs.

This was the beginning of the Franciscan Order of friars, men who were pledged solely to imitate the life of Christ and carry out His work. The monks weren't allowed to own anything but the most basic essentials and were expected to use any money they received to provide for the poor and needy.

Francis of Assisi by Ribera.

Francis of Assisi is best known today for his simple lifestyle, love for his fellow human beings, and an affection for animals. He is also thought to have conceived the first Nativity scene, a three-dimensional depiction of the events surrounding the birth of Christ. Whereas many homes today display such scenes using decorative figurines, Francis's was a "living" Nativity that used live people and animals to make the story of Jesus' birth come alive for worshipers.

Photo of church © BrokenSphere / Wikimedia Commons

A Christmas Surprise

One chilly November morning, Chang Wei announced to Mei and Li at breakfast, "Today, your mother and I are going to take our first English lesson. Uncle Ping has arranged for a teacher to come here three mornings a week. What do you think about that?"

Mei grinned at Li happily, for they had already begun to learn English from teachers and students at school. "Oh, Papa, that means Li and I can practice our English with you and Mother. Then we'll all learn faster."

"Well, I don't think we'll ever learn as quickly as you and Li, but if you help us, maybe one day we'll be able to say a few words." Wei laughed. "And since our teacher will be here right after breakfast, you will have to ride the bus by yourselves today."

"All by ourselves?" Mei said with fear in her eyes. "We can't do that, Papa. We can't!"

"No, we can't," Li echoed.

"Of course you can," Ting assured them. "You've ridden the bus many times with Papa or Uncle Ping. You know the route by now, and the bus driver knows who you are. Uncle Ping has already told the driver, Mr. Merriman, that you'll be riding by yourselves, so he'll be watching out for you."

Mei and Li knew not to argue, but they weren't at all sure about this new development.

"Now, here's your bus fare," their father said. "Walk straight to the corner and wait with the other riders. Everything will be fine. Uncle Ping will pick you up after school, as usual. Mei, you be sure to hold Li's hand."

As Mei and Li approached the bus stop, they recognized several of the regular passengers but said nothing. Some smiled at them, but others ignored them or kept reading their newspapers.

"I'm scared, Mei," Li said. "Uncle Ping always helps us, and he always pays the fare."

"Hold onto my hand," Mei said, trying to act like a responsible older sister. "Here comes the bus."

As the crowd moved as one body toward the open door of the bus, they were surprised to see the driver, Mr. Merriman, stand up and descend to the first step.

"Now everyone, please back away for just a moment," he said. "We have two very special riders today. Please allow Chang Mei and her brother, Chang Li, to board first—just for today—since this is their first solo bus ride to school."

Most of the crowd stepped aside courteously, and a few even applauded as Mr. Merriman helped Mei and Li up the steps and welcomed them aboard.

Mei and Li grinned at each other self-consciously. "Thank you, Mr. Merriman," Mei said, practicing her English.

"You're welcome, Mei," Mr. Merriman replied.

"Wow," Li whispered in Mei's ear when they took their seats, "Mr. Merriman is a nice man. I really like him."

"Me, too," Mei whispered back as she opened her Chinese-English dictionary. "Now, Li, when I point to a picture, you say the English word for it."

"Horse," Li said.

"No," Mei laughed, "cow. It's a cow."

Li laughed too, then repeated, "Cow."

Chang Wei and Chang Ting also laughed at themselves as they struggled through their first English lesson at home. "Me name Chang Wei," Wei said self-consciously.

"My name is Chang Wei," the teacher corrected with a smile.

"My name is Chang Ting," Ting said, knowing she had pronounced the pronoun correctly and included the verb. With great effort and concentration, Wei and Ting worked diligently through the lesson.

"You are fine students," Mrs. Choo said encouragingly at the end of their session. "Why, you'll be speaking perfect English in no time. Now practice with your children as much as you can each day. I will be back on Wednesday morning."

"Good-bye," Wei said proudly in English.

"Thank you," Ting added, also in English.

After Mrs. Choo left, Wei repeated, "My name Change Wei. My name Chang Wei."

"No, Wei," Ting said. "'My name is Chang Wei.'"

"Enough English for today," Wei said in Chinese. "But I like Mrs. Choo. I'm already looking forward to our next lesson on Wednesday."

"I am, too," Ting agreed. "She is very patient and kind."

"Oh, I forgot to tell you," Wei said, looking at his watch. "Mr. Blackstone told me I needed to come to work early today. He said something about a special project."

"Special project?" Ting asked. "If you work extra hours, do you think you'll be paid more?"

"I don't know," Wei replied. "But I need to be on my way. I hope to be home by midnight, but I'm not sure about that either." He kissed Ting, put on his jacket, and headed out the door.

Photo by Esra.

"Good afternoon, Wei," Chou Ling said as Wei entered the bank through the alley door. "I see you got the message. You and I have been chosen to work on a special project."

"What kind of project, Ling?" Wei asked. "And why was I chosen?"

"Well, I gave Mr. Blackstone your name," Ling answered. "I told him you were our best janitor, and I thought you'd be the best person to work with me on this project."

"Thank you very much," Wei said, embarrassed and pleased at the same time. "Will we do this project before or after my regular duties?"

"You won't be cleaning any offices tonight. You and I are in charge of decorating the bank lobby for Christmas," Chou Ling said with a twinkle in his eye. "We're going to hang wreaths, decorate the Christmas tree, and then arrange the Nativity under the tree. How's that for a special assignment?"

"Wreaths? Christmas tree? Nativity?" Wei repeated with a puzzled look. "What are those things?"

"Why, they're traditional decorations for the Christmas holiday," Chou Ling said, forgetting for a moment that Wei had never celebrated Christmas.

"I've heard of this day called Christmas. Something about a fat man with a long white beard and flying deer, right?" Wei said.

Chou Ling broke into laughter. "Oh, my, how the stories of Santa Claus travel around the world, even to China."

"Yes, that is his name, Santa Claus," Wei responded enthusiastically. "And he brings toys to children."

"Well, that's the make-believe story," Ling said, "but the real Christmas story isn't about Santa Claus. The true story of Christmas is about the birth of God's Son, Jesus."

Wei thought for a moment. "Yes, I've heard of Jesus, too. Just before I left China a man gave me a Bible. Inside he had written something about someone named Jesus, but I didn't really understand what it meant."

"Well," said Chou Ling, "after we finish our work, I can tell you more about Jesus, if you like."

By midnight, Ling and Wei had decorated the twenty-foot-tall tree, which now glittered with hundreds of twinkling lights, golden balls, and shiny red bows. They had hung two dozen wreaths throughout the huge bank lobby and two larger ones on the heavy brass entry doors. Swags of evergreen festooned the staircases and the marble pillars of the lobby.

"I've never seen anything like this," Wei exclaimed afterward. "It's all very beautiful. And it smells good—like the woods."

"Oh, it is beautiful," Ling agreed. "But it's not yet complete."

Then he carefully began to open four large wooden crates. "Here is what Christmas is really about," he said, smiling with anticipation. Ling reverently placed several Nativity figurines around the base of the tree. "Here are Joseph, Mary, the shepherds, and the wise men. And here is the Christ child," he said as he carefully placed the figure representing the infant Jesus into the manger.

"But who are they?" Wei asked. "Who is the baby? And why are there animals in the scene? Are they outdoors?"

Ling invited Wei to kneel on the floor beside him. "Do you really want to know the true story of Christmas?"

"I think so," Wei said, still absorbing the beauty of the scene.

For the next several minutes, Chou Ling explained the meaning of Christmas. "And the Jesus you read about inside the cover of the Bible, the Jesus who laid down his life for us, well, that's the same Jesus whose birth we celebrate each year at this time."

Chang Wei listened silently as he continued looking at the Nativity. Then he said, "Thank you, Ling. But it's late now. I must hurry, or I'll miss the last bus home."

"And thank you, Wei. You've become a great friend to me," Ling said with a smile. "I'm so glad you brought your family to San Francisco. And before I forget, my wife asked me to invite you and your family to our house for dinner this Saturday evening. We're having a few friends over. Do you think you would like to come?"

"Thank you, my friend," Wei answered. "We would be honored."

As the late night bus drove through the quiet streets of the hilly city, Wei was deep in thought about Ling's Christmas story. Finally, the bus stopped at the now-familiar corner near his apartment. "Good night, Mister," the driver said. "And Merry Christmas."

"Good night," Wei responded, happy to practice one of his new English phrases.

At breakfast the next morning, Chang Wei told his family about the special project he had worked on the night before. "It's all quite beautiful," he explained, sipping his tea. "I'd like to take all of you to the bank to see it."

"Papa, pretty trees are going up all over town," Mei said. "We even have one in our school. They're called Christmas trees."

"Yes, and the shops have lovely decorations, too," added Ting. "Christmas seems to be an important holiday in America."

"Oh, and we've been invited to dinner this Saturday," Wei said, taking his last sip of tea. "Chou Ling, the very nice man I work with at the bank, wants us to come to his house."

"Oh, I'd like to go," Ting replied eagerly. "We haven't met many people yet. Do tell him we'll come."

"I think people give each other gifts at Christmas," Wei said with some uncertainty. "Perhaps we should bring a gift for Chou Ling's family."

"I'll make them some egg rolls," Ting suggested. "Everyone loves egg rolls."

By Saturday evening, the city glittered with holiday decorations. As the Chang family boarded a bus to Chou Ling's home, Li asked, "Papa, who is Santa Claus? And will he bring gifts to us now that we live in America?"

"I don't know," Wei replied. "It's all confusing. Chou Ling says Santa Claus is only make-believe. But he also told me about a baby Jesus whom He says is real. Christmas is very confusing—trees, lights, Santa Claus, Jesus."

"I like all the lights," Li said enthusiastically. "And I like Santa Claus. I want lots of toys. I want a bicycle and a fire truck and . . ."

"Oh, my," Ting said, laughing. "I think our children are becoming very American already."

When they arrived at the home of Chou Ling, the family was greeted by a very cheerful crowd. "Come in," Ling said. "Come and meet some of our friends."

"Papa," Mei whispered loudly, "there's Mr. Merriman, the bus driver. What's he doing here?"

"I don't know," her father replied with a puzzled look.

"And there's Mrs. Choo, our English teacher," Ting said in surprise, pointing toward the kitchen.

"Attention, everyone," Chou Ling said. "I want all of you to meet my friend Chang Wei, his wife Ting, and their children, Mei and Li."

With welcoming smiles, everyone made the Chang family feel at home. Then, after a delicious meal that included Ting's egg rolls, Ling announced, "It's time to sing

Christmas carols. And for our new friends, I've had the English words translated into Chinese."

Mr. Merriman surprised the Chang family with his lovely voice as he led everyone in singing "O Come, All Ye Faithful":

> *O come, all ye faithful, joyful and triumphant,*
> *O come ye, O come ye to Bethlehem.*
> *Come and behold Him, born the King of angels!*
> *O come, let us adore Him,*
> *O come, let us adore Him,*
> *O come, let us adore Him,*
> *Christ the Lord.*

Wei's family listened carefully to the words of this and many other carols they had never heard before.

"So beautiful," Ting sighed. She didn't understand what the carols meant, but she enjoyed hearing and singing them.

As everyone was leaving, Chou Ling gave Mei and Li a big picture book. "It's the Christmas story," he explained. "And it's written in Chinese. I think it will help all of you understand the true meaning of the holiday."

As Ling gave Wei a parting hug, he said, "Wei, my friend, would you and your family join us at our church for a Christmas Eve service on December 24? Please?"

"We will think about it," Wei said.

"I think the Christmas Eve service will help you understand even better what it is we celebrate. I hope you will join us. Merry Christmas, Wei."

For the next two weeks, Chang Wei thoughtfully considered Chou Ling's invitation. Finally, Ting asked him, "Are we going to go to the Christmas Eve service with Chou Ling's family?"

"I've thought a lot about it," he answered. "I'm not sure why, but I think we should go. I keep thinking about people like Mr. Merriman, Mrs. Choo, and of course, Chou Ling. There's something about these people that is different from so many others we've met since coming to America. So yes, I think we should go."

Saturday evening was chilly as a heavy fog descended over the city. Waiting for the bus, the family huddled close together, trying to keep warm.

"Papa," Mei said, "I love the Christmas story book that your friend Chou Ling gave us. Will they tell that story tonight?"

"I'm not sure," her father replied as the bus approached the corner and stopped.

The old church stood on a corner near Chinatown where Chou Ling's family lived. Light shone softly through the lovely stained-glass windows and into the foggy night air. As Wei's family climbed the steps, they were greeted warmly by Ling and, to their great surprise, by Uncle Ping and Auntie Luli.

"Is this your church, Ping?" Wei asked as he hugged his brother.

"Yes, it is," Ping replied. "Merry Christmas to all of you! We're so glad you're here with us tonight."

"Please, Wei. Won't you and your family come and sit with my family?" Chou Ling asked.

Wei nodded and said, "Yes, we'd like that very much."

"We have a special guest with us who's just arrived from China," Ling explained as he led Wei's family to a pew in the middle of the church where his wife and children were already sitting. "He will bring us the Christmas message tonight. He does not yet speak English, so I'm going to translate his words into English. After the service, everyone will gather for refreshments. I'll see you then."

The service began with the singing of "O Little Town of Bethlehem." As the congregation stood to sing, several children walked to the front of the church and created a living Nativity scene in front of the altar.

"Papa," Mei whispered, "That's just like what we saw at the bank, under the Christmas tree." Wei nodded with a smile and took Mei's hand in his.

After everyone was seated, Chou Ling stood and faced the congregation.

"We have many reasons to be joyful and grateful this Christmas season," he said. "Not only are we grateful for the gift God gave us in His Son, Jesus, but we are also grateful for our church family around the world. Tonight, a member of that family who arrived from China just this week will share the Christmas message with us."

People whispered quietly as a young man walked slowly to the front of the church and stood beside Chou Ling.

"Dear friends," Ling said, "this is Fong Gui. He is an example of the true meaning of Christmas because he was willing to lay down his life for others. Please listen as he shares his story with us tonight."

The Chang family stared in disbelief at the young man who was about to speak. "Papa," Mei whispered excitedly, "isn't that the soldier who helped us hide in the storeroom before we boarded the freighter?"

Chang Wei only nodded but didn't look at Mei. His eyes were fixed on the man introduced as Fong Gui. Could this be the same man who had helped them escape?

Just before he began to speak, Gui looked directly at Wei and his family and smiled.

"It is the same man," Mei whispered.

"'This is how we know what love is,'" Fong Gui began, "'Jesus Christ laid down His life for us.'"

As Chou Ling translated the scripture into English, Chang Wei immediately recognized the words—the same words written on the inside of the Bible that Fong Gui had given them the day they left China.

"Through this great love and sacrifice," Gui continued, "we who believe in Jesus as God's Son and our Savior are welcomed as members of God's family, which is called His church. God has adopted us into His own family by bringing us to Himself through Christ. In Jesus, those of us from many, many families around the world have become members of His one eternal family."

"This is the true meaning of Christmas," he continued. "The child who was born the Son of God grew to be a man so that He might lay down His life to pay the price for our sins on the cross. Now He brings all who believe in Him into this new family, the church. This is the meaning of Christmas.

"Look around you at the people here tonight. We come from many nations, many of us from China. We come from many families, but if we have placed our faith in Jesus as God's Son and our Savior, we are one family. Even with all our cultural differences, we are still one family and one nation in Jesus Christ.

"As we celebrate the joy of being part of God's family, let us show our joy by loving others in the same way Jesus loves us. May we live to serve and, if necessary, lay down our lives for one another as Jesus laid down His life for us.

"I would like for us to close this service tonight by singing 'Joy to the World.' The joy of God's gift is not just for us who are here tonight. It is a joy to be shared in every nation of the world, including my beloved China."

The people stood and began to sing:

Joy to the world, the Lord is come!
Let earth receive her King.
Let every heart prepare Him room,
And heaven and nature sing,
And heaven and nature sing,
And heaven, and heaven and nature sing.

He rules the world with truth and grace,
And makes the nations prove
The glories of His righteousness,
And wonders of His love,
And wonders of His love,
And wonders, wonders of His love.

After the congregation sat down again, Fong Gui said, "My prayer for all nations and for each of you tonight is that your heart will prepare room for Him to be your personal Lord and King."

Gui then prayed. Then to everyone's surprise, instead of sitting down, he walked quickly down the aisle to the pew where Chang Wei's family was seated. Giving no thought to what others might think, Wei stood up to meet Gui. With tears in their eyes, the two men hugged each other.

"My dear friend," Wei cried. "What are you doing here? How did you get here?"

"I'll tell you later," Gui answered softly as he went to hug Ting, Mei, and Li who were also standing in the aisle to greet him.

"Please join us now for refreshments," Chou Ling announced to the congregation. "I hope you will all come and greet Chang Wei's family and Fong Gui."

Again, Wei said to Gui, "Please tell us how you came to be here."

"It's a long story," Gui said, "a very long story. Just know that God opened a door of escape for me after you left. The Liberation Army has captured many villages, and I, as you know, was no friend of the army. I arrived in San Francisco just last week."

"Attention everyone! Attention everyone!" Chou Ling announced. "We have another special visitor with us tonight. Fong Gui, would you do the honors?"

"Thank you, Chou Ling. Allow me to introduce my father, Fong Shan," Fong Gui said in Chinese as an older gentleman stepped forward.

"Oh!" Ting squealed. "It's Mayor Fong. Wei, it's our mayor!"

Mayor Fong walked quickly to Chang Wei's family, and again there were hugs and tears.

"I'm glad you made it to America," Fong Shan told them. "I have prayed for your family every day since you left our village."

"We'll never forget how much we owe you," Chang Wei said. "We owe you our lives. Thank you."

"There is no need to thank me. It was all arranged by your brother, Ping," Fong Shan admitted with a smile.

"Ping!" Wei exclaimed. "But how?"

"Your brother has secretly helped many people escape from China," Gui said.

"I had no idea," Wei said. "I thought he only helped us once we arrived in America because he is my brother."

"Oh, no," Gui said. "He works actively to help arrange the necessary papers on both the Chinese and American sides. And then he helps those who come here. Ever since your family left last spring, he has been working very hard to help me and my father escape as well.

Fong Shan said, "And he arranged places for us to live in America as he did for you."

"Ping is always full of surprises," Wei said, filled with new admiration for his brother. "Fong Shan, Fong Gui, I just don't know what to say. How can we ever repay you? How can we ever thank you for your kindness?"

"As I told you that day on the dock," Gui said with a smile, "you do not need to repay me or any of us. We were happy to help you, and we are very thankful you arrived here safely."

"But your family risked their lives for us—your cousin, your aunt and uncle, and your grandfather, Captain Quan. What you did was very dangerous," Wei said gravely.

"Perhaps. But when we are given an opportunity to serve, we believe it is our Christian responsibility to do so, regardless of the dangers."

"What has become of the rest of your family? Have they also escaped?"

"No. They have chosen to stay behind to help other families such as yours."

"Gui," Ting asked as she reached into her bag and took out a Bible, "do you remember this?"

"Yes, that is the Bible I gave your family on the dock in Lang Tin."

"Please, open the cover and read what you wrote to us," Ting asked, handing Gui the Bible.

After Gui read the quote from 1 John 3:16, Ting asked, "Isn't that what you said tonight in your Christmas message?"

"Why, yes it is," Gui admitted, pleased that Ting had recognized the Scripture.

"Do you and your family really believe this?" she asked.

"We do believe it, Ting, with all our hearts."

Everyone stood quietly, thinking deeply about these words from the Bible.

Finally Wei spoke. "Gui, our time in America has not been easy. We left family, friends, all our possessions, and even the nation of our birth to come here. We have often felt alone, and sometimes we have been angry. So often we have longed to be able to return to China. But you and your father . . . well, you don't seem lonely. You seem to feel at home already after just one week in America."

Fong Gui smiled. "Oh, we do miss China, Wei. We will always miss it. But we are part of a much larger family than the one we left behind. And we're part of an even bigger nation than China—we are part of God's church, a family and nation that is found around the entire world. So no matter where we are, we will always feel at home with other children of God."

Wei said, "I want my family to feel at home here, as your family does. But is the Christmas message you shared tonight for us, too? Is there room in God's family for mine?"

Gui put his arm around his friend. "The Christmas message is for all who believe that Jesus is God's Son and their Savior. It's a message for every person and family in the world who will accept it." Then with a reassuring smile he added, "Yes, I am certain, God has plenty of room in His family for yours—and for many, many more."

THINK ABOUT IT

» Which of the characters bring encouragement and blessing to Chang Wei's family as they adjust to life in America?

» What do the actions of Mr. Merriman, Mrs. Choo, and Chou Ling tell you about them?

» Why do you think Chou Ling wants Chang Wei to help him decorate the bank for Christmas? Why do you think he invites Wei's family to the Christmas Eve service at his church?

» In what ways has the Chang family seen the true meaning of Christmas lived out both in China and in America?

» According to Fong Gui, who is "God's family"? How do you think these events have changed the way Chang Wei thinks about what a family is?

» Why do you think Wei and Ting are interested in knowing more about Jesus and Christianity? Do you think they and their family will become Christians? Why or why not?

WORDS YOU NEED TO KNOW

» **Submission:** An attitude of the heart in which I give up my rights and what I want in order to joyfully serve and bless others

» **Marriage:** A relationship in which one man and one woman are united by God to share life together as husband and wife

» **Covenant:** A special agreement or promise that is not to be broken

» **Reproof:** The firm but loving words a parent uses to tell a child what he or she has done wrong

» **Honor:** To deeply appreciate, love, and respect

» **Honesty:** Truthfulness in everything I say and do

HIDE IT IN YOUR HEART

Honor your father and mother . . . that it may go well with you and that you may enjoy long life on the earth." (Ephesians 6:2–3)

Good people will be guided by honesty; dishonesty will destroy those who are not trustworthy. (Proverbs 11:3, NCV)

AMAHL AND THE NIGHT VISITORS

A Charlie Brown Christmas. Rudolph the Red-Nosed Reindeer. Miracle on 34th Street. Almost before the Thanksgiving leftovers are cold, Christmas-themed programs and movies begin to flood the television schedules. Before home video and the Internet made these programs widely available at the push of a button, millions of us sat down with our families every December to watch beloved tales of the Grinch, the Little Drummer Boy, and Ebenezer Scrooge. But the very first annual Christmas special wasn't a movie or animated program. It was an opera.

Opera is an art form in which singers and musicians perform a dramatic work combining text (called a *libretto*, or "little book") and a musical score that's often classical in nature. Although many of the most famous operas are written and performed in German or Italian, one popular opera was written in English especially for children. *Amahl and the Night Visitors* tells a Christmas story about the Magi and a young crippled

Adoration of the Magi by Bosch. The painting helped inspire Menotti to write his opera.

boy who lives near Bethlehem. The first opera written for television in America, *Amahl and the Night Visitors* was broadcast live every year from 1951 to 1963.

The story tells of Amahl, a poor shepherd boy who lives with his mother. He is lame and can walk only with a crutch. One night, as a strange bright star appears in the sky, three kings from the East stop at their house. They ask if they can rest there for the night. Amahl and his mother are extremely poor, and his mother is tempted by the gold the kings are carrying. But when they hear that it is a gift for the Christ child, she and Amahl also want to send Him a gift. When Amahl chooses to give the child his only possession—his crutch—suddenly he is healed and able to walk again!

Gian Carlo Menotti, who wrote the opera, based the story of Amahl on an incident from his own childhood in Italy. Just like the boy in the story, Menotti couldn't walk when he was a child. But after visiting a church near his village, Menotti received a blessing and was miraculously healed.

Because *Amahl and the Night Visitors* is less than an hour long and the music is relatively easy to sing, many churches and theater groups perform the opera every year, making the story of Amahl a Christmas tradition for a new generation of children and their families.

WHAT IS A FAMILY?

For better or worse, families often look much different than they did just fifty years ago. A mother and father living with the children they gave birth to is now just one possibility. Many children today are raised by single parents. Others live in blended families where one or both parents have been divorced and remarried. Many children have been adopted into new families, while others are raised by foster parents or even grandparents. Whatever your family looks like, God's reason for placing you in your specific family remains the same: to learn to love and serve others.

God created the family to be the place where we first learn to live with other people, share with others, and work together with others to accomplish the work He commanded us to do. The home was designed to be a place where members of a family care for and support one another, keep each other safe, and put each other's needs ahead of their own. It's the place where children are nurtured, taught, and given the tools to be God's hands and feet to the world. In other words, it's the place we learn to serve.

A family (and a home) cannot function properly if its members are unwilling to humble themselves and serve one another in love. A frustrating parent, a defiant spouse, a rebellious child, or a selfish sibling create disharmony in a home, causing discord and unpleasantness that can linger and fester like an open wound that refuses to heal. Instead, each family member must do his or her part to make the home a safe place to be—a place where people are built up and encouraged, never torn down or belittled.

This means that each member of the family must develop and keep an attitude of **submission**. To submit means to give up your rights and what you want in order to joyfully serve and bless others. The Bible tells us:

> *Speak to one another with psalms, hymns and spiritual songs. Sing and make music in your heart to the Lord, always giving thanks to God the Father for everything, in the name of our Lord Jesus Christ. Submit to one another out of reverence for Christ.* (Ephesians 5:19–21)

These are instructions for how brothers and sisters in Christ ought to worship together, but the same is true for how we ought to treat one another at home. Husbands and wives are to serve each other, each submitting to the other with love and respect. Children are to serve and honor their parents, submitting to them with respect and obedience. Parents are to serve their children through constant nurturing, teaching, and provision, submitting to God's will by putting the needs of their children ahead of their own wants and desires. Children are to serve one another by putting others first, helping each other when possible, and treating one another with kindness and respect.

But is this always possible? After all, people are not perfect. Sometimes they can be frustrating, perturbing, and downright difficult to live with. So how can we look past these annoyances and keep serving each other? Look at Ephesians 5:19–21 again. We do it by keeping glad hearts full of joy and thankfulness, because what's in our hearts will determine how we act toward one another (Matthew 12:34).

MAKE A NOTE OF IT
In your family, how do your parents serve each other? How do your parents serve you? How do you serve your parents? Do you have brothers or sisters? If so, how do you serve them? Do you serve only when you do things like clean your room and take out the trash? What is the most important thing about how you serve others in your family?

HOW DO HUSBANDS AND WIVES SERVE EACH OTHER?

In recent years, some people have tried to alter the meaning of marriage. Some have gone so far as to challenge this holy institution in courts of law or even pass new legislation that changes the legal definition of marriage. But God has already defined **marriage** for us as a relationship in which one man and one woman are united by God to share life together as husband and wife. And He has made it abundantly clear from the very beginning that marriage is important to His plans.

First of all, when God made Adam and Eve, He blessed them and commanded them to be fruitful and multiply and fill the earth (Genesis 1:28). On that day, God instituted the family as the best way for people to populate the earth and fulfill His plans for creation.

He then commanded Adam and Eve to "subdue" the earth and rule over every living thing. Genesis 2:15 says they were placed in the Garden of Eden "to work it and take care of it." In other words, husbands and wives

THE SWISS FAMILY ROBINSON

The classic novel *The Swiss Family Robinson* follows the adventures of a family from Switzerland that is shipwrecked during an ocean voyage to Australia. Salvaging tools and rope from the wrecked ship, the castaways sail to a nearby island where they make a home for themselves. As they explore the island, they discover useful plants and animals, build shelters, and plant crops. By the time a rescue ship finds them, the family has grown accustomed to their island home and they choose to stay.

The novel was written by Johann David Wyss, a pastor and military chaplain in Bern, Switzerland. Fascinated by Daniel Defoe's earlier novel *Robinson Crusoe*, Pastor Wyss wanted to create adventure stories for his four sons that would entertain as well as teach. Drawing upon his extensive knowledge of the outdoors, Wyss told them stories about a family like his own, modeling the boys in the book after his own sons. He chose for his setting a deserted island as a way to demonstrate survival skills and promote godly character qualities like cooperation, ingenuity, and hard work. Stranded as they are, every family member must depend on the others and on God. Each family member contributes important skills to the group, knowing that serving others to the very best of his or her ability is crucial to the survival of all.

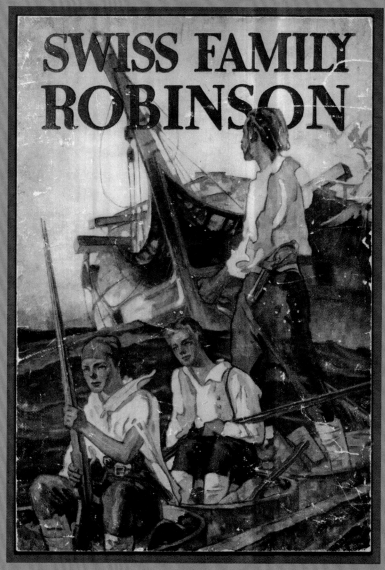

When Pastor Wyss's sons were grown, they convinced him to write down the stories he had told them as children and create a full-length novel. *The Swiss Family Robinson* was published in 1812, six years before Wyss died, and was edited by one of his sons and illustrated by another. The book became an instant favorite and has never gone out of print. Adapted and retold many times in books, movies, and television programs, the original story of the stranded family is just as fascinating and instructive today as it was when the Wyss boys first heard it.

Adam and Eve by Carolsfeld.

would work together to manage the earth and care for God's creation.

Also, as we have seen, God made people with a deep need for companionship. After creating Adam, God said, "It is not good for the man to be alone. I will make a helper suitable for him" (Genesis 2:18). And so God made Eve to be Adam's wife, and He created marriage to be a sacred institution to be treasured by husband and wife and honored by all people (Hebrews 13:4).

"For this reason," the Bible says, "a man will leave his father and mother and be united to his wife, and they will become one flesh" (Genesis 2:24). The union of a husband and wife is a holy bond, a special relationship in which a man and woman give up their individual wants and desires to love and serve one another with mutual respect and faithfulness for as long as they both are alive. No one is ever to come between a husband and wife (Mark 10:9).

As children of God, we are to show the world His glory while becoming more like Jesus every day (2 Corinthians 3:18). Likewise, a marriage reflects God's glory when a husband and wife love each other the way Christ loves us. It's not easy for two people to learn to live together peacefully under the same roof, and so a husband and wife must spend their early years together learning to be gracious and merciful toward one another. Just as God is slow to anger, abounding in love and compassion, each must be willing to forgive the other's offenses and refuse to hold on to anger (Psalm 103:7–9). And just as Christ came to serve and not be served, so a husband and wife must give themselves selflessly to each other, each meeting the other's needs with a servant's heart and humble spirit.

Let's look at three important ways husbands and wives are called by God to bless and serve each other.

HUSBANDS AND WIVES ARE CALLED TO LOVE AND RESPECT EACH OTHER

Ephesians 5:25 says, "Husbands, love your wives." The chapter goes on to say, "Each one of you also must love his wife as he loves himself, and the wife must respect her husband" (Ephesians 5:33). The apostle Peter had this to say to husbands: "Be considerate as you live with your wives, and treat them with respect" (1 Peter 3:7).

If you have a brother or sister or a best friend who lives down the street, you know that two people in a close relationship don't always get along. They won't always agree about the best way to spend their time and money or handle problems, and sometimes hurt feelings will keep them from communicating clearly with each other. This is true for husbands and wives, too. We can be thankful, therefore, that the Bible teaches people in a close relationship how to love and respect one another in a way that reflects Christ's love for us:

» Encourage the other person instead of criticizing him or her.
» Focus on the other person's strengths rather than his or her weaknesses.
» Pray for the other person instead of gossiping with your friends about his or her faults.
» Consider the other person better than yourself and put his or her interests before your own (Philippians 2:3–4).

HUSBANDS AND WIVES ARE CALLED TO SUBMIT TO EACH OTHER

In a letter to the churches of Asia Minor, the apostle Peter wrote to the men, "[Your wife] may be weaker than you are, but she is your equal partner in God's gift of new life" (1 Peter 3:7, NLT). Men and women are both created in God's image and therefore have equal value in His eyes (Genesis 1:27). Husbands are not better than their wives. Nor are wives better than their husbands. In a Christian marriage, both husband and wife are equally redeemed in our Lord and, therefore, are called to serve one another:

> *Submit to one another out of reverence for Christ. Wives, submit to your husbands as to the Lord. For the husband is the head of the wife as Christ is the head of the church. . . . Husbands, love your wives, just as Christ loved the church and gave himself up for her.* (Ephesians 5:21–25)

As we have seen, submission means to give up your rights and what you want in order to joyfully serve and bless someone else. But what about the part of this passage that says the husband is the "head," or the leader, of his wife? Doesn't that mean he's the boss? The head honcho? The top dog? The big cheese? To answer this question, we need to look closely at the second portion of this passage: "Husbands, love your wives, just as Christ loved the church and gave himself up for her."

Revelation 21:9–10 refers to the church as the "bride" of Christ. So how did Jesus love His bride? During His time on earth, did He insist that His followers wait on Him hand and foot? No, instead the Son of God served His followers by healing their wounds, feeding them physically and spiritually, comforting them in their grief, teaching them about God's kingdom, and even washing their feet! In the end, Jesus gave up His own life, enduring torture, humiliation, and death to pay the price for the sins of those whom He loved.

To be the kind of leader Jesus was, a husband (or a boss or a pastor or even a king) must serve the people he leads. Yes, the wife is called to submit to her husband as the leader of the home just as Christ submitted to the Father. But God calls the husband to submit to his wife by giving up his rights as leader and becoming a selfless servant to his wife, just as Christ served His bride, the church.

HUSBANDS AND WIVES ARE CALLED TO LIVE FAITHFULLY WITH EACH OTHER

Have you ever been to a wedding? A wedding ceremony is a celebration in which a man and a woman formally declare to the church and the community that a new family has begun. During the ceremony, the man and woman both take certain vows—that is, they make promises before God that establish their responsibilities to each other. In one traditional wedding ceremony, the minister asks the groom, or the man:

"Do you take this woman to be your wedded wife to live in the holy estate of matrimony? Do you promise to love, comfort, honor, and keep her for better or worse, for richer or poorer, in sickness and in health, and forsaking all others, be faithful only to her so long as you both shall live?"

If the groom answers, "I do," the minister will then ask the bride to make the same commitment to the groom. In other words, the newly wedded couple promises to remain together, to always love one another, to comfort one another, to honor this commitment even when life gets difficult, and to love only one another as husband and wife as long as they both live.

In the eyes of the government, the ceremony establishes a couple's legal rights and responsibilities to each other and to any children they may have. But in God's eyes, the ceremony establishes a holy union in harmony with His plan for creation. According to God, the promises made by the bride and groom are more than just words in a legally binding contract. The marriage vows represent a sacred **covenant**. A covenant is a very special agreement or promise that is not to be broken, and therefore marriage is not something to be rushed into without careful thought and wise counsel.

MAKE A NOTE OF IT
Read Ephesians 5:21–23 and Proverbs 31:10–31. Now, if you are a boy, write about or draw a picture of what you think a good husband does to serve his wife. If you are a girl, write about or draw a picture of what you think a good wife does to serve her husband.

THE GIFT OF THE MAGI

William Sydney Porter was a pharmacist and American author known by his pen name, O. Henry. As O. Henry, Porter wrote more than 300 short stories, many of which were famous for their surprise endings. One of his most enduring tales is "The Gift of the Magi," a tale of sacrificial love first published in 1905.

"The Gift of the Magi" is the story of Jim and Della, a young married couple who are short of money but desperately want to buy each other Christmas gifts. Unbeknownst to Jim, Della sells her most valuable possession—her lovely, knee-length brown hair—to a wigmaker in order to buy a platinum fob chain for Jim's prized pocket watch that was given to him by his grandfather. Meanwhile, unbeknownst to Della, Jim sells his watch to buy jeweled combs for her beautiful hair.

Although the gifts they bought have been rendered useless, Della and Jim are each pleased with the gift they've received because it represents their great love for one another. The story ends with the narrator praising husband and wife for their mutual sacrifice and comparing them to the Magi, or wise men, who gave the very first Christmas gifts (Matthew 2:1–12). O. Henry writes, "Let it be said that of all who give gifts these two were the wisest. Of all who give and receive gifts, such as they are wisest."

In other words, unselfish love is the greatest of all gifts, and those who understand this fact are wise indeed.

HOW DO YOUR PARENTS SERVE YOU?

A homemaker is a person whose main job is to take care of his or her home and children. Traditionally, the wife has been the homemaker in the family while her husband provided for the family's physical needs by hunting, farming, or working at a job. But in the island rainforests of Borneo and Sumatra, orangutans take the meaning of "homemaker" to a whole new level. Orangutans are arboreal, spending nearly all their time in the trees. Most of their day involves feeding, resting, and moving between feeding and resting sites. When evening comes around, the female orangutan begins to prepare a nest for the night for her and her youngsters. Orangutans build a new nest of leaves and sticks *every single day*, meaning that a typical orangutan mom lives in about 30,000 new homes during her lifetime.

God uses parents throughout much of the animal kingdom to provide for the needs of their young. Many animal moms and dads are known for their sacrificial devotion to their offspring, while others are famous for their ferocity in protecting their young from would-be predators. God has also given parents to human children to provide for their needs (1 Timothy 5:8) and keep them safe until they are grown, but God calls human parents to do much, much more.

Because all people are made in God's image, He expects parents to care for their children the same way He cares for each of His children. For example, parents are to love and appreciate their children because they are "a gift from the Lord" (Psalm 127:3, NLT). However, they also have a responsibility to give **reproof** and correct their children when necessary (Proverbs 29:15, NASB). Parents must encourage their children, never aggravate or discourage them (Colossians 3:21). God also commands parents to teach and train their children (Deuteronomy 6:6–7; Proverbs 22:6). Perhaps most importantly, parents must always set a godly example so that as their children grow they will know how God wants them to live (Proverbs 20:7; Titus 2:7).

You can easily remember how parents serve their children by looking at the letters in the word PARENTS:

P   Provide for their children
A   Appreciate and love their children
R   Reprove and discipline their children
E   Encourage their children
N   Never aggravate or discourage their children
T   Teach and train their children
S   Set a godly example for their children

Remember, your parents love you, though they may not always show their love with hugs and kisses or gifts. If you've been paying attention through the first few lessons, you already know there are many ways to say "I love you." By obeying God and fulfilling their responsibilities as parents, they are showing love to both you and their heavenly Father.

> ## MAKE A NOTE OF IT
> Many parents must make sacrifices in order to provide for their children's needs or to give them a better education. For some parents, this means not buying certain items for themselves so that their children can have good food and clothing. Some couples choose to make less money so that one parent can stay at home to care for the children and perhaps even teach them at home. What are some things your parents have denied themselves in order to care for you?

HOW CAN YOU SERVE YOUR FAMILY?

In the third month after God freed the people of Israel from slavery and brought them out of the land of Egypt and into the wilderness, God called Moses to the top of Mount Sinai to meet with him and give him the laws by which God's people were to live. The first ten of these laws have since become known as the Ten Commandments. The fifth of these commandments comes with a promise for those who obey it:

> *"Honor your father and mother . . . that it may go well with you and that you may enjoy long life on the earth."* (Ephesians 6:2–3)

This is a wonderful promise, but it's not always easy to give honor to someone who is always after you to brush your teeth, makes you eat Brussels sprouts, and won't let you wear your favorite pair of jeans (the ones with the cool holes in the knees) for the fifth day in a row. Parents aren't always easy to understand or easy to please, and they sometimes raise their voices in anger or frustration. They try hard, but they are not perfect.

However, our sovereign God has chosen the time and place for you to live, and He selected your parents especially for you! Because of this, you can and should honor and respect your parents—not because they are perfect, but because God is perfect. To honor your parents is to honor God and acknowledge Him as the Lord of your life.

You **honor** your parents by deeply appreciating them and showing them love and respect. Let's take a quick look at four different ways you can honor your mother and your father.

LISTEN TO YOUR PARENTS' TEACHING

Proverbs 1:8 (NLT) says, "My child, listen when your father corrects you. Don't neglect your mother's instruction." Proverbs 4:1–2 (NLT) says, "My children, listen when your father corrects you. Pay attention and learn good judgment, for I am giving you good guidance. Don't turn away from my instructions." God's words and wisdom, a heart for serving others, good manners, relationship basics, and life skills are just some of the many things your parents will pass on to you—if you will listen. You can show love and respect to your mother and father by opening your heart and giving your full attention to hear what they have to teach you.

OBEY YOUR PARENTS

Colossians 3:20 says, "Children, obey your parents in everything, for this pleases the Lord." Your parents have set certain rules for your home which you must then choose to obey or disobey. If you choose not to obey these rules, you know that there will be consequences— some form of discipline or loss of certain privileges. In much the same way, the Bible tells us that God "disciplines those he loves" (Hebrews 12:6).

On the other hand, when you make a habit of cheerfully and willingly obeying the rules set down by your parents, there is peace in your home and you will enjoy the trust and blessings of your mother and father. But it's not enough to just do what you're told. If you mumble and grumble while doing the dishes and taking out the garbage, then in your heart you are still arguing with your parents and with God. You must obey with a willing and cheerful heart for your actions to honor your mother and father.

CARE FOR YOUR PARENTS

First Timothy 5:4 (NCV) says, "If a widow has children or grandchildren, let them first learn to do their duty to their own family and to repay their parents or grandparents. That pleases God." When you were a baby, you parents did everything for you. They fed you, dressed you, held you, walked you, put you to bed, changed your diapers, and provided for all your physical needs. You could do almost nothing on your own. One day, as your parents grow older and their bodies age, they will be able to do less and less for themselves. They may need you to do for them the kinds of things they once did for you. But for now you can care for your parents simply by helping out when they're tired after a long day or perhaps feeling ill.

You can run small errands for them or do a chore they would normally do, like cook a meal for the family or clean up after dinner.

BLESS YOUR PARENTS WITH JOY

Proverbs 23:15–16 (NLT) says, "My child, if your heart is wise, my own heart will rejoice! Everything in me will celebrate when you speak what is right." King Solomon, who wrote this passage, goes on to say, "The father of godly children has cause for joy. What a pleasure to have children who are wise. So give your father and mother joy! May she who gave you birth be happy" (Proverbs 23:24–25, NLT). Do you give your parents reason to rejoice and delight in you? Here are just a few ways you can bless your parents with joy:

> » Always treat your family with love and respect at home and in public.
> » Always speak to others with kind and gentle words (Proverbs 15:4; Philippians 4:5).
> » Be a peacemaker among your family and friends (James 3:17–18).
> » Do your very best when doing even the smallest of chores (Luke 16:10).
> » Don't dwell on negative things, but think and talk about whatever is true, noble, right, pure, lovely, and worthy of praise (Philippians 4:8).

MAKE A NOTE OF IT

Read Proverbs 4:1–13. In the New Living Translation, verse 13 reads, "Take hold of my instructions; don't let them go. Guard them, for they are the key to life." What do you think it means that your parents' teachings are the "key to life"? Write about or draw a picture of something your parents have taught you that will help you live a long and godly life.

WHAT SHOULD I DO?

Being **honest** means being truthful in everything you say and do. Honesty is essential to maintaining harmony in any personal relationship. That's because all relationships are built on a foundation of trust, and when you tell even a "little" lie, you form a crack in that foundation. Every crack weakens the relationship and makes it difficult for the other person to trust you in the future.

Honesty at home is especially important for a couple of reasons. First of all, home is where you learn the patterns of behavior that tend to stay with you all your life. If, as a young person, you cannot be honest with your parents, the people who love you most and keep you safe, you will later find it hard to be truthful in your job or in friendship or a marriage. If you cannot play board games with your brother or sister without cheating, you will later find it tempting to cheat when figuring your taxes.

Your home should be the place where it's safe to be completely open and honest about your thoughts, your feelings, and your actions. When your parents ask you if you've done something you weren't supposed to do, do you always tell them the truth? It's far better to get into a little trouble for something you've done than to make matters worse by lying about it. Once you establish a pattern of dishonesty— and believe me, your parents will usually know when you're lying—you will find it harder to be truthful and your parents will find it harder to believe what you say. This mutual lack of trust will make your teen years especially difficult and even painful.

Honesty should guide each of your thoughts as well as your words and actions. That's because what you think will determine what you do and say (Matthew 12:34–35). Because you are made in the image of the One who is absolutely trustworthy, everything you do and everything you are should be based on honesty and truth. As a follower of Christ, you should always tell the truth because Jesus is truth and He lives in you (John 14:6; Galatians 2:20).

Those who are dishonest will harm their friends and loved ones, ruin relationships, and eventually destroy themselves. Proverbs 11:3 (ICB) says, "Good people will be guided by honesty. But dishonesty will destroy those who are not trustworthy."

A Prayer

Dear God, thank you for my family. Please give me a gracious and humble heart and help me look for ways to serve each member of my family. Help me to honor my parents every day and obey them cheerfully. Help me to always be truthful in everything I think and say and do. In Jesus' name I pray. Amen.

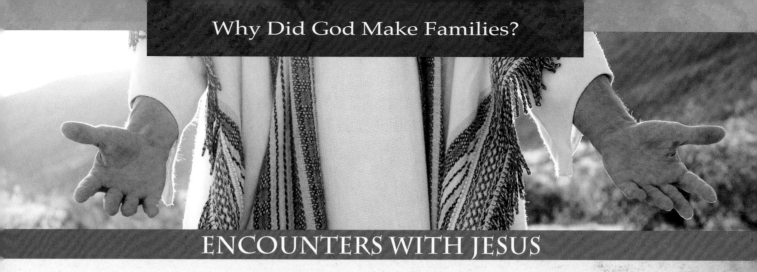

ENCOUNTERS WITH JESUS

LOOK OUT BELOW!

Thomas lay in bed listening to the sounds of Capernaum waking up around him. His wife, Hava, moved quietly about the next room preparing breakfast. Outside, the goat bleated plaintively, calling for Thomas's son to milk it. Donkeys clopped rhythmically along the street, pulling creaking carts.

The ruins of Capernaum in the early 1900s.

The beginning of a new day always made Thomas achingly sad. Once he had been a strong man, a fisherman, able to provide for and protect his family. Now he couldn't even roll over in bed by himself.

The tremors had begun a year ago, worsening little by little. First, he had lost control of his hands. This put him out of work, for a fisherman who couldn't handle a rope or a net was useless. Soon he couldn't stand without support and was confined to bed. Then the paralysis set in, and he could no longer sit up in bed without help. Now, months later, he could barely swallow and had to be fed by his wife or children. A tear worked its way down Thomas's cheek. He felt so helpless as his remaining vigor slipped away day by day.

His youngest daughter, Tirzah, crawled onto the pallet with him, tousled and sleepy. "Don't cry, Abba," she said, running a stubby little finger down the path the tear had left on his cheek. "We still love you." She snuggled up against him, using his shoulder for a pillow, and promptly fell asleep again.

Hava found them that way when she and her brother Aaron came in to help Thomas get ready for the day. Aaron stopped by every day, morning and evening, to help his sister care for Thomas. After bathing Thomas, Aaron and Hava dressed him warmly and moved his pallet close to the fire to drive off the winter chill. Tirzah was appointed nursemaid, to feed him warm broth and make sure her abba was comfortable.

While Tirzah played nearby, and Hava and the older children scattered across Capernaum to earn or beg what coins they could to pay for food, Thomas was left alone with his thoughts. The rabbis taught that physical suffering was the result of sin. This day as every day, Thomas lay on his pallet, unable to move more than his eyes and lips, and wondered what sin he had committed that was grievous enough for God to cause his body to waste away like this.

He knew the townspeople wondered the same. Although they helped his family when they could—out of duty to provide for the poor—they avoided contact with him and his family whenever possible, as if his sin would rub off onto them. What Thomas found hardest to bear was the way his family suffered because of his affliction. As the weather grew colder, Thomas grew more fearful that neither he nor his family would survive to see the spring.

A commotion outside in the street shook Thomas from his thoughts. Excited voices mingled with running feet. Then a fist pounded on the door. Before Tirzah could open it, her uncle Aaron burst in excitedly.

"Thomas! Peter and Andrew have returned, and they've brought Jesus of Nazareth!" Aaron said breathlessly. "He is the one I told you of. They say he has healed blind men and lepers. Maybe . . ."

Thomas fought against the paralysis weighing down his tongue. "Take me to him," he whispered.

"I'll go find some men to help me carry you. If necessary, I'll take you to him on my back." Aaron disappeared as quickly as he had come.

For a moment Thomas was caught up in hope. Was it possible? Could he be the man he once was? But on the heels of hope came a crushing dread. What if his sins were too great for him to be healed?

Hava came running in a few minutes later. "Husband, did you hear? Aaron is on his way here." She gave him an exuberant kiss on the forehead and hurried to gather warm clothes to wrap him in.

Aaron didn't bother to knock this time but opened the door and entered in one motion. He carried two long poles and several coils of fishing rope. "Let's make you as comfortable as possible," he said.

Hava pulled the blanket off the children's bed and helped Aaron secure it to the poles to make a litter. Then they padded the litter with cloth and tied ropes to it, front and back. Wrapping Thomas carefully in his own blanket, they laid him on the makeshift bed.

As they finished, three of Aaron's friends arrived to help carry Thomas to see Jesus. Benjamin and his two younger brothers, all fellow fishermen, had spent time listening to Jesus' teachings and were among the few who were always quick to help Thomas and his family.

"This is the day, Thomas," Benjamin said. "Tonight you will return home a new man.

Just see if you don't." He joined Aaron at the head of the litter, while Benjamin's brothers carefully lifted the foot.

Throwing her cloak over Thomas, Hava wrapped Tirzah up and followed the men into the cold, damp morning. Despite the added weight of the litter and blankets, the four men were easily able to carry Thomas's fragile body through the streets. Just seeing their cheerful faces lifted Thomas's spirits. He was blessed to have such good friends and a loving family. As he watched the grey clouds pass overhead, Thomas was caught between a hope that reached to the skies and a despair deeper than the greatest abyss. What if Jesus took one look at him and turned him away, seeing only the sins that darkened his soul and withered his body? Yet there was no other hope for him and his family. If this failed, they were all doomed. It was just a matter of time.

The streets became more crowded and the going tougher as the little group made its way through the city. As they turned onto the street where Peter's house was, they ran into a crush of people hoping to see Jesus. At the head of the litter, Aaron and Benjamin pushed through the crowd. Behind them, little Tirzah was jostled by the press of bodies and slipped out of her mother's arms. Thomas saw Hava catch her, just as the crowd closed around him, separating him from his wife and child.

Aaron and Benjamin pressed onward until they reached the outer doorway of the house. "Please, let us through!" Aaron shouted.

The people around him shushed him urgently. "Quiet!" one man hissed. "Don't you know there are important men of the law from Jerusalem in there? They have come to question Jesus about his teachings."

Another man, annoyed at the interruption, poked his head out the door. "This is not the time to ask for a healing. Come back in a few days, when the teachers of the law have gone home."

Aaron and Benjamin looked at each other, then at Thomas. Thomas could only return their look with pleading eyes. Finally, Aaron said decisively, "We will take him to the roof." Benjamin and his brothers nodded. They didn't know what Aaron had in mind, but they were willing to hazard almost anything for the hope of getting Thomas and his family the miracle they so desperately needed.

Moving slowly through the crowd and trying not to draw so much attention to themselves, the four men carried Thomas around the edge of the building to an outside staircase that led to the roof. No one took notice of them as they mounted the stairs.

Typical house in the Holy Land around 1900.

Peter's house had several ground-floor rooms surrounding a large courtyard that was currently packed with people listening intently to what Jesus and the religious leaders were discussing. The courtyard was covered by a simple roof of clay tiles. On hot summer days the tiles shaded the courtyard from the sun; in the winter they kept the walkways dry.

Making their way to a spot near the tiled opening at the center of the roof, Aaron and the brothers set Thomas down. "What do we do now?" Benjamin asked.

"We lower him through the roof," Aaron said, taking off his outer garment and climbing over the wall that surrounded the opening. "It's the only way we'll be able to reach Jesus."

"But you'll make a scene!" one of the brothers said.

Benjamin faced his brother. "I am convinced this man has the power to heal Thomas. If you have any doubt he is a messenger of God, perhaps you should leave now. Otherwise, stay and see a miracle."

His brother set his chin and said resolutely, "I believe."

Aaron knelt beside Thomas. "I believe as Benjamin does—Jesus is sent by God. But there are others down there who will not be pleased by what we are about to do. Do you still want to see him, come what may?"

"Please," Thomas whispered.

Smiling, Aaron nodded once and stood. Grasping Benjamin's hand for safety, Aaron climbed over the wall and onto the tiled roof. Carefully, he began removing the baked clay tiles, one by one, and handing them back over the wall to the brothers, who stacked them in neat piles. Aaron tried to work quietly, but Thomas soon heard a growing murmur from the crowd downstairs.

By the time Aaron had removed enough tiles to uncover the framework of latticed branches supporting them, Jesus and the Pharisees had stopped talking, their attention drawn to what was happening above them. All eyes were on Aaron, Benjamin, and his brothers as they cleared away enough of the woven branches underneath the tiles to admit the litter, then positioned themselves at the four corners of the hole. Working together to keep Thomas level and secure on the litter, they lowered him by ropes through the exposed framework of the roof.

Thomas held his breath as he descended. He knew he was making a spectacle of himself and his loyal friends in the process, all on the slim hope that Jesus would pardon this interruption and have mercy on him.

As the litter neared the ground, hands reached out from below to help steady it and bring Thomas safely to the floor. The crowd waited, holding its collective breath. What would the rabbi do? What would the Pharisees say?

Christ Heals a Paralyzed Man by Bida.

In that moment, Thomas turned his eyes toward Jesus, the question he most wanted to ask sticking in his throat. The compassion he saw on Jesus' face only made him wonder: Why should such a one as Jesus ever take the time to speak with him, let alone grant his greatest desire and heal his feeble body?

Jesus rose from his seat and approached the litter. Kneeling, he spoke to Thomas. "Friend, do not be afraid. Your friends have great faith. Your sins are forgiven."

Peace such as he had never known washed over Thomas, dissolving the worry and shame that weighed him down. This was more than he had dared to hope for! Even if he remained paralyzed for the rest of his life, he would never be the same.

In the utter joy of the moment, Thomas almost missed the reaction of those around him. The faces of the Pharisees looked horrified, as though Jesus had spoken blasphemy.

Turning to the Pharisees, Jesus asked them, "Why do you think such things in your hearts? Tell me, which is easier: to say to the paralyzed man 'Your sins are forgiven' or to say 'Get up and walk'? Watch and I will prove to you that the Son of Man has the authority on earth to forgive sins."

Jesus turned back to Thomas and said, "Stand up, pick up your mat, and go home."

Without a thought, Thomas sat up, then got to his feet unassisted. As he stood, the pain in his joints and the numbness in his hands and feet faded away. He could feel the strength flowing through his once-withered muscles. For the first time in months, he could breathe easily. Bending without effort, Thomas picked up his limp litter and wrapped the ropes around it. His body responded as if no time at all had passed between his youth as a strong fisherman and this moment.

With tears of joy streaming down his face, Thomas lifted up his voice and praised God, who had given such power to Jesus. Making his way through the crowd, which now parted before him like grain before a wind, he left Peter's house. He was anxious to share his miracle with Hava and Tirzah and thank Aaron and Benjamin and his brothers for their faith and loyalty. As he passed, many were gripped with wonder and awe, and they praised God, exclaiming, "We have seen amazing things today!"

TAKE A CLOSER LOOK

» Read the biblical accounts of these events in Matthew 9:2–7, Mark 2:1–12, and Luke 5:17–25, and compare them to the story you've just read.

» Why did Thomas's friends have difficulty getting their friend into Peter's house to see Jesus? What other ways might they have tried?

» Thomas could barely speak, and the Gospels do not tell us that he spoke at all to Jesus. How do you think Jesus knew the greatest desire of this man's heart?

» What was Thomas's greatest need—physical or spiritual healing? How did Thomas respond when Jesus said his sins were forgiven?

» The Pharisees were appalled at Jesus' words. How did Jesus prove to them He had the authority to forgive sins? How was this proof of His power and authority? What did this healing reveal about His love and compassion?

» Identify everyone who served Thomas in this story. How did they serve him?

THE HOUSE OF TRUTH: THE TENTH PILLAR

You have learned that God created the family to be the place where we first learn to live with other people, share with others, and work together with others to accomplish the work God commanded us to do. The home was designed to be a place where members of a family care for and support one another, keep each other safe, and put each other's needs ahead of their own. It's the place where children are nurtured, taught, and given the tools to be God's hands and feet to the world. In other words, it's the place we first learn to serve.

In this lesson, you erected the second pillar in your Servanthood Wall:

BIBLICAL TRUTH 14:

God made the family where we are to serve one another.

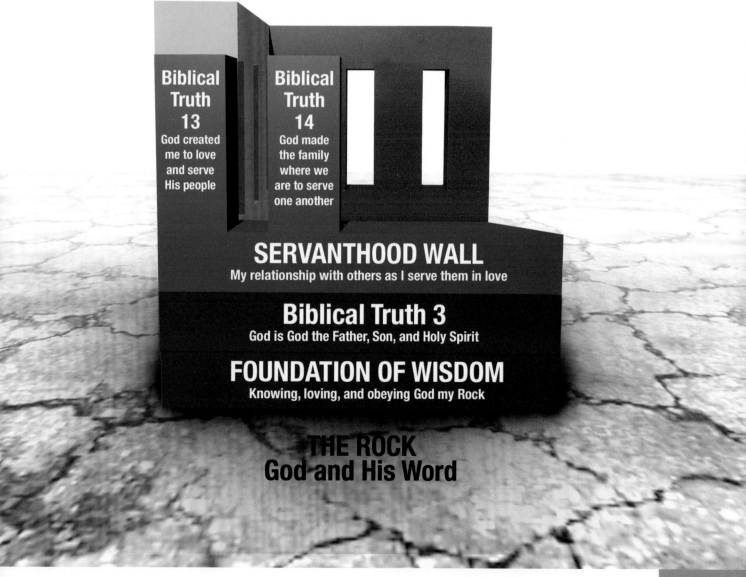

Biblical Truth 13
God created me to love and serve His people

Biblical Truth 14
God made the family where we are to serve one another

SERVANTHOOD WALL
My relationship with others as I serve them in love

Biblical Truth 3
God is God the Father, Son, and Holy Spirit

FOUNDATION OF WISDOM
Knowing, loving, and obeying God my Rock

THE ROCK
God and His Word

WHAT CAN I DO FOR MY COUNTRY?

HE MAKES NATIONS GREAT, AND DESTROYS THEM; HE ENLARGES NATIONS, AND DISPERSES THEM.

JOB 12:23

THE BIG IDEA

You have learned that God made people to live in relationship with one another. From the beginning He made us to need each other, love each other, and share our joys and sorrows with each other. He created Adam and Eve to love one another unselfishly and to help one another. Because people were given the responsibility of caring for and ruling over the entire earth and everything in it, God commanded Adam and Eve to have children and, eventually, fill the world with people (Genesis 1:28). As the number of people on the earth increased, together they would be able to obey God's command to take care of the earth.

So Adam and Eve had children, their children had children, and their children's children grew up and married and had families of their own. As the years went by, the earth became populated by more and more people and their families. But where do you think all these people lived? Do you suppose everyone built homes near the Garden of Eden where Adam and Eve lived in the suburbs? This certainly would have made family reunions easier to organize, but could the people obey God's command to fill the earth if they all stayed together in one small place? No, that would be impossible.

At first, however, people did not bother to obey God's commands. Indeed, the thoughts of most of them were "only evil all the time" (Genesis 6:5). So God sent a great flood to wipe mankind from the face of the earth. But He saved for Himself one righteous man, Noah, along with Noah's wife, his three sons, and their wives. When the floodwaters receded, God blessed Noah and his family and sent them out into the world, saying once more, "Be fruitful and increase in number and fill the earth" (Genesis 9:1).

And so the sons of Noah went their separate ways and began families. As the families

Noah's Sacrifice by Koch.

moved to new places, they formed tribes or communities. As the tribes grew larger, they formed nations (Genesis 10:31). Each nation had its own large area of land, and the families within each nation worked together to develop and protect the land.

Woven into the fabric of creation are three basic institutions, or groups, that God made to help us live in relationship with one another. These three institutions are the family, the nation, and the church. You now know that the family is where we first learn to serve our neighbors in love. It's also where we are taught God's commandments, where we find out who we are as God's children, and where we learn how to live in ways that will honor and glorify God. Because the family is the primary institution God uses to build His kingdom on earth, the family is the number one target for our enemy, the devil. Satan will do everything he can to destroy or cripple marriages and the institution of the family.

Why? In part because Satan is keenly aware that strong, godly families contribute to the growth, stability, and harmony of a nation, and Satan is determined to thwart the righteous development of nations on earth in order to gain territory for himself. Two or three generations of weak, broken families whose children do not love righteousness and do not learn to love and serve their neighbors will contribute more to the downfall of a nation than any invading enemy.

In this lesson, you will learn that God not only raises up the nations in which families are to live and serve others, but He also pulls down the nations in His timing to accomplish His purposes in history. You will learn what God intends for nations and their leaders to do for their citizens, as well as what He commands us to do to serve our city, state, and national governments. And you will see how, in His Word, God provides righteous principles that require all governments and their citizens to promote justice and secure peace for themselves and one another.

We will tell the next generation the praiseworthy deeds of the LORD, his power, and the wonders he has done. He decreed statutes . . . and established the law . . . which he commanded our forefathers to teach their children, so the next generation would know them, even the children yet to be born, and they in turn would tell their children. Then they would put their trust in God and would not forget his deeds but would keep his commands. (Psalm 78:4–7)

» You will understand the origin and purpose of nations as God created them.

» You will recognize the purpose of laws and why we must follow them.

» You will identify four ways God commands us to serve those who are in authority over us.

MCGUFFEY'S READERS

If you lived in the nineteenth century, you would probably have learned to read using McGuffey's Readers. These textbooks taught basic skills like reading and spelling but also taught students how to live a moral life.

The author of these textbooks was William Holmes McGuffey, a Presbyterian minister born in 1800. McGuffey began his career as a teacher at age fourteen, traveling to frontier schools and teaching for a few months at a time. Certified to teach Latin, Greek, and Hebrew, he spent the rest of his life as a professor and president of several colleges and universities in Ohio and Virginia.

In 1835, McGuffey was asked to write a series of textbooks for teaching children to read. After a year of researching and writing—and trying out his lessons on the neighborhood children—McGuffey completed the first two readers, which taught basic reading skills and vocabulary. Volumes three and four quickly followed and taught grammar on intermediate and advanced levels. Later, McGuffey's brother Alexander helped compile another two volumes that introduced students to good literature.

McGuffey also included religious instruction in his books. He believed that moral education was just as important as reading or arithmetic. He wanted to train children to be good as well as smart because he believed this was the only way to grow and maintain a healthy society.

Soon after McGuffey's Readers were first published, they became standard textbooks in schools across America. By the 1920s, nearly one hundred years later, McGuffey's Readers had sold more than 120 million copies, although some later editions of the readers did not include the religious themes. Even today, many homeschooling families still use McGuffey's Readers because of the way they combine reading skills and moral teachings within an interesting and easy-to-follow system.

A BOOK, A BELL, AND A CUP

As the late spring sun began slipping behind the Appalachian Mountains, the budding oaks of the Shenandoah Valley below cast their long afternoon shadows across the banks of Stony Creek. A soft, warm haze, scented by freshly plowed earth and wisps of smoke from a nearby smokehouse, draped lazily over the valley. Only the lowing of a small herd of cows plodding faithfully homeward for their evening milking disturbed the stillness of the landscape.

I loves this time a' day, Hattie thought to herself as she leaned against a large oak near the creek. Most days after finishing her many chores, she was allowed this short time to play and explore the farm where her grandparents, her parents, and she had been born. But Hattie looked forward to these late afternoons by the creek for a special reason—a secret reason.

I wonder what new words I's gonna learn today, Hattie pondered as she caught sight of her friend running down the path that led from the big stone house on the hill. "You is a sight, Emma Jane," Hattie called, laughing. "Yo' pigtails flyin' out behind you while you tryin' to keep that McGuffey's Reader from fallin' outta yo' apron."

Both girls giggled as Emma Jane untied her apron and carefully removed the well-worn reader.

"Hattie," said Emma Jane, still catching her breath from running, "if I ever get caught down here or anywhere else tryin' to teach you to read, we'll both be in a heap-a trouble."

"I knows," Hattie replied, her smile giving way to an expression of seriousness, even fear. "I don't never tell nobody what we be doin' down here by the creek."

"Nor I," said Emma Jane reassuringly. "Now, we don't have much time before supper, so let's get started."

Emma Jane sat down on the grassy bank next to Hattie as they both leaned against the tree. She opened the reader so both girls could see the page.

Haltingly, Hattie read the first line. "Frank . . . has . . . a . . . pretty . . . boat."

"Good," Emma Jane said encouragingly. "Now read the next one."

Hattie smiled as she gained confidence, slowly reading all the words on the page.

Just then the familiar clanging of the dinner bell reminded both girls that it was time to scurry home.

"Your mama rings that bell loud enough for all Augusta County to hear," Emma Jane teased. "Same time every day."

"She been clangin' it long as I can remember," said Hattie. "C'mon, hurry. And be sure to hide the reader, Emma Jane. We can't let nobody know."

But as Emma Jane tried to secure the book under her apron, the reader slipped from her grasp and slid down the sloping bank toward the creek. She rushed to the water's edge just in time to rescue it, but not in time to keep her shoes from sinking into the soft, muddy bank.

"Emma Jane Williams, what yo' mama gonna say when she sees you?"

"Don't worry about it, Hattie. Everything will be fine," Emma Jane said as she tucked the reader under her apron. "Now hurry home or we'll both be in trouble."

When she reached the back porch of the house, Emma Jane sat down on the steps to remove her muddy shoes. She didn't see Winnie coming down the path from the cook house.

"Where yo' shoes, Miz Emma Jane?" Winnie asked as she carried a loaf of freshly baked bread to the warming kitchen, Emma Jane trailing behind her

"And how did you get that mud on the hem of your skirt?" asked Emma Jane's mother.

"Um . . . Hattie and I were down by the creek, and I slipped on the muddy bank," Emma Jane replied, careful not to lie about her whereabouts but avoiding the subject of what they had been doing.

"Well, no matter. A little dirt on your hem won't be the end of you," Mrs. Williams said. "Now hurry and set the dining table. Your father and Moses are back from Turner's Store. He'll be up from the barn soon as the wagon's unloaded."

"Yes, Mama," replied Emma Jane, scurrying in her stocking feet down the hall and into the parlor. Carefully, she slipped the reader from under her apron and placed it on the shelf next to her other school books. Then she crossed the hall into the dining room and began her evening chore of setting the table.

Emma Jane set a plate for her father at one end where he always sat and then arranged the silverware, napkin, and glass exactly as her mother had taught her. Next she set her mother's place at the opposite end, followed by her own place to the left of her father's. Finally, following a new family tradition established by her father, she set a place for her older brother, Zachary, on her father's right, just as she had every evening since he left for the military academy three months earlier. She set his place with pride, knowing he was preparing to serve his country. But she also set it with sadness because she missed her brother and the constant teasing she had often complained about.

"Papa!" cried Emma Jane with a smile as Dr. Thomas Williams opened the front door. She ran to him, and he swept her up into his long arms and swung her about.

"Looks like I made it home just in time," Dr. Williams said. "Something smells delicious, as always."

"Of course it's delicious," replied Sarah, his wife, as she carried a platter of sliced ham and sweet potatoes out of the warming kitchen into the dining room. "Winnie's the best cook in the valley." Setting the platter down, she gave her husband a warm hug. "You and Moses must be exhausted. Did you buy all the seed we'll need for spring plantin'?"

"I think we'll have enough. Moses assures me it's good seed and that he'll have the horses harnessed and ready to turn the sod at daybreak. But come now, enough about work. Let's eat."

"I miss Zachary," said Emma Jane wistfully as they sat down.

"We all do," her father said, "but military service is an honorable profession, and we've given him our blessing. He'll be home come summer to help with the farm work— long enough for you to tire again of his teasing, I'm sure."

Emma Jane began to giggle but stopped herself as her father began to pray.

"Dear Father, we thank thee for our family. We ask thee to protect Zach while he's away. We thank thee for the food thou hast set before us. And thank thee for Winnie and Moses and for their service to us. In Jesus' name. Amen."

After supper, Dr. Williams retired to his study as he did each evening and lit the oil lamp on his desk. In preparation for his next six-day circuit, he carefully reviewed the list of patients he was treating in the valley. Then he opened his medicine cabinet and began packing his saddlebag with ointments and medicines.

"Winnie," Mrs. Williams said as she and Emma Jane helped clear the table, "Hattie's birthday is comin' up, isn't it?"

"Yes'm, Miz Sarah. It's jus' around the corner—eight more days iffn' I got my countin' right. She ten this year, jus' two years younger than Miz Emma Jane."

"That's what I thought. You know, Dr. Williams and I want this to be a special birthday for Hattie."

"Why, Miz Williams, all her birthdays been special," said Winnie as she carried the last of the dishes into the warming kitchen. "You always remember her birthday."

"But ten is a very special birthday," said Mrs. Williams.

Emma Jane asked, "What's gonna be so special, Mama?"

"Well," she replied, taking a deep breath and lowering her voice almost to a whisper, "your father and I think Hattie should learn to read."

"Read?" gasped Winnie. "That's 'gainst the law! Ever since that slave rebellion back when I's a child, it's a crime to teach a slave to read. Please, Miz Williams, don't do nothin' to get us all in trouble!"

"Winnie," Mrs. Williams replied lovingly but firmly, "you're not slaves anymore. You know that Dr. Williams freed your whole family when his father died and he inherited the farm ten years ago. Why, we think of you as family. You remember when Dr. Williams served in the Mexican War as a civilian doctor and Moses accompanied him?"

"I do remember. Them was hard days, hard days indeed."

"Dr. Williams hasn't forgotten either. He wouldn't have survived without Moses. And you surely remember how your dear sons, Ned and Samuel, helped Thomas's father keep the farm goin'. And you were right there to help bring Emma Jane into the world!"

"Yes, there are risks in these parts of teaching even freedmen to read. But once

Hattie knows how, a whole new world will be opened to her. And most importantly, she'll be able to read the Bible. I know no Northerner or Southerner who'd object to Bible readin'. Dr. Williams says times are changin', not only here in the South but in the North, too. He says there are turbulent times ahead . . . but no need to talk about that now."

"I don't knows what to say, Miz Sarah," Winnie said, still uncertain about the whole idea. "But I knows one thing for sure—I can keep a secret like nobody else on this earth."

Emma Jane, who always felt uncomfortable when the subject of slavery came up, had been listening intently. She was happy that her family was willing to take risks to teach Hattie to read. But how could her mother teach Hattie to read without finding out that she already knew how? And how could she, in good conscience, keep meeting with Hattie every afternoon under the old tree, knowing that a gift of reading lessons was forthcoming as a birthday surprise?

"Mama, how will you teach her?"

"Hattie will come to the warming kitchen each morning for an hour, and I'll teach her using a McGuffey's Reader, just the way I taught you."

"Tha— that's wonderful, Mama," Emma Jane managed to say as her heart raced. "I'm sure Hattie will learn quickly."

"Now remember, this is a surprise. So don't go sayin' anything to Hattie about it."

"Oh, I won't, Mama," Emma Jane promised sincerely despite her worries.

"Now, say goodnight to your father and head up to bed. I've got some sewin' I need to finish for your father before he leaves in the mornin'."

The next morning, Moses haltingly addressed Dr. Williams about the family's birthday surprise for Hattie. "I ain't sure that's a wise thing to do. 'Nuff people in this here valley already s'picious 'bout the kind way you treat us Negro folk, Dr. Williams. If they finds out Miz Sarah's teachin' Hattie to read, why, who knows what they might do?"

Moses knew the Williams family loved him, Winnie, Hattie, and their two sons who left the farm to go north when they were given their freedom. Nevertheless, their relationship bore the strain of a society divided over the institution of slavery. Both

155

Winnie's and Moses' parents and grandparents had served as slaves for two generations of the Williams family. And even after Dr. Williams had granted them freedom, Winnie and Moses had chosen to remain on the farm and continue the only work they had ever known. In fact, Dr. Williams had put Moses in charge of the farm, realizing that as a doctor he could not manage it alone. This unconventional arrangement between a freedman and his former master had raised eyebrows in the valley, but most folks' respect for the doctor and his service to their community took precedence over their political differences.

"No one needs to know, Moses. It'll be our secret," Dr. Williams reassured him. "And a day's comin' when we won't need to do this sort of thing in secret. We just have to be patient and, above all, keep on prayin' for this divided nation of ours."

With no further discussion, Dr. Williams mounted his horse and headed north toward New Market.

That morning Emma Jane was having a difficult time concentrating on her lessons. "Pay attention, Emma Jane," her mother scolded. "Read that passage again." With some effort, Emma Jane managed to read the selection aloud with fewer stumbles. Still, her mind wandered throughout her lessons. All she could think about was how to tell Hattie that afternoon that she would have to stop teaching her to read.

"Emma Jane Williams, I think that's enough for today. You don't seem quite

yourself this mornin'. Now I need you to try on a new dress I'm makin' Hattie for her birthday. She's already nearly as tall as you."

"Oh, Mama," said Emma Jane, "you always think of the best surprises for birthdays. A new dress *and* readin' lessons! Hattie will be so happy."

"Tomorrow, I'm goin' to ask Moses to hitch up the wagon and take me to Turner's Store," her mother said. "I understand Mr. Turner has received some new school books, including a new printin' of McGuffey's Readers. I want Hattie to have a brand-new one, one she can use to teach her own children someday."

"But, Mama," Emma Jane interrupted. "I want Hattie to have *my* reader. I don't need it anymore, and I think it'd be special for her—you know, since we've been friends for so long."

"But it's tattered and, the last time I saw it, even a bit muddy. I think she'd like to have a new one."

"Mama, please. I know Hattie, and I just know she'd like mine better," Emma Jane insisted.

"Well, you might be right. But if she seems disappointed, assure her it was your idea and that I'll be happy to buy her a new one."

"And one more thing, Mama," said Emma Jane. "You and Papa are plannin' to surprise Hattie with readin' lessons and a new dress. So I've been thinkin' about what I could do to surprise her, too. Something really special!"

"What kind of surprise do you have in mind?"

"Mama, I want to invite Hattie, Moses, and Winnie to have a special birthday dinner with us in our dining room."

"Oh my, Emma Jane. Just the readin' lessons have Winnie and Moses on edge. But eatin' with us . . . well, I'm not even sure they'd agree to it. We need to be sensitive, you know, to their feelings about what's considered acceptable."

"Please, Mama, let's at least ask. And there's one more thing. You know how every year on my birthday you set my place with the silver cup Colonel Lee and his wife gave you when I was born?"

"Of course. You always love hearin' your father tell about servin' as a young doctor and meetin' Colonel Lee in the Mexican War before you were even born."

"That's why the cup's so special. And I just know it will make Hattie's birthday special, too."

"Well, I do think we need to wait and ask your father about this when he gets home next week. You know, it wouldn't be kind or Christian to put others in an uncomfortable position."

"I know, Mama. I don't want them to feel uncomfortable either, just special. Anyway, after I try on the dress, may Hattie and I go down to the creek together?"

"I don't think so. Winnie told me this mornin' that Hattie has a bit of a fever. And besides, I could use your help sewin' the buttons on Hattie's new dress."

Emma Jane, though concerned that Hattie was not well, felt a momentary relief. For until Hattie was better, their discussion about the reading lessons by the creek could be delayed, giving Emma Jane more time to find an answer to her dilemma.

Winnie didn't ring the dinner bell that evening. Instead, at supper time, she brought a simple meal of beans and cornbread into the warming kitchen. "Miz Sarah," she explained, "with Hattie bein' sick and Dr. Williams bein' gone, I jus' fixed you somethin' easy."

"I understand," Sarah replied sympathetically. "Does Hattie need anything?"

"No, Miz Sarah. I jus' gonna give her some chicken broth and keep a wet rag on her forehead. She be better come mornin'."

"It's cozy here in the warmin' kitchen," said Emma Jane as she and her mother ate their meal, "but it's lonely without Papa and Zachary. I miss settin' the table. And I'm a little worried about Hattie."

"I understand how you feel. We don't often think about the things and people so familiar to us—that is, not until we don't have them. But your father will be home in a few days, and Hattie will get better soon. And we have her birthday to look forward to. Now, off to bed. I'll wash up the bowls and be upstairs shortly to say our prayers."

The next few days went by slowly for Emma Jane. Hattie, while not getting worse, was still too ill to play, and Emma Jane grew more worried by the day about her mother and father's birthday gift of reading lessons for Hattie.

Early Saturday morning, Emma Jane awoke to the clanging of the dinner bell breaking the quietness. Jumping out of bed and rushing to the window, she saw Winnie down below announcing Dr. William's homecoming.

"It's Papa! He's back!" shouted Emma Jane.

Dressing quickly, she rushed downstairs, out the back door, and down the path to the barn where Moses was already helping unsaddle her father's horse.

"How's my girl?" Emma Jane's father asked as he lifted her off the ground and twirled her around.

"Oh, Pa! I missed you so much!"

The return of her father lifted Emma Jane's spirits immensely. That afternoon, Dr. and Mrs. Williams called Emma Jane into the parlor to discuss the plans for Hattie's birthday.

"It's just two days away," Mrs. Williams said thoughtfully. "I've almost finished the dress, and Winnie's planned a special dinner. She's even planned a surprise of her own for Hattie—an apple stack cake for dessert."

"Sounds like everything's done then," said Dr. Williams.

"Well, not quite, dear," said Sarah. "Emma Jane has a few ideas of her own that we need to discuss with you. Emma Jane, tell your father what you have in mind."

One by one, Emma Jane explained the three surprises she insisted would make Hattie's birthday even more special—giving Hattie her used McGuffey's Reader instead of a new one; inviting Hattie, Moses, and Winnie to eat with them in the dining room; and setting Hattie's place with the silver birthday cup from Colonel Lee.

"Well, I think your surprises are creative and most generous," replied Dr. Williams slowly as he evaluated the merits of each. "I'm pleased you're thinkin' so much about making others happy. I think Hattie will like the gift of your reader. But, Emma Jane," he cautioned, "don't be surprised or disappointed if they refuse to join us for dinner. That might make them very uncomfortable, and if they say no, we must not insist."

Emma Jane nodded, knowing without needing to be told that eating a meal together at the same table with Hattie, Winnie, and Moses would cause a stir among their neighbors should they ever find out. Yet she believed in her heart that the birthday surprises would be a success—all except the discovery that Hattie already knew how to read.

Early the next morning Winnie graciously but with unease accepted the invitation to dinner, knowing that the Williamses had extended it sincerely and lovingly.

"Oh, that's wonderful," exclaimed Sarah. "Now, Winnie, we've lots of work to do."

On the morning of the birthday, Winnie took special care in preparing the apple stack cake for Hattie, knowing it was also Dr. Williams's favorite. Later, Emma Jane helped Winnie polish the silver before setting the places at the table.

"Winnie," Emma Jane asked politely, "could you get down my silver cup from the cabinet?"

"Why, whatever for, Miz Emma Jane? It's not yo' birthday."

"I know, but I'm settin' Hattie's place with it. Mama and Papa said it's all right. It's very special to me, so I want to share it with

Hattie today."

"I knows that cup, and I remember when it come here from Colonel Lee after you was born. And I knows lots a good about Colonel Lee from Moses and yo' Pa. But what I don't knows is about lettin' Hattie use that special cup."

"But it's part of our surprise," Emma Jane insisted.

Winnie nodded with a frown and hurried back to the cook house, everything spinning around in her head. "It's too much, too much," she kept repeating under her breath.

There was no dinner bell that evening because everyone was already up at the old stone house making preparations—everyone except Hattie, who had been instructed to wait for Moses to come for her.

Just before seven o'clock, Sarah Williams lit the oil lamps and candles in the dining room while Winnie, wearing her Sunday dress, set the platters of food on the buffet.

"Moses, it's time to get Hattie," Mrs. Williams said warmly.

Hattie entered the dining room shyly and smiled with embarrassment as everyone shouted, "Happy birthday, Hattie!"

"Now, everyone sit down," Mrs. Williams instructed. "This is goin' to be a special evening."

Dr. Williams offered a prayer of thanks for the meal. Winnie served the food, then sat down next to Moses. Quietly, everyone began eating. Soon, however, the room was noisy with conversation. Dr. Williams told stories about his circuit ride, while Moses shared his hopes for good summer crops. And everyone talked about how they missed Zachary and how good it would be to see him at the table come summer.

Hattie kept stealing glances at the silver cup beside her plate but did not attempt to drink from it. Finally, Emma Jane looked directly at Hattie and with a kind but commanding voice said, "Hattie, my surprise for your birthday is to share my special cup with you. So please don't just look at it. Use it."

"Thank you, Emma Jane," Hattie said, grinning shyly. Then she took a sip of sweet tea, her favorite drink.

"Now before dessert," announced Dr. Williams, "Mrs. Williams, Emma Jane, and I have a special gift for you, Hattie."

Sarah rose and left the room, returning with a small package wrapped in delicate floral paper. "Happy birthday, Hattie," she said, placing the gift in the child's hands.

"Thank you, Miz Sarah," Hattie said softly, staring at the package.

"Open it, Hattie," whispered Winnie.

Emma Jane sat nervously, knowing that the moment she was dreading had arrived. Carefully, Hattie tore back the paper.

"Oh, my!" she exclaimed. "It's Emma Jane's McGuffey's Reader! I mean . . . it's a book!"

Emma Jane felt a knot forming in her stomach, her clammy hands grasping the underside of her dining chair.

"Why, how did you know it's a McGuffey's Reader?" asked Mrs. Williams in surprise. "And how did you know it's Emma Jane's?"

"Well, I . . . I jus' heard Emma Jane talkin' about her reader. I just supposin' . . . this be it." Then she paused, knowing she had lied. With tears forming in her eyes, she glanced at Emma Jane, who stared directly at her but said nothing. Then, after what seemed an eternity to Emma Jane, Hattie burst into tears. "Oh, Dr. Williams, Miz Williams. Oh, Ma and Pa! I can't lie no more. I jus' can't."

Emma Jane got up from her chair and hurried to Hattie's side. Putting her arms around her, she swallowed hard. "It's my fault, not Hattie's. It was my idea to teach her to read. I'm the one to blame." Then she began to cry, too.

"So that's the real story behind the mud splatters on the cover," exclaimed Dr. Williams. "I do declare, Emma Jane! You do seem to be one step ahead of your mother and me on some issues, and I guess this is one of them. Hattie, don't you worry for one moment. If you've already begun to read, Mrs. Williams's job of teachin' you will be that much easier. And Hattie, may God bless you with many, many more happy birthdays!"

Emma Jane, seeing that the crisis had passed, wiped her tears, hugged Hattie, and returned to her chair.

Winnie, who had said nothing throughout this conversation, rose from her chair and announced, "This is too much excitement on one night for anybody on God's good earth. My goodness, Hattie! I thought I was the bes' secret-keeper in the world, and you done kep' one better than I ever could." As she started toward the warming kitchen, she announced, "I think it's high time for some apple stack cake!"

Everyone burst into laughter as Winnie scurried off to the warming kitchen, and Hattie took another sip of sweet tea from the birthday cup.

APPLE STACK CAKE

Apple Stack Cake is a traditional dessert that has been made by cooks throughout the South for generations, especially in the Appalachian region. Because the cake uses basic ingredients, it was a favorite treat for birthdays, holidays, weddings, and family get-togethers.

To keep fresh apples from going bad, pioneers would slice them into thin pieces and lay them out in the sun to dry. Then the dried apples would be put away for the winter. Later the apples could be cooked in water to plump them up and bring back their flavor.

Although this recipe uses fresh apples, you can substitute a pound of dried apples for the filling, if you have them. To make it taste just right, the cake needs to be made the day before, so the apple flavor soaks into the cake layers. Be careful, though: The finished cake is heavy!

Photo: thebitenword.com

Old-Fashioned Apple Stack Cake

Cake:

½ cup butter
½ cup sugar
1 egg, well beaten
½ cup molasses
½ cup milk
3 ½ cups flour
½ teaspoon baking soda
½ teaspoon salt
1 teaspoon ginger

1. Preheat oven to 350 degrees.
2. Cream butter and sugar together. Add egg, molasses, and milk.
3. Mix together flour, baking soda, salt, and ginger.
4. Add dry ingredients to the wet ingredients. Mix thoroughly. Divide dough into 6 equal parts.
5. Roll out dough like pie crust and place into 9-inch pie pan. (Reuse pan or use multiple pans.)
6. Bake each layer for 10 to 12 minutes until golden brown. Cool.

Filling:

6 tart apples, peeled, cored, and thinly sliced
1 to 2 cups water
2 cups brown sugar
1 teaspoon cinnamon
1 teaspoon allspice
¼ teaspoon cloves

1. Cook apples with just enough water so they don't stick and burn.
2. When soft, mash apples with a potato masher. Add brown sugar and spices.
3. Continue cooking until mixture is very thick, like apple butter.
4. Spread filling between each cake layer, then chill for 24 hours.
5. To serve, slice into thin pieces.

THINK ABOUT IT

» Our story is set in the spring of 1860, one year before the start of the U.S. Civil War, also known as the War Between the States. In which state do Emma Jane and Hattie live? How do you know?

» Why do Emma Jane and Hattie keep their reading lessons a secret? Why do you think it was illegal in that time and place to teach a slave to read? Hattie's family has been freed by Emma Jane's father, so they are no longer slaves. Why do you think some of their neighbors might still believe it's wrong for Hattie to learn to read?

» Moses and Winnie are no longer slaves. Why do you think they've chosen to stay on the farm and serve the Williams family?

» What are some of the ways Emma Jane chooses to serve Hattie?

» What is the significance of the story's title, "A Book, a Bell, and a Cup"?

» How do you think the coming war will affect Emma Jane and her family? Why?

WORDS YOU NEED TO KNOW

» **Nation:** A group of many people who share a common language, culture, traditions, and history

» **Government:** The leaders God has chosen to guide and serve a nation by making and enforcing good laws for its citizens

» **Citizen:** A person who is a member of a nation because he or she was born there or was adopted by law from another nation

» **Laws:** Rules that protect a nation's people and tell them how to live peacefully among themselves and with others

» **Justice:** The righteous, unbiased enforcement of laws that are good and fair

» **Tax:** Money citizens pay to their government so it can provide services for the people

» **Loyalty:** A character trait you show by being faithful to another person or a group with whom you have a relationship

HIDE IT IN YOUR HEART

Pray for rulers and for all who have authority so that we can have quiet and peaceful lives full of worship and respect for God. (1 Timothy 2:2, NCV)

He who pursues righteousness and loyalty finds life, righteousness and honor. (Proverbs 21:21, NASB)

GOD RAISES UP NATIONS AND THEIR LEADERS

When is a nation not a country? After all, don't the words *nation* and *country* mean the same thing? Not exactly. Although the terms are often used interchangeably, a **nation** is a large group of people who share a common language, culture, traditions, and history. A country, on the other hand, is defined largely by its political and geographical boundaries. To put it simply, the word *nation* refers to a people, while *country* refers to a land.

Today, there are nearly 200 independent countries in the world. Each of these countries has a sovereign government, meaning that no other country has power over its territory. Also, each has clearly defined borders, even if one of its borders may be disputed by an adjoining country. For example, although Pakistan, India, and China disagree as to which of them owns an agricultural region known as Kashmir, all three countries are nevertheless easily identifiable on a world map.

However, not all nations with governments and borders are considered countries. A number of territories such as Bermuda, Hong Kong, and Puerto Rico have distinctive cultures but belong to other countries. For example, icy Greenland is home to more than 56,000 people mostly descended from Eskimos or early Scandinavian settlers. Greenland has its own constitution and a democratic government. Yet by law it is part of the kingdom of Denmark.

One thing all nations do have in common is that God has brought them into existence in His timing in the place of His choosing, and they will rise and fall according to His will for His glory and purposes. Acts 17:26 says, "From one man he made every nation of men, that they should inhabit the whole earth; and he determined the times set for them and the exact places where they should live."

Of the greatest civilizations of the past, many no longer exist as the world once knew them—the Babylonians, the Phoenicians, the Mayans, the Persians, the Ancient Greeks, the Macedonians of Alexander the Great, the Romans, and more. All were brought down and laid low in God's timing, but in His wisdom He allowed the influence of these peoples to live on through certain artistic, mathematical, linguistic, philosophical, medical, and technological advances that were passed along to other cultures. Job 12:23 says that God "makes nations great, and destroys them; he enlarges nations, and disperses them."

Not only does God control the rise and fall of nations and countries, but He also chooses the men and women who will rule over the people of a nation. The prophet Daniel said, "Praise the name of God forever and ever, for he has all wisdom and power. He controls

Detail from *The Battle of Milvian Bridge* by Romano.

the course of world events; he removes kings and sets up other kings" (Daniel 2:20–21, NLT). The apostle Paul wrote, "The authorities are God's servants, sent for your good" (Romans 13:4, NLT).

Does this mean that all kings and queens will fear and obey the Lord God Almighty? Does this mean all presidents and prime ministers will always make wise decisions? Does this mean legislators will always make laws that are just and right? No. Nevertheless, we can trust that God is using those in authority over us to accomplish His good purposes in history. Even rulers who do evil can be used by God. For example, under the rule of the Pharaohs, God strengthened through hardship (and eventually blessed with wealth) the people who would become the nation of Israel. Later, when Israel turned away from God, the Lord used Nebuchadnezzar II of Babylon to bring about His judgment against His chosen people (Jeremiah 25:9).

Regardless of whether a person has risen to a position of national leadership by democratic election, the overthrow of the established government, or royal succession, we can know that because God is always good and just, He appoints our leaders and orchestrates world events in keeping with His goodness, justice, and plan for creation. And one day, when Jesus returns, all the nations of the earth will acknowledge His authority over them: "The whole earth will acknowledge the LORD and return to him. All the families of the nations will bow down before him. For royal power belongs to the LORD. He rules all the nations" (Psalm 22:27–28, NLT).

> *My great concern is not whether God is on our side;*
> *my great concern is to be on God's side.*
> **Abraham Lincoln**
> 1809–1865

A GOVERNMENT MUST SERVE ITS CITIZENS

The United States' Declaration of Independence begins, "We hold these truths to be self-evident, that all men are created equal, that they are endowed by their Creator with certain unalienable rights, that among these are life, liberty, and the pursuit of happiness—that to secure these rights, governments are instituted among men . . ."

In other words, governments do not exist to expand their territory by waging war against their neighbors. They do not exist so that a few men and women can wield power or grow wealthy by trampling the rights of citizens and oppressing those they have been chosen to lead. Nor do governments exist to dictate to citizens what they may say, how they are to raise their children, how they are to spend their money, what they are to believe, or how they are to worship.

Governments exist to protect their citizens' rights and to provide them with security, basic services, administration, order, and justice. A **government** is made up of leaders God has chosen to guide and serve a nation by making and enforcing good laws for its citizens. Because God creates nations and raises up their leaders, their governments have a responsibility to rule wisely and make laws that reflect the just character of God. But what about those leaders who do not know God or choose not to seek Him? The Bible says, "The heavens proclaim his righteousness; every nation sees his glory" (Psalm 97:6, NLT). God's character has been etched into everything He made, including people, who are made in His image, so a nation's leaders have no excuse for not knowing His good and just nature (Romans 1:20). Therefore, even leaders who don't seek Him know in their hearts that just laws are good and right and essential to a nation's survival (Proverbs 29:4).

Before we go any further, let's define some terms. A **citizen** is a person who is a member of a nation or country. You are a citizen of your country either because you were born in that country or you were adopted by legal means from another nation. As a citizen of your country, you have both rights and responsibilities as defined by the nation's laws.

Laws are rules that protect a nation's people and tell them how to live peacefully among themselves and with others. Because we live in a fallen world, laws are created and enforced for our own good and protection as well as for the good of society in general. Just as when God placed Adam and Eve in the garden of Eden and gave them a single law for their protection (Genesis 2:17), so godly laws provide us with security, both protecting us from harm and freeing us to enjoy all that is truly good and beautiful. Ideally, a country's laws are created by people who fear God and love justice and mercy.

Justice is the righteous, unbiased enforcement of laws that are good and fair. Our Lord is a righteous God who loves justice (Psalm 11:7), and He commands His image-bearers to live and serve one another with respect, goodness, and fairness (Jeremiah 22:3). Those who are chosen to rule must do likewise: "He who rules over men must be just, ruling in the fear of God" (2 Samuel 23:3, NKJV). Presidents, kings, and lawmakers must be fair and establish justice in their nations by making good laws and enforcing them with wisdom, righteousness, and respect for all citizens.

One of the definitions of the word *just* is "deserved." You may have heard the phrase "just deserts." This means that fair and impartial laws come with deserved consequences for those who choose to disobey the law. When a person "breaks," or violates, a law, he or she may be required by the nation's court system to pay a fine, perform community service, or go to prison, depending on the severity of the crime that was committed. Because some laws come with harsh penalties for breaking them, it is extremely important that the government provide a fair trial to every person who is accused of a crime, whatever his or her status, wealth, race, lifestyle, or religion. Deuteronomy 1:17 (ICB) says, "When you judge, be fair to everyone. Don't act as if one person is more important than another."

In 1892, Baptist minister Francis Bellamy composed what he called "The Pledge of Allegiance" in celebration of the 400th anniversary of Christopher Columbus's arrival in the Americas. First published in a popular children's magazine, the pledge was formally adopted by the United States Congress as the national pledge in 1942. The wording has changed four times over the years, the most recent being the addition of the words "under God" in 1954. Today, the Pledge of Allegiance goes like this:

Photo: Frank Vincentz

I pledge allegiance to the flag of the United States of America, and to the republic for which it stands, one nation under God, indivisible, with liberty and justice for all.

Notice the final six words: "with liberty and justice for all." These words speak to the heart of what God intends every nation should provide its citizens—*all* of its citizens. If a nation is to be truly free and allow righteousness to flourish (Proverbs 14:34), liberty and justice cannot be limited to a privileged few, nor can it be denied to a less powerful segment of society. The poet Emma Lazarus—whose sonnet "The New Colossus" is inscribed on a plaque mounted on the pedestal of the Statue of Liberty—once said, "Until we are all free, we are none of us free."

MAKE A NOTE OF IT
Draw or collect pictures of several services a government provides to its people. Where do you think the money comes from to pay for each of these services?

THE SPACE RACE

During the 1950s and '60s, the United States and the former Soviet Union competed to see which would be the first to explore the frontiers of outer space. Both countries spent millions on the space race because each believed that winning the race was vital to the protection of its citizens and their way of life. At first, the Soviet Union pulled ahead, launching Sputnik, the first man-made satellite, on October 4, 1957, and then sending the first human—cosmonaut Yuri Gagarin—into space on April 12, 1961.

Earthrise by William Anders.

Determined not to fall behind, the United States kicked its space program into high gear. In 1962, President John F. Kennedy promised that before the end of the decade, America would put a man on the moon and bring him safely home. After nearly a dozen manned space missions, Apollo 11 touched down on the surface of the moon on July 20, 1969, and astronaut Neil Armstrong became the first human to step on another world.

Reaching the moon was an important achievement for the United States, but the victory did not come without sacrifice. In 1967, the first Apollo crew died when a fire started inside their spacecraft during a test. This tragedy changed the way future spacecraft were built and flown.

A great number of the household conveniences we enjoy today are a direct result of the space race. Many of the technologies developed for the space program have been adapted for everyday use in kitchen appliances, food packaging, power tools, video games, health care, even in athletic shoes. Micro-technology developed for use in space has changed the way we keep time, listen to music, and keep in touch with one another.

The space race even had a profound impact on ecology, as people were able to see our planet for the first time from space. The photo *Earthrise*, taken by Apollo 8 astronaut William Anders in 1968, showed the planet Earth rising above the surface of the moon. This image became instantly famous and inspired many people to become better stewards of the earth's resources.

HOW CAN YOU SERVE YOUR COUNTRY?

Every four years, the United States of America holds a November election in which its citizens vote and select a president to lead their country for the next four years. The following January an inauguration is held, during which the elected president takes an oath to faithfully carry out the duties of the office and to preserve, protect, and defend the Constitution of the United States. Traditionally, the newly sworn-in president then delivers a speech called the inaugural address. One of the most memorable of these speeches was delivered on January 20, 1961, by John F. Kennedy, the youngest man ever elected to the presidency.

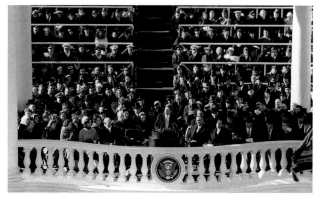

John F. Kennedy giving his inaugural speech.

In his speech, Kennedy called on a new generation of Americans to put the needs of others ahead of their own. He said that every citizen must be prepared to make sacrifices if our nation and the world were to emerge victorious in the struggle against tyranny, poverty, and disease. "And so, my fellow Americans," he said, "ask not what your country can do for you—ask what you can do for your country. . . . Let us go forth to lead the land we love, asking His blessing and His help, but knowing that here on earth God's work must truly be our own."

So what can you do for your country? The Bible tells us that Christians have the following responsibilities to their nation and its laws:

1. Submit to the authorities.
2. Obey the laws of the land.
3. Show respect to everyone.
4. Pray for those in authority.

Let's take a closer look at each of these responsibilities.

SUBMIT TO THE AUTHORITIES

The apostle Peter said, "Submit yourselves for the Lord's sake to every authority instituted among men: whether to the king, as the supreme authority, or to governors, who are sent by him to punish those who do wrong and to commend those who do right" (1 Peter 2:13–14). Romans 13:1–2 (NCV) says, "All of you must yield to the government rulers. No one rules unless God has given him the power to rule, and no one rules now without that power from God. So those who are against the government are really against what God has commanded."

We submit to authorities by honoring them and acknowledging their right to rule over us. Another way we submit to the government is by paying our taxes. A tax is money citizens pay to their government so it can provide services for the people, such as a military, courts, police, firefighters, libraries, parks, and roads. Government officials are also paid out of our taxes. Romans 13:6–7 (NCV) says, "This is also why you pay taxes. Rulers are working for God and give their time to their work. Pay everyone, then, what you owe. If you owe any kind of tax, pay it. Show respect and honor to them all."

Jesus summed it up this way: "Render to Caesar the things that are Caesar's, and to God the things that are God's" (Matthew 22:21, ESV).

OBEY THE LAWS OF THE LAND

Government leaders are responsible for establishing and enforcing laws that promote justice, maintain order, and protect the life and liberty of every citizen. Traffic laws, for example, are designed to keep all drivers and their passengers safe on the roads. Copyright laws protect the rights of authors and artists to copy, distribute, or adapt their work. Free speech laws protect the rights of citizens to express their beliefs peacefully without fear of being silenced by a government that disagrees with them.

Christians are commanded to obey the laws that have been set down by those whom God has placed in authority over us. Titus 3:1 (NLT) says, "Remind the believers to submit to the government and its officers. They should be obedient, always ready to do what is good." But what about when a law is ungodly or unjust? What if your country passed a law making it illegal to worship Jesus Christ or pray to God?

The Bible makes it clear that when a man-made law conflicts with God's laws, we are to obey God's laws first. When Peter and the apostles were arrested by the authorities for preaching the gospel, an angel of the Lord opened the doors of the jail during the night and

said to them, "Go, stand in the temple courts and tell the people the full message of this new life." At daybreak the apostles entered the temple courts, as they had been told, and began to teach the people. The authorities came to them once more and said, "We gave you strict orders not to teach in the name of Jesus." Peter responded, "We must obey God rather than men!" (Acts 5:17–29).

Paul and Agrippa by Surikov.

SHOW RESPECT TO EVERYONE

First Peter 2:17 says, "Show proper respect to everyone: Love the brotherhood of believers, fear God, honor the king." Good laws usually come down to mutual love and respect among citizens. Indeed, Jesus said that all of God's law could be summed up in two commandments: "Love the Lord your God with all your heart and with all your soul and with all your mind" and "Love your neighbor as yourself" (Matthew 22:37–40). If all people faithfully followed these two commandments and treated one another with kindness and respect, they would be the only two laws anyone ever needed.

MAKE A NOTE OF IT

Read Acts 5:12–42. Peter and the apostles showed their faith and courage by choosing to preach the gospel in violation of an ungodly law. The authorities had them flogged, or whipped, for their disobedience and commanded them again not to speak in the name of Jesus. Yet the apostles rejoiced because they had been counted worthy of suffering for His name's sake, and "they never stopped teaching and proclaiming the good news that Jesus is the Christ." Did the apostles do the right thing when they disobeyed the government authorities? Why? What can you expect the authorities to do if you choose not to obey their laws? What does Matthew 5:11–12 say about being persecuted for obeying God?

THE PEACE CORPS

The Peace Corps was created as a way to promote peace and friendship throughout the world. In 1961, President Kennedy signed an executive order creating a volunteer organization that would provide technological training to underprivileged countries, as well as help promote cultural understanding between America and other nations.

Peace Corps volunteers are usually college graduates who devote at least two years of their lives to serving and teaching abroad. Nearly half of the Corps' assistance goes to countries in Africa, while other programs bring education and expertise to Latin America, the Caribbean, Asia, and island nations in the Pacific.

Recently, the organization celebrated its fiftieth anniversary. In the past five decades, more than 200,000 Peace Corps volunteers have assisted people around the world in areas such as farming and agriculture, conservation, park and wildlife management, and health and sanitation. They also help with short-term projects, such as cleaning up after a natural disaster or helping people become better prepared to survive floods, volcanoes, or tsunamis. With the rise of computers, the Peace Corps now offers programs on computer literacy, business development, and information technologies.

A similar organization, dedicated to helping encourage volunteerism within the United States, is called AmeriCorps. Founded in 1993 by President Bill Clinton and later expanded by President George W. Bush, AmeriCorps focuses on issues within the United States such as education, poverty, and disaster relief. AmeriCorps volunteers often work with faith-based organizations, public agencies, and groups like Habitat for Humanity and the American Red Cross to assist low-income communities or help local governments with infrastructure improvement, urban and rural development, and energy conservation.

PRAY FOR THOSE IN AUTHORITY

In his letter to Timothy, the apostle Paul wrote, "I urge, then, first of all, that requests, prayers, intercession and thanksgiving be made for everyone—for kings and all those in authority, that we may live peaceful and quiet lives in all godliness and holiness" (1 Timothy 2:1–2). As Christians, we are to pray for our nation's leaders even if we don't agree with all their policies and decisions.

How should you pray for those in authority? Remember to give thanks for the authorities because they are God's servants and are sent for your good (Romans 13:4). Ask God to grant to your nation's leaders the wisdom and courage to do what is right. Ask Him to give them the strength to defend our liberties and protect and safeguard our homes and our families. Finally, ask God to give the authorities the vision to guide our nation into the paths of peace, justice, and righteousness.

WHAT SHOULD I DO?

Loyalty is a character trait that you show by being faithful to another person or a group with whom you have a relationship. Loyalty is a commitment you make to love, honor, and support a friend or a government even in tough times. The three Persons of the Trinity exhibit perfect loyalty. Their eternal love for one another and the oneness of their fellowship show us the kind of relationship God wants us to experience with Him, with our families, and with our fellow Christians. He expects us to be loyal, to stick together "through thick and thin," to remain faithful in loving and serving Him and others. "He who pursues righteousness and loyalty finds life, righteousness and honor" (Proverbs 21:21, NASB).

Patriotism is a love or devotion we show to our country. We demonstrate patriotic loyalty to our country by obeying its laws (Matthew 22:21), participating in civic duties such as voting or serving in government, praying for our leaders, and by submitting to the authorities God has placed over us (1 Peter 2:17).

A PRAYER

Dear God, thank you for the nation where I live. Thank you for choosing the leaders of our government. Give them the wisdom and courage to do what is right. Help them to love freedom and justice and to protect our homes and our families. And please give me the desire and the ability to love and serve my fellow citizens. I ask these things in the mighty name of Jesus. Amen.

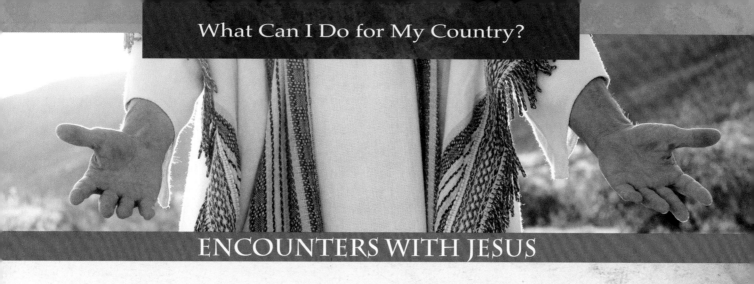

ENCOUNTERS WITH JESUS

THE KINGDOM OF GOD BELONGS TO SUCH AS THESE

Shoshanna loved the feast of Passover. The holiday always seemed full of warmth and good feelings, a time when all the Jews gathered as equals to celebrate God's faithfulness in delivering them from slavery long ago, making Shoshanna proud to be a member of the Hebrew nation. She also loved that Passover arrived in springtime, her favorite season of the year. The land was green, flowers bloomed, and the whole earth seemed to be awakening from a gray, wet winter and looking forward to the warm summer sun.

This was a special Passover for Shoshanna's family. This year Shoshanna's mother and baby brother were going with her father on his annual pilgrimage to Jerusalem. And because Shoshanna was now ten and old enough to help along the way, her father had said that she, too, could go. She felt as if she knew Jerusalem from her father's stories, but this would be her first time to see the grand city and its glorious temple. Her father said that the temple building and its walls were made of pure white marble and decorated with gold. He always spoke of the temple in a reverent tone. Shoshanna could hardly wait to see it for herself!

Because of the expense required for all four of them to make the trip from Galilee to Jerusalem and back again, Shoshanna had been going to work with her mother for the past month. Shoshanna's mother was employed as a servant in the home of Eli, a wealthy and influential businessman in the city of Tiberius. Because of its position on the southwestern edge of the Sea of Galilee, Tiberius was an important trade city that connected Jerusalem and the cities of southern Judea with the region of Galilee and, eventually, the Mediterranean.

Tiberius in the early 1900s.

This year, however, Master Eli wasn't well enough to travel to Jerusalem, so his twenty-five-year-old son Solomon was making the journey with friends. That meant Shoshanna's mother and the other servants needed to prepare the feast for Eli's family at home while also getting food ready for Solomon and his friends to take with them on their journey.

Although Shoshanna was too small to help with work involving sharp knives or hot ovens, she was the perfect size to run errands and do other small tasks for the servants. She could also help with cleaning the house, since a Jewish home had to be spotless for the Passover feast. As she worked, Shoshanna couldn't help being a little envious of Master Eli and his family and all the fine things they owned. Her own family's small house had a dirt floor, and she had to share a bed with her three younger sisters. Her father said that being rich couldn't make a person happy, but Shoshanna liked the warm fires, soft blankets, and colorful mosaics in Master Eli's house. His daughters had beautiful clothing and warm winter cloaks. They enjoyed bread made from the finest wheat flour, fresh fish every day, and more olives and grapes than they could eat. After a day of smelling such food, Shoshanna found it difficult to be satisfied with the coarse barley bread and dried salted sardines she ate at home.

Because of their status, Master Eli's daughters would marry well and move to other elegant houses. Their brother, Solomon, had been studying the Torah since he was a boy and had become a leader in the local synagogue. Eventually, he hoped to become a member of the Sanhedrin in Jerusalem. The Sanhedrin was a council of powerful religious leaders who made important decisions about how Jews were to live.

Only one thing made Shoshanna think twice about wanting to change places with Master Eli's daughters. Watching the family interact at meals, Shoshanna thought that they were all too worried about what other people thought of them. Solomon, in particular, was concerned with rigidly following all the rules the Jewish leaders set down about how to eat, how to wash, how to pray, and whom to talk to. Shoshanna wondered if this was what it took to please God.

When she was alone with her father, she asked him about it. "Does following the rabbis' rules please God?"

Her father sat quietly for a moment, then said, "Following the rules the rabbis have given us is good. They have studied the law God gave Moses, and their teachings help us keep that law. It is our tradition and our obligation to God." He stretched his feet toward the fire and pulled Shoshanna close. The chill of winter had passed, but the nights were still cool. "It's like this: What would happen if you disobeyed me?"

Shoshanna didn't have to think about this long. "I would be punished, of course," she said.

"That's true," her father replied. "You obey me to avoid punishment, and that pleases me."

"But father, I obey you for another reason, too. I obey you because I love you." Shoshanna stretched up tall to give her father a kiss on the cheek.

He laughed and snuggled her close. "I love you too, Shoshanna. Very much."

Road to Jerusalem, early 1900s.

One week before the Passover feast, Shoshanna and her parents packed their things in cloth bags and started out on the road to Jerusalem. Such an adventure! Her sisters were too young to walk such a long way, so they stayed with relatives. Because the road was rough and dusty, Shoshanna tucked her sandals into her satchel and walked barefoot whenever she could, wanting to have her sandals clean when they reached Jerusalem.

Their journey took them south along the Jordan River valley, surrounded by distant peaks and rocky wilderness. They kept to the main road along the east side of the river because the region of Samaria claimed the western side. Shoshanna's father said that the Samaritans were outsiders—Jews who long ago had intermarried with Canaanites and fallen from the true way of worshiping God. The rabbis in Jerusalem had decreed that all Jews should avoid speaking or dealing with Samaritans.

As Shoshanna and her parents neared Jerusalem, the crowds became larger. But the people were merry and cheerful, singing songs and telling stories and jokes. Although Shoshanna often helped with the baby, her mother generally let her roam freely to play with the other children, trusting the many mothers and fathers among the travelers to keep an eye on them all.

When the noonday sun began to beat down on the travelers, most stopped by the side of the road to rest and wait for the heat to die down. Sitting next to her mother as they ate day-old flatbread, Shoshanna listened to the conversations around her. Her mother and some of the other women from Tiberius chatted good-naturedly. Beyond, a group of boys played a game in the dirt with stones. And near the side of the road sat a man surrounded by fishermen and laborers who listened intently to him. As Shoshanna watched, a few synagogue leaders who were also traveling to Jerusalem for the feast stopped and began to debate with the man.

As they talked, whispers began to circulate among the crowd. "I think that is the teacher Jesus," one of the women told Shoshanna's mother. "They say he can heal the sick."

Another woman chimed in. "I heard that he can even make the deaf hear and the blind see. Not even the rabbis can work such miracles."

Shoshanna thought he looked very ordinary. She was sure she could pass him on the road and never notice him. Yet there was something about his face and voice that captured her attention. She wanted to get closer to him, but she wasn't exactly sure why.

As the sun sank a little lower in the sky, people began to stand and gather their things to continue the journey. Within a few hours, night would fall, bringing the beginning of another day. The travelers would want to be safely camped by then.

Seeing that the men with Jesus were preparing to start out again as well, Shoshanna's mother grabbed her hand and pulled her to her feet. "Come with me," she said. "Maybe the teacher Jesus will bless you and Jonah."

Walking up behind Jesus and his followers, Shoshanna's mother waited until the men from the synagogue had walked away. Then she humbly approached Jesus, holding out little Jonah. "Sir, would you please bless my son?" she asked.

Jesus turned and saw the three of them, with other mothers at their heels, eager to take advantage of this opportunity. They all wanted a blessing for their children from the holy man. Jesus smiled at the sight of Shoshanna's squirming baby brother.

But one of his followers stepped between them. "I am sorry, mother, but the master cannot be disturbed. We have far to go before the Passover and no time for children."

Frightened by the man, Shoshanna ducked behind her mother, trying to become invisible. She looked at her dusty, mud-streaked hands and clothing. She thought the man was probably worried that she was too dirty to see Jesus.

In the frozen silence, Jesus stepped forward and placed his hand on the man's arm. "It is you who are wrong," he said firmly. "Let the little children come to me. Do not stop them, because the kingdom of God belongs to little ones such as these." He reached for Jonah, smiling at Shoshanna's mother. Timidly, she handed the baby to Jesus, still unsure whether it was all right.

Cradling the baby boy, Jesus spoke to his companions. "The truth is that whoever does not enter the kingdom of God like a little child will not enter it at all." Placing his large, calloused hand on Jonah's fuzzy little head, Jesus tenderly spoke a blessing over him. Then he handed the baby back to his mother and beckoned the other children to come close, touching and blessing them one after another.

Shoshanna watched as the line of mothers and children slowly shrank. She, too, desperately wanted a blessing from Jesus, but she felt so dirty. She tried to find a clean section of her robe to wipe her hands on but couldn't seem to make much progress. When the last child had been blessed by Jesus, Shoshanna still hadn't gathered up enough courage to step forward for the blessing she wanted so much.

The men with Jesus tried to usher him back onto the road. But Jesus sat and waited, looking in Shoshanna's direction. Seeing her peek out from behind her mother's skirts, he smiled a warm, friendly smile that made Shoshanna happy all over. Suddenly she forgot that her hands were dirty. Not frightened or ashamed any longer, Shoshanna ran to him and hugged him, then put her hands into his.

Leaning toward her until their foreheads touched, Jesus spoke a special blessing over Shoshanna. When he was done, Shoshanna felt clean inside and out, as though she sparkled from head to toe. She didn't know much about the kingdom of God, but she knew that if Jesus was going to be there, she wanted to be there too. Impulsively, she stretched up and kissed him shyly on the cheek. He smiled and put his hand on the top of her head before she slipped away, back to her mother.

As Jesus and his companions set out down the road, Shoshanna followed close behind. She wanted to be near Jesus as long as she could. Suddenly, a young man ran up to them and knelt at Jesus' feet. She recognized the man as Solomon, Master Eli's son. Shoshanna crept closer to where she could see and hear everything.

Solomon looked up at Jesus earnestly. "Rabbi," he begged, "what good thing must I do to gain eternal life?" Shoshanna saw that his fine robes were getting dirty from kneeling in the middle of the road, but he didn't seem to care.

Jesus looked at Solomon soberly, as if measuring both him and his question. "Why do

you ask me about what is good? No one is good—except God alone." Looking at the young man like he was seeing into his soul, Jesus said, "If you still want to obtain eternal life, you must keep the commandments."

"Which ones?" Solomon asked eagerly.

"Don't murder, don't commit adultery, don't steal, don't lie. Honor your father and mother. And, above all, love your neighbor as yourself," Jesus replied.

Solomon seemed disappointed by Jesus' answer. "But I have kept all of these commandments since I was a boy. What else must I do?"

Jesus looked at him steadily. "You still lack one thing. Go sell all your possessions, give the money to the poor, and you will have riches in heaven. Then come and follow me."

Shoshanna gasped, thinking about all the nice things in Master Eli's house. If Solomon only sold the things he himself owned—his furniture, clothing, and horses—the money raised would be enormous! But then Solomon would be poor himself, and this would destroy his dreams of becoming an important man.

Picturing Master Eli's grand house all empty and cold, Shoshanna was suddenly grateful for her small house, with its dirt floor and scratchy blankets. It wouldn't be hard at all for her to give up these few things to please Jesus!

Solomon's face fell like a dark cloud passing over the sun. It was clear from his hurt expression that he thought Jesus had asked too much of him. He had come seeking the key to greatness from someone he respected, and Jesus had told him he must give up all his riches and, with them, his dreams. Standing, Solomon walked sorrowfully away.

Watching him go, Jesus remarked to his companions, "I tell you the truth, it is very hard for a rich person to enter the kingdom of heaven. In fact, it would be easier for a camel to pass through the eye of a needle than for a wealthy man to enter the kingdom of God."

Shoshanna giggled at the thought of several men trying to shove a camel through the tiny hole in a needle. Then she caught herself and stopped, remembering Solomon's profound sadness.

One of Jesus' companions asked him, "Who then can be saved?"

The Rich Young Man by Bida.

Jesus turned to him. "For people, it is impossible. But with God, all things are possible."

As Jesus and his followers resumed their journey, Shoshanna stood thinking about everything she had seen and heard that day. She knew in her heart that the blessing she had received from Jesus was more precious than anything owned by Solomon and his sisters. Yet Solomon had turned and walked away from Jesus.

Suddenly, it was very important to Shoshanna to find Solomon and convince him to come back. Following Jesus, she was certain, was so much more valuable than money, things, or titles! Urgently, she searched the crowd for Solomon, weaving in and out of the stream of people headed for Jerusalem. She had to tell him that he had made a mistake, that there was still time. She believed it with all her heart.

But Solomon was nowhere to be found.

TAKE A CLOSER LOOK

» Read the biblical accounts of these events in Matthew 19:13–26 and Mark 10:13–27 and compare them to the story you've just read.

» Why does Shoshanna envy Eli's family? What do they have that her family does not?

» Why is Solomon careful to follow God's law and all the rules set down by the Jewish leaders? Why do you think he wants to someday join the Sanhedrin?

» Read Matthew 23 and 1 Corinthians 13:1–2. Why is it not enough to obey the "letter of the law," or just what is written in the law? What is the "spirit of the law," and why is it important? Is it easier or harder to obey someone you love? Why?

» What do you think Jesus means when He says, "Anyone who will not receive the kingdom of God like a little child will never enter it"?

» Jesus and the apostles did not teach that all followers of Christ must sell everything they have and give the money to the poor. Why do you think He says this to the rich young man? Why does He tell his disciples that it's difficult for a rich man to enter the kingdom of heaven?

WHY CAN'T WE ALL JUST GET ALONG?

FOR WHERE YOU HAVE ENVY AND SELFISH AMBITION, THERE YOU FIND DISORDER AND EVERY EVIL PRACTICE.

JAMES 3:16

THE BIG IDEA

The 1950s are often remembered as a time of peace and prosperity in America, happy days of malt shops, hula hoops, pony tails, ducktails, poodle skirts, and penny loafers. Yet in Hollywood it seemed the world was coming to an end every other week. Audiences were flocking to movie theaters to see low-budget thrillers with titles like *It Came from Beneath the Sea, The Beast from 20,000 Fathoms, It! The Terror from Beyond Space, The Blob,* and *The Thing from Another World.* On the big screen, humanity was under constant threat of annihilation by colossal insects, radioactive behemoths, and malevolent beings from outer space bent on claiming our planet for their own.

Why were 1950s movie-goers so fascinated with tales of mass destruction and alien invasion? Because these movies played upon a nagging fear that maybe life in America wasn't as rosy as it appeared on the surface. The evening news was dominated by stories of racial unrest, growing tension between the United States and the Soviet Union, the new hydrogen bomb, and claims by a little-known senator from Wisconsin that Communists had infiltrated the federal

government. Science-fiction thrillers gave a face to Americans' fears with oversized enemies that could be clearly identified and eventually defeated, usually in less than an hour and a half of screen time.

Look again at the movie titles and you'll see that the threat appeared to come from somewhere else. Beneath the sea. Beyond space. Another world. But the origin of many of the monstrous mutations in these movies could often be traced to mankind's own actions. Some of the creatures, as in *The Fly*, were the results of strange experiments gone terribly wrong. Some, like the gargantuan ants of *Them!*, were unforeseen consequences of the testing of atomic bombs.

The best of these movies, however, recognized the biblical truth that the greatest threat to our peace and safety does not come from alien blobs or giant bugs. The most terrible danger to men, women, and children lurks within the hearts of people themselves. What is this creeping menace that can wreak havoc in our homes, destroy lives, and bring down entire civilizations? The Bible calls it sin.

Expulsion from the Garden of Eden by Cole.

Before Adam and Eve chose to disobey God, they could never have imagined the horrible consequences of sin. They couldn't even begin to comprehend the end of life. But the moment they chose to put their own desires first, ahead of God's commandments, death and destruction entered creation and became the way of all things. People had been given a choice between right and wrong and chose to do wrong. With this willful act of disobedience, sin came into the world and destroyed people's perfect home, perfect bodies, perfect lives, and their perfect relationship with God.

Since the Fall, all people have been separated from God by their sin (Romans 3:23). Because they do not live in harmony with God, they do not live in harmony with themselves. And because people do not live in harmony with themselves, they find it impossible to live in harmony with each other. Even among loving families and friends there is never perfect harmony. Sometimes the best of friends argue among themselves. Brothers and sisters sometimes fight with each other. Sometimes parents do not stay married, and children do not always obey and honor their parents.

Not only are friends and families affected by the Fall, but sin creates problems for every nation. Look around our country and you will see many of God's blessings. You will see many citizens who know and love God and who strive to help our nation provide justice for all people. But you don't have to look far to see the ravages of sin in our cities and our nation.

People commit crimes against others. Government leaders argue with one another, leading to poor decisions and, sometimes, unjust laws. Nations want what other nations have, which leads to unfriendly relations and sometimes war.

All sin is destructive, but in this lesson we will focus on one sin that is responsible for much of the disharmony we experience in our families and among friends and nations. That sin is envy. When we envy what other people have or are, we often act selfishly, thinking only

HARRIET BEECHER STOWE

Harriet Beecher Stowe was born in Connecticut in 1811, the seventh of thirteen children. Her parents were deeply religious and taught their children they could make a difference in the world. Harriet's seven brothers, including Henry Ward Beecher, all became ministers. Her oldest sister was a pioneer in education for American women, while her youngest sister was cofounder of an organization to win voting rights for women. Harriet believed her purpose in life was to write about social injustice.

In 1851, she began writing *Uncle Tom's Cabin* as a serialized story for an antislavery magazine. The story was soon published as a book and took the country by storm, eventually becoming the best-selling novel of the century.

The book tells the story of Uncle Tom, a middle-aged slave who is sold by his master. While traveling downriver with a slave trader, Tom rescues Eva, a white girl, from drowning and is bought by her father. Tom and Eva become good friends, and when Eva becomes sick, she convinces her father before she dies to free Uncle Tom. But her father is killed before he can arrange it, and Tom is sold to a cruel master, Simon Legree, who is determined to destroy Tom's faith. In the end, Tom is killed for helping two other slaves escape. As Tom is dying, he forgives the two overseers who have savagely beaten him. Humbled by the character of the man they have killed, both men become Christians. The truth of Uncle Tom's faith lives on.

The publication of *Uncle Tom's Cabin* fanned the flames of an already tense national issue. Abolitionists, people who wanted to make it illegal to own slaves, praised the novel for exposing the evils of slavery. However, Southern slave owners were outraged, calling the novel slanderous and false.

Reflecting on the novel years later, Harriet Beecher Stowe said in her journal, "I wrote what I did because as a woman, as a mother, I was oppressed and broken-hearted with the sorrows and injustice I saw; because as a Christian I felt the dishonor to Christianity; because as a lover of my county, I trembled at the coming day of wrath."

In 1862, during the early years of the Civil War, Harriet met with Abraham Lincoln. According to popular legend, President Lincoln said upon meeting her, "So this is the little lady who started this great war."

of ourselves. Then in order to get what we want, we commit more sins that hurt other people. Greed, quarreling, lying, stealing, cheating, slander—these are just a few of the formidable fiends that will poison your relationships, sap your faith, and undermine your character. And every one of them comes from within the human heart.

WHAT YOU WILL DO
» You will learn how envy leads to many other sins against others.
» You will recognize the destructive effects of sin on families and nations.
» You will be encouraged to demonstrate kindness as a means of building harmony in your family, among your friends, and with others.

THE VISIT—SUMMER 1860

"Thank you, Moses," said Sarah Williams as Moses unloaded the wagon filled with the supplies he had purchased that morning at Turner's Store. "And was there any mail?"

"Jus' one letter, Miz Sarah," replied Moses as he reached inside his satchel and handed her an envelope.

"Why, I declare! It's from my brother Thad in Pennsylvania. What a surprise!" she exclaimed as she hurried up the back steps into the warming kitchen. "I just can't believe it."

"Believe what?" asked Emma Jane, who was sitting with Hattie at the long oak table that served as the desk for their reading lessons.

"We just received a letter from your Uncle Thaddeus. Whatever could have inspired him to write?"

As her mother began reading the letter silently, Emma Jane watched her face intently, trying to decipher the message. Her mother's smile assured her the letter contained good news, but then her raised eyebrows and audible gasp seemed to indicate the news was not so good after all.

"Tell us, Mama!" exclaimed Emma Jane, unable to contain her curiosity any longer. "What's Uncle Thaddeus writing about?"

"The whole family's comin' for a visit!" Sarah replied with astonishment.

"Oh, Mama! Will I finally get to meet them—Uncle Thaddeus, Aunt Elizabeth, and all my cousins?"

"Yes, my dear, *all* of them! And much sooner than you can imagine!"

"What do you mean?"

"I mean next week—the whole lot of them—Uncle Thaddeus, Aunt Elizabeth, and your cousins David, Martha, Sallie, and little Peter. How can we possibly be ready by then?"

Emma Jane didn't share her mother's concerns about the timing of the visit. All she could think of was the excitement of finally meeting the relatives she had only heard about.

"Is they comin' by wagon, Miz Sarah?" asked Hattie who had also been listening.

"No, Hattie," chuckled Sarah. "They're takin' a train from Lancaster to Baltimore, a steamer down Chesapeake Bay to Potomac Creek, another train to Richmond, and another from Richmond to Waynesboro."

"And how will they get from Waynesboro to our farm?" asked Emma Jane.

"Uncle Thaddeus says they'll take a stagecoach from the train station in Waynesboro to Turner's Store, and he wants your father and Moses to pick them up there."

"Mama, doesn't Uncle Thaddeus work for the railroad?"

"Well, he doesn't exactly *work for* the railroad. I'd say he's more like an *owner* of the Pennsylvania Railroad, or at least one of the owners."

"Is they rich folk?" asked Hattie.

"Well, let's just say that Uncle Thaddeus has been very successful in business. But more importantly, he's a wonderful brother. Now, Emma Jane, you listen to Hattie read the last part of the lesson for today while I go find your father and Zachary. We have a heap of things to do before next week."

Cadets at Virginia Military Institute. Photo by Mgirardi.

Zachary, who was home from Virginia Military Institute for the summer, had exchanged his cadet's uniform for farming overalls. He, his father, and Moses were down by the barn where they were adding carefully measured amounts of skimmed milk, lime, iron oxide, and linseed oil to a large copper vat.

"I'm definitely choosing a military career over farming!" Zachary exclaimed as he stirred the sticky red mixture they would use to paint the faded barn.

"I understand, Son," his father responded with a hearty laugh. "Keeping this old home place up is hard work. But I think you'll appreciate it bein' in good shape when you inherit it after your mother and I are gone."

"Thomas," shouted Sarah as she ran toward the barn. "Company's comin' next week, and lots of it! Thad, Elizabeth, and the children will be here a week from today! How can we possibly be ready by then?"

"That's great news. Great news, indeed! Don't worry—Zach's here, and we have Moses and Winnie," he replied reassuringly.

Zachary wiped red dust from his forehead and said, "I haven't seen Cousin David since we were kids in little britches. I promise I'll try to be nice to him in spite of our rivalry—you know how it is between VMI and West Point cadets!"

Sarah Williams smiled, but her mind was elsewhere already making preparations for the visit. She hurried back to the house and gathered Winnie, Hattie, and Emma Jane around the kitchen table to begin making plans. First, there were the sleeping arrangements, which would include pallets for the youngest two children in the guest bedroom with Thaddeus and Elizabeth. Emma Jane said she wouldn't mind sleeping on the floor if it meant getting to know her cousins better. Next, Sarah and Winnie chose menus and made a list of additional supplies for Moses to purchase at Turner's Store. What initially had seemed an impossible task soon appeared manageable, and Sarah's excitement and joy over her brother's visit took the place of her initial panic.

The days passed quickly as everyone helped with the preparations. Late in the afternoon on the day of their expected arrival, Zachary bounded onto the back porch, opened the door, and announced, "They're here! I see the dust bein' kicked up behind the wagon. Looks like all of Pennsylvania's arrivin' in the valley at the same time."

Amid hugs, introductions, and exclamations, the Thaddeus Johnston clan had arrived, all six of them and a small mountain of baggage. After much pleasant laughter and expressions of welcome and relief, Sarah led the guests up the wide staircase to the bedrooms and explained the sleeping arrangements, while the men lugged the bags to the appropriate rooms. As Winnie began the unpacking, Sarah announced happily, "Everyone, I know you must be exhausted from your travels. Wash up and rest before dinner. Winnie's prepared a very special meal for you. Dinner's at eight o'clock in the dinin' room."

That evening Winnie served platters of venison and roast pheasant and bowls of steaming creamed onions, peas and celery, and sweet potato pudding around the festive table. Thomas Williams proudly announced, "I've often thought how good it would be to have extended family together 'round this table. What a joyous occasion this is, a joyous one indeed!"

The conversation meandered pleasantly from the Johnstons' journey to the weather, from the health of the crops to how much the children had grown since the adults had last seen them. Zachary and David sparred amiably about the merits of VMI versus those of West Point, while Emma Jane asked Martha and Sallie countless questions about life in Pennsylvania. After dinner the adults, along with Zachary and David, adjourned to the parlor, while Emma Jane led the girls and little Peter down the path to Winnie and Moses' cabin to find Hattie.

Without intending to change the tone of the conversation so dramatically, Thaddeus Johnston's face looked grave as he turned to his brother-in-law and said, "I tell you, Thomas, I don't know what's happening to this country. Seems like tensions between North and South are growing worse by the day. All the dissension about whether the western territories should be added to the Union as slave states or free states—it's got all of Washington on edge."

"And not just Washington, Uncle Thad!" Zachary said. "Right now free states and slave states are represented equally in Congress. But Southerners are opposed to legislation that would admit new states to the Union only if they enter as free states. Such a condition would change the balance of power in Washington. And if that happens, most Southerners believe the abolitionists' position would prevail, outlawin' slavery once and for all."

"And that's the way it should be," David Johnston asserted forcefully as he leaned forward at the edge of his chair.

Zachary flinched at David's remark but clenched his jaw, trying to contain his anger. "I didn't say I'm in favor of slavery. I read *Uncle Tom's Cabin* same as you. But what I am in favor of is the right of each state to decide the question for itself. The federal government does not have the authority to tell these new states how to govern their territory."

"Well, that's easy for you to say—you've already got your chattel. Seems to me you're just using the states' rights argument to justify slavery."

Zachary's face reddened. Jumping to his feet, he shouted, "Moses and Winnie are not slaves! They're freedmen. My father freed them years ago. They're like family to us. Moses and Winnie made a choice to stay here on our farm and work. And we pay them, I might add!"

"Well, they sure *look* like slaves," David retorted. "I don't see *them* living in a nice big house like this. And it seems to me like Winnie does all the cooking and serving and Moses does all the—"

"That's enough, David!" Thaddeus said sternly. "We didn't come here to vent our political differences, if indeed we even have any. I'm sure your Uncle Thomas and Aunt Sarah don't like slavery any more than we do. And I'm also certain that they and other progressive Southerners will play an important role in bringing about a peaceful resolution to these volatile issues."

In an attempt to bring the evening to a peaceful close, Sarah rose from her chair, trying to hide her discomfort. She said, "I'm sure you're all terribly exhausted. Why don't we turn in for the night? We have so much to catch up on in the days ahead!" Then, forcing as sincere a smile as she could, she looked at David and said, "Besides, Emma Jane and I need to *help* Winnie finish cleanin' up and prepare a few things for breakfast in the mornin'."

"I agree with you, Sarah," added Elizabeth, grateful for the chance to change the subject. "We are tired, but we enjoyed this evening more than you can guess. Be sure to tell Winnie how much we enjoyed the delicious dinner."

Shortly after breakfast the next morning, Hattie knocked on the door to the back porch. "Is you ready for my readin' lesson, Miz Sarah?"

"Oh, Hattie! In all the commotion yesterday, I forgot to tell you there won't be any lessons for you or Emma Jane all week. I just want you children to get to know each other and have a good time. After you and Emma Jane finish your mornin' chores, why don't you show Martha, Sallie, and Peter around the farm?"

"I likes that idea, Miz Sarah," Hattie replied with a grin as she ran to make quick work of her chores.

Soon the four girls and little Peter were exploring Hattie and Emma Jane's favorite hideaways. As they passed the barn where Zachary and Moses were painting, Martha saw that her brother David was up on the scaffold with them. "What are you doing way up there?" she asked.

"What's it look like?" snapped David. "I'm helping paint the barn. Some vacation this is turning out to be."

Sensing that this was not the time for them to linger, Emma Jane suggested they walk down to the creek by the old oak tree. Sitting in the shade, the children listened as Emma Jane told the story of Hattie's secret reading lessons and how frightened she and Hattie were that someone would find out. Of course, retelling the story made them all laugh, especially since it had a happy ending.

"My brother David says that slavery's a bad thing," said eight-year-old Sallie carelessly, causing the laughter to stop suddenly.

"Sallie," Martha said, rebuking her little sister. "Mama told us not to talk about that while we're here."

Hattie looked away from the others, pretending to be studying something crawling in the grass.

"It's all right, Sallie," said Emma Jane. "Slavery's *not* a good thing. And our family doesn't own slaves, do we Hattie?"

Hattie didn't say anything but only shook her head without looking up.

"I'm really sorry, Emma Jane," Martha said, wanting them all to be happy again. "Sallie overheard our parents talking about Zachary and David's argument last night in the parlor. Oh, I do wish all this talk about slavery and the differences between the North and the South would just go away."

"I do, too. Besides, that's all grown-up talk," Emma Jane said as if trying to convince herself that, indeed, there was nothing to worry about.

"I like you a lot, Hattie," Sallie said kindly as she began to understand that it had been her comment that made her new friend so uncomfortable.

"I likes you, too. And I jus' wants us all to be friends, jus' like me and Emma Jane."

They were interrupted just then by the clanging of the dinner bell announcing that lunch was ready. Martha and Sallie were startled by the sound, and even little Peter turned in the direction of the noise with alarm.

"What's that?" Martha asked. "It doesn't sound like a church bell."

"Why, that's the dinner bell! Ain't you ever heard one before?" Hattie asked with surprise.

"We don't have dinner bells in the city, at least that I know of," explained Martha with a laugh.

"Well, let's get goin'. Last one home is a smelly rotten egg," Emma Jane challenged as she darted up the hill.

Winnie's hearty lunch of fried chicken, grits, crispy fried okra, and black-eyed peas cooked slowly with a ham hock was mostly new to the Johnstons. And after everyone had enjoyed a serving of Winnie's peach cobbler, Zachary and David helped themselves to seconds and thirds until it was gone.

"Winnie," David said sincerely, hoping to mend the hurt feelings his heated remarks the night before had surely caused, "I'd say that's just about the best meal I've ever eaten."

"I's happy you liked it," she replied with a good-natured grin. "You cadet boys need all the good food you can git while you home for the summer!"

"You can say that again, Winnie," Zachary exclaimed as he recalled some less-than-appetizing meals he'd endured at the military academy.

That afternoon, Uncle Thaddeus joined Thomas, Zachary, David, and Moses in painting the barn, while Sarah, Elizabeth, and Winnie sat in the shade of the back porch shelling nearly a bushel of peas from the garden. In the sticky June heat, Peter napped restlessly on a cotton pallet that Aunt Sarah had placed on the cool stone floor of the kitchen. Emma Jane and the other girls retreated to the front veranda with glasses of lemonade.

"I love it here," Martha said wistfully as she looked across the corn fields to the Blue Ridge Mountains that seemed to shimmer in the afternoon haze. "I wish we lived closer."

"Me, too," Emma Jane agreed sincerely. "And maybe after gettin' to know each other better, our brothers might get along, too."

At seven o'clock that evening, the dinner bell sounded again. "I'm beginning to love that sound," Martha said as she and Emma Jane finished setting the dining room table, "because it means it's time for more of Winnie's good cooking."

"Well, child, don' be disappointed if it ain't be like the spread we had at dinner las' night or lunch today," Winnie said, laughing robustly as she rounded the corner with a large, steaming bowl. "We's only havin' peas and cornbread, smoked ham, and fresh tomatoes. Yo' mama told me if y'all keep on eatin' like you has been, there's no way you gonna fit on the train goin' home. Now, I can use some help carryin' the rest of the fixins' up from the cook house."

The dinner conversation was more pleasant than it had been the night before. Zachary and David continued to spar about the superiority of their schools, but they were each careful to avoid exchanges regarding their political or social views.

Thaddeus and Thomas, however, were engaged in an intense but quiet conversation that to Emma Jane seemed strained, though not disagreeable.

"I agree with you, Thad," Emma Jane heard her father say with conviction, "I don't like the divisions in our nation any more than you do. But I tell you, if Abraham Lincoln is elected president in November, and if he succeeds in negotiatin' legislation to keep slavery out of all the new territories as he's pledged to do, we could see a wedge driven through the heart of our country that splits us like a rail."

"And that split, Thomas," replied Thaddeus, "would come at a great price—the price of war, I do believe."

Thomas Williams bowed his head in agreement as a hush fell over the table. Emma Jane glanced at Martha and Sallie and then at Zachary and David. She didn't want the joy of the visit to be spoiled by such talk. She wanted to hear only about good things, not about a war that even she sensed could destroy, or greatly damage, all she loved—her family, her friends, their farm, the beautiful valley, and of course, their nation, which she had learned was founded on the declaration that all men are created equal.

Finally, Thomas addressed everyone at the table. "In the midst of this joyful reunion of our families, we can't ignore the truth that we all face uncertain times ahead. As much as we would prefer to shield you children from these discussions, we fear that a time is comin' when we won't be able to. But please know—all of you—that Sarah and I and Thaddeus and Elizabeth are committed to prayin' for our nation, and, of course, for our families. Our differences over the issues facin' us are not as great as we might think, even if we have different views about how to resolve them. We must trust God to see us through these times, and we must look to Him for wisdom and guidance."

"But, Papa," said Emma Jane, "if war does come between the North and the South, what would that mean for our family? I mean, David's at West Point, and Zachary's at VMI. Wouldn't they be on different sides? Would they have to fight each other? That just can't happen, can it, Papa?"

This question startled them all, not because they hadn't yet thought about the divisions and destruction such a war could cause. Rather, Emma Jane's question forced them to think about the unthinkable—how war between the North and South would affect each family member seated around the table. Would cousins David and Zachary be required to take up arms against each other? Would a war drive a deep and lasting wedge between their families? No one could give a simple answer, nor did anyone attempt to do so.

Breaking the uncomfortable silence, Uncle Thaddeus said, "Dear Emma Jane, dearest family. All of our hearts are heavy tonight as we think about what seems inevitable unless God Himself intervenes. Even among ourselves there are conflicting opinions about how our nation might avoid such a catastrophe. Personally, I want to see slavery abolished, but I know our nation is so divided over this issue, it's more than likely to split in two. Zachary feels strongly about preserving the rights of the states, a belief that some will misunderstand as an endorsement of slavery. Exactly where he will stand should war come, I cannot know for sure. He will have to act on his own conscience. As for you, David, I believe you're committed to maintaining the Union, but not at the cost of enslaving your fellow man. And if it is inevitable that war should pit cousin against cousin and brother against brother, heaven help us all. But I know one very important fact: Each of us seated around this table is a faithful Christian, and each of us deeply loves our God and each other. My prayer is that our love will bind our hearts together and preserve our family and even our nation should the storms of war rage against us."

Emma Jane swallowed hard as tears ran down her cheeks. David got up from his chair and walked over to Zachary and embraced him as they both wept unashamedly. "I love you, Zach—even if you are a VMI cadet," David said, trying to bring a little humor to this sober moment.

"And I love you, too, David," Zach replied earnestly.

Uncle Thaddeus asked everyone to hold hands as he led both families in prayer. As he prayed, Emma Jane experienced a strange, fluctuating mixture of fear and hope, joy and sadness. *Oh, God*, she prayed silently as her uncle prayed aloud, *please don't let war come. Please let all of our family times be like this where everyone loves each other.*

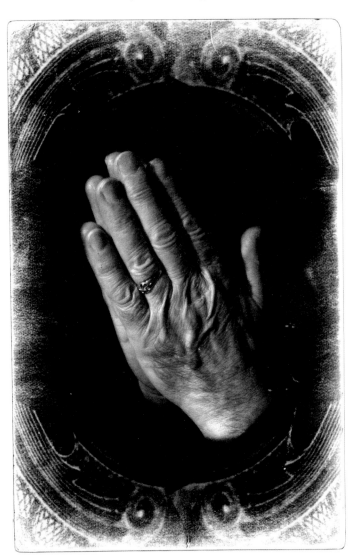

In the remaining days of the Johnstons' visit, all the activities and outings, while joyful, were clouded by the looming specter of war. Yet no one talked of it again, as if everyone wanted to enjoy and savor the blessings of the visit, knowing this could be the last time they would all be together.

THINK ABOUT IT

» What is slavery? Did you know that many people around the world are enslaved even today? Do you think owning another person is right or wrong? Why? Why do you think a person would want to own other people?

» Many Americans believe that the federal government has taken more power than our founding fathers intended when they wrote the Constitution. In fact, the issue of states' rights has been around since our nation declared its independence from Great Britain. Read the Bill of Rights as a family and discuss why many people think it's important to limit the power of the federal government.

» The emotionally charged issues that divided the North and South at this time were like kegs of gunpowder ready to be ignited by the first side to light a match. Why do Zach and David become angry at each other after dinner? Why does David say that Winnie and Moses look to him like slaves? Why is Zach offended by David's words?

» Why does the talk of war make the younger children uncomfortable? Why do you think Hattie grows quiet when Sallie brings up the subject of slavery?

» The United States Military Academy, where David attends school, is in West Point, New York, a Northern free state. Virginia Military Institute, where Zach attends school, is in Lexington, Virginia, a Southern slave state. What do you think David and Zach will do if war is declared? What do you think might happen if they find themselves facing one another in battle?

WORDS YOU NEED TO KNOW

» **Envy:** The sin of not loving others because they have something I want and do not have

» **Contentment:** A deep, lasting peace and satisfaction that comes from knowing and loving God more every day

» **Kindness:** Loving acts of service and courtesy I give to others

HIDE IT IN YOUR HEART

For wherever there is jealousy and selfish ambition, there you will find disorder and evil of every kind. (James 3:16, NLT)

Make sure that nobody pays back wrong for wrong, but always try to be kind to each other and to everyone else. (1 Thessalonians 5:15)

THE SHENANDOAH VALLEY

The Shenandoah Valley lies in western Virginia, between the Blue Ridge Mountains on the east and the Allegheny Mountains on the west. Watered by the Shenandoah River, the valley is green and fertile, surrounded by beautiful peaks and dotted with natural caverns.

The word *Shenandoah* comes from the native tribes who lived there before the valley was settled. One popular legend says the name means "Daughter of the Stars." According to the legend, the valley was so beautiful that the stars promised to meet there once every thousand years. Another story says that George Washington, who had surveyed parts of the valley, named it after an Oneida Indian chief, Oskanondonha, who brought food to the starving soldiers at Valley Forge, Pennsylvania, during the winter of 1777.

Settlers began to arrive in the valley during the 1730s, many of whom were German and Scotch-Irish. The valley provided a buffer for the rest of Virginia against attacks during the French and Indian War. The Warriors Road, used by the Indians to travel north and south through the valley, later became known as the Great Wagon Road as it brought settlers into the area. U.S. Route 11 now follows much the same path.

During the Civil War, the Shenandoah Valley was known as the "breadbasket of the South," as the area provided much of the grain for the Confederate Army. The valley also provided an ideal route for Confederate soldiers to travel north between Union lines. During the early years of the war, the valley was under the control of the Confederate Army. But by 1864 the Union Army began conquering strategic sites and burning fields and food supplies to hamper the Southern war effort.

Today, the Shenandoah Valley remains as beautiful as when the first settlers arrived, its natural scenery now dotted with historical sites.

Photo by USDA.

THE HEART OF THE PROBLEM

When God created the world, He gave people everything they needed to work together and live peacefully with one another. Man and woman were made in God's image to live in perfect harmony with God, with themselves, and with each other. Before the Fall, Adam and Eve were perfectly at ease with one another. They worked hand in hand tending the garden and helping one another as needed. They never argued or fought or misunderstood one another. Neither was jealous of the other's status, looks, or abilities.

But then Adam and Eve ate from the forbidden tree, and they immediately began pointing fingers. When God confronted them with their guilt, Adam accused both his wife and God for putting him in a difficult position and causing him to sin: "The woman you put here with me—she gave me some fruit from the tree, and I ate it" (Genesis 3:12). Eve turned around and blamed the serpent: "The serpent deceived me," she said. "That's why I ate it" (Genesis 3:13, NLT). Tragically, blame is only one of the many sins that produces disharmony among people.

A destroyed Iraqi tank from the Gulf War. Photo: JO1 LEE BOSCO.

The Bible tells us, "When Adam sinned, sin entered the world. Adam's sin brought death, so death spread to everyone, for everyone sinned" (Romans 5:12, NLT). Every person born since the Fall has inherited a sinful nature, and every one of us has sinned as a result (Romans 3:23; 1 John 1:8). And the corrosive effects of sin touch every part of our lives, hindering our ability to honor God, love our neighbors, and serve one another in humility.

Today, our world is plagued by hunger, poverty, cruelty, violence, and hatred. "Wars and rumors of wars" and nation rising against nation are daily headlines (Matthew 24:6–7). Sins the apostle Paul warned us of seem almost fashionable:

There will be terrible times in the last days. People will be lovers of themselves, lovers of money, boastful, proud, abusive, disobedient to their parents, ungrateful, unholy, without love, unforgiving, slanderous, without self-control, brutal, not lovers of the good, treacherous, rash, conceited, lovers of pleasure rather than lovers of God.
(2 Timothy 3:1-4)

This could be the description for just about any weekly episode of "reality" television. That's because we are surrounded by brokenness, arrogance, quarreling, disease, and death, which are the inevitable fruits of sin in our world.

Yet despite all the evidence to the contrary, many of us cling to the belief that people are basically good inside. We want to believe that nations and individuals will one day see the error of their ways, choose to do the right thing, and set aside their differences, thereby ushering in a new age of harmony and world peace. Some think governments should step in and force people to do what is right, while others believe that amazing new advances in technology will solve the world's problems. But despite all our laws and technological sophistication, it seems all we do is invent new ways to cheat one another, belittle one another, and kill one another.

Christ on the Cross by Mengs.

The truth is that people cannot save themselves. This book is about doing good works, but good works alone cannot save us from sin (Ephesians 2:8–9). Big government and science won't save us because they don't address the real issue. Just as an illness cannot be cured by treating the symptoms without addressing the underlying cause, so the world's ills cannot be dealt with unless we go to the heart of the problem. Sin is the true source of our many difficulties. It's like a cancer eating away at our families, marriages, and nations. But sin resides in the heart (Luke 6:43–45), and no amount of time, reasoning, or research can change the human heart.

But there is good news! God has provided the perfect remedy to everyone who will receive it. He sent His one and only Son to live as our example and then die to pay the price to redeem us from sin. In doing so, Jesus made it possible once more for us to live in harmony with the Father and with our brothers and sisters in the Lord. The fact is that only the Holy Spirit can change a person's heart, and only the blood of Jesus Christ can wash away our sins. That is why He has sent us into our neighborhoods, our cities, and the ends of the earth to share this good news and make disciples of all who are willing to follow Him (Matthew 28:19; Acts 1:8).

ENVY KILLS

An ancient Greek writer tells the story of a statue erected to Theogenes (thee-AH-jen-ees) of Thasos, one of history's first professional athletes and a man renowned for his extraordinary strength and swiftness. Theogenes is said to have been victorious in more than 1,300 athletic contests and was undefeated as a boxer for more than twenty years. When a statue of Theogenes was erected in his honor, one of his oft-defeated rivals was so overcome with envy that he went every night and threw himself against the statue in an attempt to topple it from its pedestal. Ultimately, he was successful. Alas, the statue fell upon the jealous man and he was crushed to death.

Envy, or jealousy, is the sin of not loving your neighbors because they have something you want and do not have, and it's among the deadliest of sins. Proverbs 14:30 says, "A heart at peace gives life to the body, but envy rots the bones." The apostle James identified envy as the source of much of the disharmony we experience with others:

What is causing the quarrels and fights among you? Don't they come from the evil desires at war within you? You want what you don't have, so you scheme and kill to get it. You are jealous of what others have, but you can't get it, so you fight and wage war to take it away from them. (James 4:1–2, NLT)

Cain and Abel. Photo: I, Sailko.

It should come as no surprise then that the very first murder was the result of envy.

Cain and Abel were the sons of Adam and Eve. When they grew up, Abel became a shepherd, while Cain became a farmer. At harvest time, Cain brought to the Lord a gift from among his fruits and vegetables, whereas Abel gave to the Lord "the best of the firstborn lambs from his flock" (Genesis 4:4, NLT). God was pleased with Abel and his offering, but He did not accept Cain and his offering. This made Cain extremely angry and envious of his brother.

In his play *Othello*, William Shakespeare called jealousy "the green-eyed monster." Indeed, God warned Cain that sin is "crouching at the door," fangs bared, eager to devour its prey:

"Why are you so angry?" the LORD asked Cain. "Why do you look so dejected? You will be accepted if you do what is right. But if you refuse to do what is right, then watch out! Sin is crouching at the door, eager to control you. But you must subdue it and be its master." (Genesis 4:6–7, NLT)

Sadly, Cain allowed envy of his brother to consume him. Cain lured Abel out to the field and killed him there. And the Lord sentenced Cain to wander the earth, a fugitive all the rest of his days.

Of course, sin that injures someone else does not just happen out of the blue. Sins that visibly hurt other people begin as hidden sins of the heart. Envy and selfishness, for example, fester like an infection in a person's thoughts and lead to all sorts of malicious behavior. James 3:16 says, "For where you have envy and selfish ambition, there you find disorder and every evil practice."

Jesus taught that murder, stealing, lying, and speaking evil of others all begin in a person's thoughts (Matthew 15:18–19). He said:

A good tree does not produce bad fruit, nor does a bad tree produce good fruit. . . . Good people bring good things out of the good they stored in their hearts. But evil people bring evil things out of the evil they stored in their hearts.
(Luke 6:43–45, NCV).

> *Envy takes the joy, happiness, and contentment out of living.*
> **Billy Graham**

In other words, people say and do the things that are already in their hearts. Therefore, it's important that you guard your heart carefully and do not allow envy and selfishness to gain a foothold there.

Do you count your blessings daily and think about the many things God has done for you? Or do you often find yourself thinking about things you *don't* have? Do you look longingly at your neighbors' shiny new truck? Do you wish you lived in a bigger house with a larger, nicer yard like the one across the street? Do you read novels that make you long for supernatural powers? Do you watch actors and singers on TV and wonder why God didn't make you faster, stronger, and richer or prettier, slimmer, and more talented? CAUTION: This is just the kind of thinking that leads to dissatisfaction and greed and will cause you to do things that harm yourself and others. As Proverbs 4:23 (NCV) says, "Be careful what you think, because your thoughts run your life."

MAKE A NOTE OF IT
Write a short story or draw a cartoon about a monster called Envy who tries to convince you to be unhappy about something you don't have, and show what you do to defeat him.

HOW TO DEFEAT ENVY
Have you ever seen a horse poking its head through a narrow opening in a fence and stretching its neck just to eat from a patch of grass growing on the other side? It's rather comical when that same horse is standing in a field of lush green grass yet seems to think the grass beyond the fence is some kind of rare delicacy. That horse is going through an awful lot of effort to obtain its prize when a perfectly wonderful meal has been right under its feet the whole time!

You and I are a lot more like that horse than we care to admit. There's an old saying that goes "The grass is always greener on the other side of the fence." What this means is that we tend to look at our neighbors and envy them, thinking they are happier than we are because they don't experience the same kinds of problems we're dealing with. Of course, this perception is almost always false because every family has its own set of problems. But when we let ourselves get caught up in thinking about our own difficult circumstances—our

THE DAY THE EARTH STOOD STILL

The classic 1951 science fiction movie *The Day the Earth Stood Still* tells the story of an alien's visit to the planet Earth. When an extraterrestrial spaceship lands in Washington, DC, the world panics. A humanoid alien and his enormous robot emerge from the ship, and the alien, Klaatu, announces that he has only peaceful intentions. But a frightened soldier fires his rifle, wounding the alien. Klaatu is taken to a hospital and treated with care, though he is kept under guard. He says that he has an important message for the people of Earth and requests a meeting with representatives from every nation.

However, this seemingly simple request proves anything but simple. The leaders of the world's nations do not trust one another and cannot agree where the meeting should take place. Frustrated by their stubbornness, Klaatu escapes from the hospital so that he can get out among the people and try to understand the cause of "these strange, unreasoning attitudes."

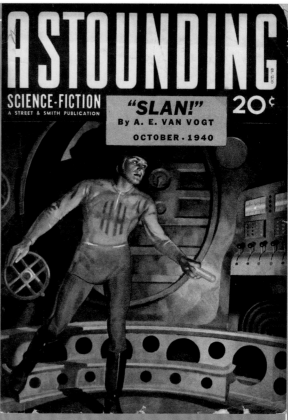

October 1940 issue of *Astounding Science Fiction* in which the short story "Farewell to the Master" first appeared. This story was adapted for the 1951 film *The Day the Earth Stood Still.*

He takes a room at a local boarding house using the name "Mr. Carpenter." There he meets a single mother, Helen, and her son, Bobby, who show him kindness though he is a stranger. Klaatu also meets an eminent scientist in whom he chooses to confide. He warns the professor that if the people of Earth cannot find a way to resolve their differences and live in harmony, they may have to be eliminated before they discover space travel and threaten the peace of other planets. The professor promises to gather the world's greatest scientists so they can convey this vital message to their respective nations.

But before the meeting can take place, Helen and the man she has been dating discover the true identity of Mr. Carpenter. Klaatu reveals to Helen his reason for coming to Earth, and she offers to help in any way she can. But her friend, Tom, is interested only in himself and how famous he will become when he turns the spaceman over to the army. Helen tries to stop him. "Tom, you mustn't!" she says. "You don't know what you're doing! It isn't just you and Mr. Carpenter. The rest of the world is involved!" In a fit of exasperation, Tom replies, "I don't care about the rest of the world!"

Throughout Klaatu's visit, this stranger in a strange land is met with a telling variety of attitudes. A few people, such as Helen and Bobby, offer him hospitality, friendship, and assistance. Some, like the soldier who panics and shoots him, give in to their fears and mistrust and make harmful choices. But Tom represents our very worst tendencies as humans born into sin. He is driven by ambition and greed, and his selfishness puts at risk the lives of every person on the planet. Now that you have spent time studying servanthood, how do you think you would respond?

struggles, our shortcomings, our failures—it's easy to look at other people and think, *If only I had his money (or her looks or their name), I wouldn't be in this mess.*

If anyone ever had reason to complain to God about his circumstances, it was the apostle Paul. He had been a second-generation Pharisee, a respected and highly educated man, yet now he was languishing in a dungeon in Rome because of his faith in Jesus Christ. Nevertheless, he was perfectly at peace. He wrote to his friends:

> *I have learned to be content whatever the circumstances. I know what it is to be in need, and I know what it is to have plenty. I have learned the secret of being content in any and every situation, whether well fed or hungry, whether living in plenty or in want. I can do everything through him who gives me strength.*
> (Philippians 4:11–13)

Saint Paul by El Greco.

Contentment is a deep, abiding peace and satisfaction that comes from knowing and loving God more every day. Are you content in your life? If not, what do you think will make you happy? A bigger family car? A nicer wardrobe? Your own smartphone? A Florida vacation? Do you really think possessions can make you happy? Let's see what Paul had to say about possessions.

Paul had once owned many nice things when his name was Saul. He had been raised the son of a Pharisee and well-to-do tentmaker. Educated in Jerusalem by the finest teachers, Saul also enjoyed the privileges of Roman citizenship. Yet for his all riches and education and status, he could not find peace. And so, against the advice and urging of his mentor (Acts 5:34–39), Saul zealously hunted down and persecuted the followers of Christ (Acts 8:1–3). But then Jesus Christ met Saul on the road to Damascus (Acts 9:1–19), changed his name, and set him on a new path.

Now that he had lost everything, Paul no longer looked for *things* to make him happy:

> *I consider everything a loss compared to the surpassing greatness of knowing Christ Jesus my Lord, for whose sake I have lost all things. I consider them rubbish, that I may gain Christ.* (Philippians 3:8)

Paul had learned that the constant pursuit of possessions and accomplishments led only to disillusionment and despair. Joyously, he had instead discovered the threefold secret to lasting contentment:

1. Trust in Jesus Christ.
2. Be thankful in all circumstances.
3. Give love and comfort to others.

TRUST IN JESUS CHRIST

We can find contentment in the same place we find salvation: in Christ. He is the only answer to sin, and He is the only answer to our need for peace (John 14:27). Paul's relationship with God did not depend on what he did or did not have. His peace was based not on his circumstances but on knowing and trusting Jesus:

> *My old self has been crucified with Christ. It is no longer I who live, but Christ lives in me. So I live in this earthly body by trusting in the Son of God, who loved me and gave himself for me.* (Galatians 2:20, NLT)

> *[The Lord] said to me, "My grace is sufficient for you, for my power is made perfect in weakness." Therefore I will boast all the more gladly of my weaknesses, so that the power of Christ may rest upon me. For the sake of Christ, then, I am content with weaknesses, insults, hardships, persecutions, and calamities. For when I am weak, then I am strong.* (2 Corinthians 12:9–10, ESV)

Keep in mind that contentment doesn't come overnight. As you build your relationship with God through prayer, Bible study, and worship, you will learn to trust God more and rely on yourself less. When you trust in Christ, He will give you the strength to be content in any situation you encounter. Remember and pray the words of the psalmist: "Whom have I in heaven but you? And earth has nothing I desire besides you. My flesh and my heart may fail, but God is the strength of my heart and my portion forever" (Psalm 73:25–26).

BE THANKFUL IN ALL CIRCUMSTANCES

The book of Philippians is a letter from Paul thanking the church at Philippi for a "care" package they had sent him in prison. Have you sent a thank-you note to anyone recently? Thankfulness is a very important quality to have, whatever your situation. Paul instructed us:

Do not be anxious about anything, but in everything, by prayer and petition, with thanksgiving, present your requests to God. And the peace of God, which transcends all understanding, will guard your hearts and your minds in Christ Jesus. (Philippians 4:6–7)

In everything give thanks; for this is God's will for you in Christ Jesus. (1 Thessalonians 5:18, NASB)

When you think of what God the Son has done for us—stepping down from His throne to live among us and teach us, then allowing Himself to be killed in the most humiliating way possible to pay the penalty for our sins—how can your heartfelt response be anything but gratitude? We must be thankful to God each day for who He is, for everything He created, and for His infinite goodness toward us.

GIVE LOVE AND COMFORT TO OTHERS

When we go through life discontented—grumbling, whining, doubting God, and thinking only about ourselves—we tend to hold tightly to the very things God wants us to give to others, including our time, our talents, and our treasure. But in the economy of God's kingdom, we must give away that which we hope to gain:

Give freely and become more wealthy; be stingy and lose everything. The generous will prosper; those who refresh others will themselves be refreshed. (Proverbs 11:24–25, NLT)

For example, God gives us comfort so that we can pass it on to others who need it:

Praise be to the God and Father of our Lord Jesus Christ, the Father of compassion and the God of all comfort, who comforts us in all our troubles, so that we can comfort those in any trouble with the comfort we ourselves have received from God. (2 Corinthians 1:3–4)

Jesus said, "It is more blessed to give than to receive" (Acts 20:35). Indeed, giving defined the ultimate expression of love: "For God so loved the world that he *gave* . . ." (John 3:16). When you look beyond your own problems to focus on meeting the needs of those around you, you will go a long way toward taming the beast crouching at the door. A true servant is happy just to serve, and envy has no place in his or her life.

The grass is not, in fact, always greener on the other side of the fence. Grass is greenest where it is watered. When you cross over fences to serve your neighbors with love and humility and share with them living water (John 7:38), you make the grass greener wherever you go.

MAKE A NOTE OF IT

Think of someone who has blessed you recently and write a thank-you note to that person. This could be your Sunday school teacher, your mailman, or even the lady at the ice cream shop who served you with a smile.

WHAT SHOULD I DO?

No matter how old you are or what your talents are or how much influence you wield, you can begin to make a difference in this world simply by being kind to the people around you. **Kindness** is an outward expression of love that helps to create harmony among people. Simple acts of thoughtfulness and courtesy flow from an unselfish attitude and reflect to the world Jesus' own selfless service to others.

> *The more any gracious heart can bring itself to be in a contented disposition, the more fit it is for any service of and for God.*
> **Jeremiah Burroughs**
> 1600–1646

If you doubt the power of kindness to change the world, think about what life is like in your own home when family members are kind to one another. No family is perfect, of course, and we all have disagreements from time to time. But when brothers, sisters, and parents are considerate toward one another, when they go out of their way to help one another, when they speak kindly to one another, doesn't that make your home a peaceful place to live? Doesn't it make you want to be kind to other people?

But what about when someone is unkind to you? Should you set aside kindness and courtesy and teach the other person a lesson? Of course not. The Bible says, "Make sure that nobody pays back wrong for wrong, but always try to be kind to each other and to everyone else" (1 Thessalonians 5:15). Think what the world would be like if no one returned "evil for evil" but instead did everything possible to live in peace with all people (Romans 12:17).

A PRAYER

Dear God, thank you for everything you have done for me. Thank you for all your wonderful gifts! Help me not to be stingy with your gifts but to share them freely with my family and friends and people who need them. Show me when I am being selfish or envious, and help me guard my heart against sin. In Jesus' name I pray. Amen.

ENCOUNTERS WITH JESUS

THE WOMAN WHO WAS FORGIVEN MUCH

Rivka felt the townspeople watching her as she made her way toward the house of Simon the Pharisee. No one spoke to her, but the accusations in their eyes made their disdain for her clear enough. Her many sins were widely known, and the people of the village gave her a wide berth as she passed, as though just being near her would blacken them too.

Once she had been married and respectable. Rivka's husband had deeply loved and cared for her. But when a strain of fever passed through the region, Rivka first lost her parents and then her husband to the illness. Suddenly, she was left with no one to support her. With few respectable means of earning a living open to her, she had begun entertaining Roman soldiers for money.

She no longer worried about starving, but she had no friends and no family and was not welcome at public gatherings. Many of her former acquaintances believed it would have been better for Rivka to have died with her husband than to consort with Gentiles and live in sin. Worse, she believed they were right. She was now damaged, tainted, and disreputable. She had traded her soul for the comfort of knowing she would have food, clothes, and a roof over her head.

Rivka had become used to being shunned by the townspeople. She had learned to avoid meeting people's eyes or listening too closely to their comments as she passed, and if she kept her head down and went quietly about her daily tasks, most of the time they would just leave her alone. However, the guilt and shame never left her. The choices she had made weighed on her like heavy chains, and she was certain God no longer heard her prayers.

But that was yesterday. Now everything was different.

This morning Rivka had risen early and gone to listen to the teacher known as Jesus of Nazareth. At first she had stood apart from the crowds but had steadily inched closer to hear the teacher's message. That's when her whole life had changed.

For a few moments she forgot she was standing amid a crowd of people who hated her.

Jesus' words poured grace and hope and peace into her soul, and her heart leapt in response. "Come to me, you who are weary and burdened, and I will give you rest," the teacher had said. "Take my yoke upon you and learn from me, for I am gentle and humble in heart, and you will find rest for your soul. For my yoke is easy and my burden is light." Then Jesus had turned and looked in her direction. Rivka's eyes met his, and she was suddenly certain that he knew everything she had ever done, knew every one of her sins, yet loved her anyway.

Tears began streaming down her face. Rivka sank to her knees, desperate to trade her heavy burden for the new life that Jesus promised. Not caring if anyone nearby was listening, Rivka fell on her face and poured out her sins, confessing them to God and humbly asking for his forgiveness.

When Rivka at last raised her face to heaven, believing that God had answered her prayers, she felt clean all the way through. The tremendous weight of guilt and shame had lifted from Rivka's soul, and her heart was filled with a joy she hadn't known in years. She could barely contain the hope and gratitude that flooded her soul.

Once she recovered herself and looked around, the light was fading and the crowd had begun to disperse. Urgently, Rivka searched the many faces around her to find Jesus. Nothing in her life was ever going to be the same again, and she had to thank him, to show him she had changed. But Jesus was nowhere to be found.

Rivka began asking passersby if they knew where Jesus had gone. The only answer she received from most of them was silence, but the looks on their faces made it clear: Even if they knew where Jesus was, they weren't going to tell her. After all, a sinner such as she had no business talking with common folk, let alone approaching an honored teacher.

Not caring what they thought, Rivka continued to ask after Jesus. Finally, a stranger answered, "He accepted an invitation to dinner with Simon the Pharisee at his home."

Rivka knew of Simon. He often invited traveling rabbis and teachers to his home. Simon enjoyed a reputation for hosting intellectuals who came to discuss religion and the issues of the day. Rivka thought he probably also appreciated the chance to show off his wealth. No one in the village had so large a house or such lavish taste in food and decorations.

Thanking the stranger profusely, Rivka hurried in the direction of the Pharisee's house.

These kinds of dinners were usually open to the public, a sort of open forum where anyone who wanted could come and listen to Simon and his fellow teachers debate with their guests. If she arrived early enough, perhaps she could find a place along the wall close to where Jesus would be seated.

Rivka knew she risked humiliation going to an event like this. People managed to ignore her in public places like the market, where they expected to have to mingle with the lowest members of society. But to appear at a prominent Pharisee's home, when he was hosting a well-known teacher, was coming dangerously close to crossing the line. Any religious man of such prominence would go to great lengths to protect his good name from being sullied by contact with her kind. Perhaps, though, Simon's pride would provide her some protection, for surely a man who was eager to be known far and wide as a paragon of hospitality wouldn't cause a scene by having her thrown out.

As she threaded her way through the narrow streets, Rivka thought about how she might express her gratitude and devotion to Jesus. She didn't dare speak to this man of God, but she could perform the duties of a servant for him. No doubt Simon's servants would wash Jesus' feet when he first arrived, but she could still perfume them. This gesture of devotion and humility didn't seem like enough after what he had done for her, but it was the best she could think of.

Detouring through the market, Rivka stopped at a stall that sold scented oils. There were many varieties, ranging from the finest of Egyptian perfumes to the most basic scents derived from local flowers. Rivka carried only a few coins, but without hesitation she spent them all to purchase her favorite blend, myrrh mixed with the essence of roses and almond blossoms. Nearly every woman of her village carried an alabastron, a vial filled with scented oil to use after bathing or to disguise bodily odors after a hot day. Now Rivka filled hers with the purchased scent. She tied the vial around her neck and used her headscarf to cover the lower part of her face, as she would if the day were dusty. She then hurried on her way, determined that no one would prevent her from reaching Jesus.

When Rivka arrived at Simon's house, she quietly blended in with the servants as she made her way to the large gathering room. The room was one of the largest she had ever seen, as tall as it was wide and long. The high ceiling kept the lower half of the room cool and provided plenty of room for elaborate wall paintings. Even the floor was covered in colorful mosaics. Circling the room until she came to the head of the low table, where Simon would sit, she chose a place along the wall just behind the position where the most honored guest

would recline. Then she waited, as other interested onlookers began to line the walls.

The servants moved about her, lining the low table with soft cushions and decorating it with the finest cups and plates. Rivka ignored the few inquisitive glances she received. Nothing else mattered. Jesus would be gone by morning, taking his message to others like her throughout the region. She had only this one chance to serve him.

Platters of food started to arrive, causing Rivka to remember she hadn't eaten since breakfast. She rarely dined so well as Simon's household seemed to. Soon the table was filled with steaming flatbread made from the finest wheat, fish prepared several different ways, a dish of spicy lamb roasted in its own juices, and mounds of olives, grapes, dates, and figs.

Another onlooker joked to his friend, "If only we had been invited to sample the food as well as the conversation!" Then a hush near the door heralded Simon's entrance, followed by his guests, including other important men of the town who had a standing invitation to any of Simon's dinners.

Rivka watched Jesus approach, her heart welling up once more with the emotion she felt at the moment of belief. She felt tears running down her cheeks. She praised God silently, thanking him for his mercy in accepting and cleansing a sinner like her.

She watched as Jesus and the other dinner guests reclined on the cushions. Each man lay on his left side, propping himself up on his left elbow and reaching for food or drink with his right hand. The feet of the diners pointed away from the food. Servants freely moved along the other side of the table, refilling empty glasses with wine and bringing more food to the table as needed.

Amid the grandeur of Simon's house and the ostentatious clothing of his guests, Jesus and his friends looked like common laborers. Even before she had taken up with Gentiles, Rivka was used to religious leaders whose trappings made it hard for an ordinary person to come near to God. But Jesus made it seem easy. He called everyone to come to the Father, regardless of their social status or the depths of their sinfulness.

Christ at the House of Simon the Pharisee by Subleyras.

Rivka waited anxiously for the benediction to be said and the meal to begin. When Simon had blessed all under his roof and at his table, he tore a piece of bread into chunks and passed them around the table.

Now was her chance.

But looking down at Jesus' bare feet, Rivka saw that they were still dusty from the road, as if they had been merely wiped with a dry towel instead of properly washed. Yet the feet of the Pharisees on either side of Simon were cleaned and oiled. Simon had saved his most lavish regard for his peers, men he apparently considered more important than a mere carpenter from Galilee.

How could Simon think Jesus unworthy of honor? He had changed her life in a way that was too dramatic to put into words. Rivka's tears of joy turned to tears of sorrow, and she bent her head and wept openly. As she did, her headscarf fell to the ground, revealing her identity to the other guests.

In the midst of her silent weeping, she noticed that her tears were falling on Jesus' feet. She freed her hair from its braid and used it to carefully wipe away the moistened dust. Then, untying the alabastron from where it hung around her neck, she slowly applied the scented oil to Jesus' feet, kissing them again and again, thanking him silently for each sin he had forgiven. Even after the last drop of oil fell from her vial, she continued rubbing the oil into his skin as if he were the richest of royalty.

Rivka gradually became aware of the room around her once more. It was utterly silent, everyone transfixed by the scene of her devotion. Simon's face was especially eloquent, contempt curling his lip as he glared at the

Photo by Joseolgon.

teacher and the sinner. His thoughts seemed to echo loudly in the large room: *If this man were truly a prophet, he would know how sinful this woman is.*

Rivka bowed her head over Jesus' feet once more, afraid she had brought shame to Jesus by her display of gratitude and reverence. She couldn't bring herself to look up again.

In the silence, Jesus spoke. "Simon, I have something to say to you."

"Say it, Rabbi," Simon answered.

Rivka held her breath. Would Jesus ask Simon to have her removed? To her surprise, Jesus simply began telling a story. "A certain man loaned money to two people—five hundred pieces of silver to one, and fifty pieces of silver to the other. When neither man was able to repay, he kindly forgave them both, canceling their debts. Now which of these two will love him more?"

Simon and the rest of his guests sat frozen for a moment, no doubt trying to work out where Jesus was leading the conversation. Then Simon answered, "I suppose the one who owed him more money."

"Your judgment is correct," Jesus replied. Then sitting up and facing Rivka, Jesus asked, "Do you see this woman, Simon?"

Rivka was startled. She was used to being socially invisible. Now Jesus had brought her into the middle of the conversation. She sat back on her heels and watched Jesus' face, determined to bear the painful scrutiny of the crowd. She kept telling herself that Jesus was the only reason she was here.

Jesus said, "When I came into your house, Simon, you didn't wash my feet. But this woman has washed them with her tears and dried them with her hair. You didn't greet me with a kiss of welcome, but she hasn't stopped kissing my feet since I arrived. You didn't anoint my head with oil, but she anointed my feet with perfume."

Hearing his words, Rivka felt more tears well up and drip down her cheeks. Jesus understood exactly what she had been trying to do with her act of devotion. She could barely breathe as relief flooded through her, washing away any trace of shame or regret.

"Her sins—which are many—have been forgiven, so she has shown me much love." Jesus paused, catching Simon's eye. "But someone who has been forgiven only a little will love only a little."

Simon sucked in his breath at these words. Feeling the rebuke of one of their own, the important men around the table began murmuring about how this man claimed to be able to forgive sins, something only God could do. But Jesus sat still, calm in the center of controversy.

Looking into Rivka's tear-stained face, Jesus said gently, "Your faith has saved you. Go in peace."

Rivka bent over his feet one last time, overcome by his generosity. Picking up her empty vial, she stood as peace flooded her heart. Her sins had been wiped away as completely as if they had never even existed.

Walking slowly out of the house, Rivka realized that she had never felt so alive or so whole. The crowd parted before her—not in disgust this time, but in awe of Jesus' authority.

TAKE A CLOSER LOOK

» Read the biblical account of these events in Luke 7:36–50 and compare it to the story you've just read.

» Rivka is burdened by guilt and shame. What is a burden? What is shame? What do you think it's like to feel shame?

» Read Matthew 11:25–30. What is a yoke? What does Jesus mean when he says "My yoke is easy and my burden is light"?

» How do you think the people at the dinner felt when they recognized the sinful woman? How do you think Simon the Pharisee felt?

» How did Rivka serve Jesus? How did Simon not serve Jesus?

» How did Jesus serve Rivka? What does His service to the sinful woman tell us about how you and I must serve others who are sinful?

Supper in the House of Simon Pharisee by Moretto da Brescia.

THE HOUSE OF TRUTH: THE ELEVENTH PILLAR

You have learned that disharmony among people and nations is the result of our sinful nature and cannot be repaired without the redeeming work of Jesus Christ. In this lesson, you erected the third pillar in your Servanthood Wall:

BIBLICAL TRUTH 15:

Sin causes disharmony among people.

Biblical
Truth
13
God created
me to love
and serve
His people

Biblical
Truth
14
God made
the family
where we
are to serve
one another

Biblical
Truth
15
Sin causes
disharmony
among
people

SERVANTHOOD WALL
My relationship with others as I serve them in love

Biblical Truth 3
God is God the Father, Son, and Holy Spirit

FOUNDATION OF WISDOM
Knowing, loving, and obeying God my Rock

THE ROCK
God and His Word

WHO IS GOD'S FAMILY?

> THEREFORE, AS WE HAVE OPPORTUNITY, LET US DO GOOD
> TO ALL PEOPLE, ESPECIALLY TO THOSE WHO BELONG TO THE
> FAMILY OF BELIEVERS.
>
> GALATIANS 6:10

THE BIG IDEA

How big is your family? Do you have brothers? Sisters? A grandparent who lives with you? Did you know there's a couple in Arkansas famous for having nineteen children, all of whose names begin with the letter J? Whether you have a dozen siblings or you're an only child, you, too, are part of a large family. As a follower of Christ, you have millions of brothers and sisters. They come in all shapes, sizes, and ages. Your family is made up of students, parents, farmers, construction workers, musicians, zookeepers, world leaders, and executives of major corporations. And together you can change the world.

As we have seen, when Adam and Eve gave in to Satan's temptation in the Garden of Eden and disobeyed God, all of creation was thrown into a state of disharmony. No longer would men and women know the joy of personal fellowship with God. No longer would they be at perfect ease with themselves, with one another, or with the earth. But before God created the world, He had a plan to restore His creation. Do you remember the promise God made to Adam and Eve after they sinned? He said that a descendant of Eve would one day "crush" the head of Satan and defeat him (Genesis 3:15). This was the first announcement that God's own Son, Jesus, would come to set things right once more.

The Bible says, "The Son of God came for this purpose: to destroy the devil's work" (1 John 3:8, NCV). He came into the world as a child, born to the virgin Mary, a descendant of Eve. Jesus lived a sinless life and then willingly died on the cross to pay the debt we owe for our sins. When Christ died on the cross and was resurrected, Satan's power was broken and harmony in our human relationships once again became a very real possibility.

Satan could neither destroy Jesus nor keep Him in the grave, and he cannot prevail against the children of God (Matthew 16:18). Who are these people whom Satan can no longer destroy? All of us who believe in Jesus as God's Son and our Savior! We have been adopted as members of God's new family and restored to fellowship with God. God is our Father, and we are His children (Romans 8:15). Jesus is our big brother and our King (Hebrews 2:11). Together, we are the church.

As the church, we are to work together in unity of faith and purpose to bring the message of God's salvation to every corner of a hungry and hurting world. No individual among us can accomplish this on his or her own. Indeed, God made us to depend on one another. Together, we're more effective, we can overcome bigger problems, and we can help one another when one of us becomes tired or discouraged.

It's said that no two snowflakes are alike, and this is very likely true considering the vast number of water molecules in a typical snowflake and the fact that snowflakes grow at different rates and form different patterns depending on changing atmospheric conditions. Likewise, every person in the church is unique. We are individually gifted by God and shaped by our experiences and the family and social conditions in which we grew.

Snowflakes are fragile, delicate things, but when enough of them stick together they can bring a city to its knees or transform a barren landscape into a winter wonderland. In the same way, you and I may feel like we can't make much of a difference in this world as individuals. But working together we have the ability to transform our culture and change our world. The people of this world are desperate for love and a sense of belonging. So when they see God's family "agreeing wholeheartedly with each other, loving one another, and working together with one mind and purpose" (Philippians 2:2, NLT), they will know that God is the source of our love (John 17:23), and they will thirst for the living water (John 7:38).

What You Will Do

» You will understand how people are born and adopted into God's new family, the church.

» You will examine the meaning of fellowship and its role in building unity among God's family.

» You will explore God's plan for reaching the world through His church.

» You will be encouraged to forgive others when they hurt you or are unkind to you, just as Christ has forgiven you.

Stonewall Jackson

Thomas J. Jackson, nicknamed "Stonewall" because of his steadiness in battle, was one of the Confederacy's most revered commanders during the Civil War. Born in Virginia in 1824, Jackson was orphaned at a young age, then passed around among relatives. These hardships gave him an appreciation for hard work and self-discipline. In 1842, he was accepted to the United States Military Academy at West Point, though he barely passed the entrance exams because of his inadequate schooling. Nevertheless, he was one of the hardest working cadets and graduated in the top third of his class.

His ceaseless determination won him more field promotions than any other officer during the Mexican-American War (1846–1848). Upon returning home, he accepted a position at the Virginia Military Institute in Lexington, Virginia, where he taught for ten years. After losing his first wife and son in childbirth, Jackson married again in 1857. While in Lexington, Jackson organized and taught regular Sunday school classes for blacks, and he was revered by both slaves and freedmen in town.

When the Civil War broke out, Jackson was given the rank of brigadier general in the Confederate Army and eventually took command of the Shenandoah Valley regiments. He earned his famous nickname at the first battle of Manassas on July 21, 1861. As the Confederate lines began to falter under a heavy Union assault, Jackson's brigade provided crucial reinforcements. A fellow general exhorted his own troops to hold their line by shouting, "There is Jackson standing like a stone wall. Let us determine to die here, and we will conquer. Rally behind the Virginians!" In battle after battle, Jackson and his soldiers distinguished themselves and contributed to other important Confederate victories at Manassas, Fredericksburg, and Chancellorsville.

The night after the battle of Chancellorsville, Stonewall Jackson was mistaken for an enemy and shot by his own sentries. He was taken to a nearby plantation, where his left arm was amputated, but his doctors missed the early signs of pneumonia. As Jackson lay dying, Lee sent a message to Chancellorsville, saying, "Give General Jackson my affectionate regards, and say to him: He has lost his left arm but I my right."

An eccentric but brilliant commander, Jackson's loss was devastating for the South. Today, his likeness appears alongside those of Jefferson Davis and Robert E. Lee on the enormous carving on Stone Mountain in Georgia.

THE WAR—1861 TO 1865

Emma Jane's memories of the Johnstons' summer visit were bittersweet. She recalled with delight exploring the farm with her cousins, reading books together on the veranda, and catching fireflies after dark. Yet her recollections of Zachary and David's heated discussion about slavery, as well as the dining table conversation about the potential for war, overshadowed her happier memories.

      For the rest of the summer before Zachary's return to school, Emma Jane spent as much time with him as she could, enduring his teasing while wondering what life would be like without him if war came. Zachary and Moses finished painting the barn just in time to begin cutting and baling the summer hay. Emma Jane, her mother, Winnie, and Hattie worked equally long days picking and preserving fruits and vegetables for the coming winter months, leaving little time for lessons or play.

      "I'll miss you, Emma Jane," Zachary said affectionately on the morning he was to leave. "Most of all, I'll miss celebrating your thirteenth birthday next month. Why, you'll be all grown up next time I see you!"

      "Well, I won't miss you and your teasing one bit," Emma Jane responded, trying to keep herself from crying.

      "Now hurry, Zach. Your father already has the horses saddled," their mother said half-heartedly as she, too, tried to mask her worry over her son's future.

"We'll take the Valley Pike as far as Staunton, where I'll begin another two-week circuit," Dr. Williams said as he and Zachary mounted their horses. "Should be there before dark, and tomorrow Zach should make Lexington by late afternoon if he gets an early start."

"You two be careful now," Moses said as Hattie, Winnie, Sarah, and Emma Jane waved tearful good-byes. "And there'll be more hay to cut next summer, Zach, so don't you be gettin' yo' self in trouble."

"Now, that's enough good-byes," Mrs. Williams said, wiping her tears. "We've got work to do around this place. Why, we've lessons to read, pickles to make, and heaven only knows how Moses will manage the farm by himself!"

As much as they would miss Zachary, the family welcomed the arrival of fall and familiar routines. For Emma Jane, resuming her studies and spending time with Hattie brought a sense of security. And looking forward to her October birthday distracted her from worrying about Zach and David and the possibility of war.

Unlike Hattie's tenth birthday with its many unconventional surprises, Emma Jane's thirteenth birthday was celebrated quietly. Winnie polished the silver birthday cup as usual and baked Emma Jane's favorite blueberry pie. Hattie embroidered Emma Jane's initials on a small handkerchief. Her parents' gift of a delicately engraved silver locket and a letter from Zachary were more than enough to create a memorable birthday.

But familiar routines and birthday memories could not shield Emma Jane or her family from the reality of the rising tensions tearing the nation apart. One chilly evening near the end of October, Dr. Williams lit a fire in the parlor. He settled into his favorite chair and began reading *Harper's Weekly*, which usually arrived at Turner's Store a full week or more after its publication. Emma Jane, who was careful not to disturb her father's reading, curled up on the sofa to read *Jane Eyre*, while her mother resumed her needlepoint.

"Says here Lincoln stands a good chance of winnin' this election," Dr. Williams announced, abruptly breaking the silence, "and that worries me. Some say he's an abolitionist; others say he's just very committed to maintainin' the Union. Either way, some Southern states are vowin' secession if he's elected."

"What's secession, Papa?" Emma Jane asked, gathering from her father's tone of voice that this wasn't a good thing.

"It means that some states are threatenin' to break away from the United States and start their own country."

"But that would mean two nations instead of one, wouldn't it?"

"Indeed it does, and that could mean war."

"But if there's a war, Zach would have to fight. And I don't want him to fight."

"Nor do I. Nobody wants war, including Uncle Thaddeus and Aunt Elizabeth. I'm sorry, Emma Jane, for bringing this up again. I know it makes you uncomfortable. But I'm deeply concerned, as are all the people around these parts."

Dr. Williams's concerns were well founded. Abraham Lincoln was elected president on November 6, 1860, and he swore to preserve the Union. Then on December 20, South Carolina became the first state to make good on its threats to secede. By the end of February, just before Lincoln's inauguration, Mississippi, Florida, Alabama, Georgia, Louisiana, and Texas had joined South Carolina in forming the Confederate States of America. They chose Jefferson Davis, an influential United States senator, to be their president.

Campaign button for Abraham Lincoln.

"Where's this all leadin' us, Dr. Williams?" Moses asked as the two men unloaded seed for the April planting. "Will Virginia join the Confederates? And what's all this feudin' gonna mean fo' us and yo' family?"

"I suspect Virginia's leanin' toward the Confederacy. As for us, well, I just don't know. I'm not in favor of secession any more than I'm in favor of slavery. I'm torn about this whole states' rights issue, just like Zachary. But if war comes, as a doctor I couldn't turn my back on any soldier in need, Union or Confederate."

War did come. Through telegraph and couriers, word spread quickly through the Shenandoah Valley that on April 12, 1861, Confederate troops attacked Union defenses at Fort Sumter, South Carolina, forcing their surrender two days later. Then on April 17, after Lincoln's call for thousands of volunteers to fight, Virginia seceded from the Union.

"Oh, I hope there's a letter from Zach today," Sarah Williams cried expectantly as she and Emma Jane hurried down the path to the barn. Dr. Williams was dismounting his horse after his third ride to Turner's Store in as many days, and Sarah hugged him anxiously.

Thomas smiled, reached into his satchel, and pulled out a letter. "We've received news from Zach," he said.

"Oh, read it, Papa, read it," begged Emma Jane.

Dear Father, Mother, and Emma Jane,

I take pen in hand, praying this letter finds you well and prospering. I miss you all, though I find little time to write. By the time you receive this, most of the corps will probably be in Richmond where we have been assigned the duty of drilling Confederate army recruits. We do not know what other duties we will be required to perform, as orders may change depending on the direction of the war. We leave tomorrow under the command of Major Thomas J. Jackson, one of our professors. He's an artillery instructor and a tough drill master. Rumor has it he shall return to active duty after we arrive in Richmond.

I'm sure you've heard the news that Colonel Lee resigned his commission with the Union army and will take command of Virginia's forces. You know of his love for this country, but he said he couldn't take arms against members of his own family and his fellow Virginians. I feel that way too. I do not want to fight, but I do believe in states' rights. And I know I could never fight against my neighbors.

Father, I told Major Jackson that you are a doctor. He said both military and civilian doctors would be greatly needed should the war escalate, but I sincerely hope it does not come to that.

I will write again from Richmond. I love you all very much. Please give my regards to Moses, Winnie, and Hattie. Please do not worry about me. Hoping you are well and will continue well, I remain,

Your son and brother,
Zachary

General Robert E. Lee.

Although Zachary's letter relieved the family's concerns about his well-being, it did little to calm fears that war would spread beyond South Carolina into the Shenandoah Valley. On an early July afternoon, these fears were justified by a letter Dr. Williams received from the Confederate States Department of War, requesting civilian doctors to volunteer their services to the Confederacy. Of immediate concern was the potential

Soldiers at the ruins of Manassas Junction.

of engagement between Union and Confederate armies near Manassas Junction, Virginia, only twenty-five miles southwest of Washington. Union troops were preparing to march on Richmond, the Confederate capital, hoping to put a quick end to the war, while Confederate troops were massing in large numbers in the northern Shenandoah Valley and in the countryside around Manassas Junction. Confrontation seemed inevitable, and preparations included recruiting physicians to care for the wounded.

"I must go, Sarah," Thomas said with somber conviction after reading the letter to her. "How God will use me, I don't know, but I must go."

"But you have patients here who need you," cried Sarah. "And what will happen to us if you don't . . . ?"

The words caught in her throat, knowing that talk of dying would make the situation even more unbearable.

"Oh, Papa, please don't go," Emma Jane pleaded, knowing nothing would change her father's resolute decision.

"I'll be home soon, and God will protect us all."

With her father away, Emma Jane kept track of the days in her diary:

July 15, 1861. Father left for Manassas Junction today. We're all sad. Dear Jesus, please take care of him, and please stop this war. I'm glad Zach is safe in Richmond, but we miss him very much.

July 30, 1861. Today we heard that many soldiers were wounded or killed at Manassas Junction. I wish we'd hear from Father. I pray he's alive and not hurt. I don't feel much like studying these days. Hattie doesn't either.

August 27, 1861. Still no word from Father. I'm worried, and so is Mother. We're happy to still have Moses, Winnie, and Hattie here with us.

Doctor tending to wounded Confederate soldiers.

On a warm September afternoon, Dr. Williams arrived home unexpectedly. His homecoming was joyous yet tearful. To Emma Jane, he seemed like a different man than the one who had left three months earlier. Not only was he gaunt, but he was also withdrawn. He spoke little of the battle, saying only that it was much worse than the newspapers reported. He spoke briefly about the primitive, makeshift hospitals and the lack of supplies, and he wept as he spoke of his inability to save the most seriously injured. "I did the best I could under the circumstances. Dear God, what has befallen our nation?"

Dr. Williams remained home the rest of that year. He saw only a few patients nearby in the valley and devoted most of his time to regaining his strength and helping Moses with the daily demands of the farm. An occasional letter from Zachary, the celebration of Emma Jane's fourteenth birthday, and the peacefulness of the farm contributed to his physical and emotional recovery.

For Emma Jane, everything had changed. The war had taken both her father and brother from her. Although she did not doubt her father's love, he no longer readily laughed. Family conversations always gravitated toward the war, concerns about the future, and Zachary's well-being. Even his interactions with Moses and Winnie became less frequent, pertaining mostly to maintaining the farm. Emma Jane and Hattie continued their lessons but without the enthusiasm and laughter that had filled the warming kitchen two years earlier.

With much of the South still planted in cotton, the fertile farmland of the Shenandoah Valley became the breadbasket of the Confederacy. The Williamses and their neighbors were urged to convert their pastureland to food crops to support the army. Because they understood the need to feed the troops, the farmers bore the burden of extra costs for seed as well as extended days of grueling work, planting, weeding, and harvesting. Even Emma Jane and Hattie worked long, hot hours in the fields with their fathers.

1862 lithograph of the Battle of Winchester.

Unfortunately, the relative peace of the valley did not last. In March 1862, just before spring planting, Confederate forces engaged the Union army near Winchester, bringing a major battle line within eighty-five miles of the Williams farm. By May, as spring crops pushed their tender shoots through the fertile soil, Union troops pushed like tendrils of iron deep into the valley, drawing ever closer to the farm.

"I cannot sit by and do nothing," Dr. Williams announced when he heard news of battles near Harrisonburg, Cross Keys, and Port Republic. "Why, these people are our neighbors. Some are my patients!"

Sarah Williams did not try to dissuade her husband from volunteering that summer to help save lives on the battle front. Emma Jane sensed that his absence this time would be much longer than before.

That evening, Emma Jane and her mother ate supper with Moses' family in the warming kitchen. Mrs. Williams asked Moses to pray for her husband and Zachary and all who were bearing the distresses of war. Then, without prompting, Hattie asked if she could read the twenty-third psalm. "Of course," Mrs. Williams answered. "We all need to hear words of peace in times like these."

Before going to bed, Emma Jane wrote again in her diary:

June 16, 1862. Father has left again. We are all sad. I thank thee, O God, that thou art our Shepherd and will lead us through the valley of the shadow of death.

That summer passed slowly. In early October, just before Emma Jane's fifteenth birthday, the family received a letter from Dr. Williams, assuring them he was safe though exhausted and deeply discouraged by the ongoing war. They also learned that in August he had accompanied the man now known as General "Stonewall" Jackson into a second engagement at Manassas Junction and was with his Second Corps in the bloody battle at Sharpsburg, Maryland.

October 10, 1862

My Dearest Loved Ones,

I remain safe, unlike the thousands I have watched die on these wretched fields. You must have heard by now that Lee's invasion of Maryland was thwarted at Sharpsburg, forcing him back into Virginia. Surely that was the bloodiest day in America's history. The Union victory, dear ones, gave Lincoln the confidence to deliver an ultimatum: Unless the Confederate States rejoin the Union by the first of January, he will issue a proclamation forever freeing all slaves held in these Southern states. Of course, many of our neighbors will scorn anything Mr. Lincoln says, and all this means nothing unless the Union wins the war.

I question whether either side can endure much longer, and Confederate supplies seem inadequate to the task. But I do have some good news. Near Sharpsburg, I had the unexpected joy of a brief reunion with General Lee. Emma Jane, I told him how you celebrate your birthdays with the silver cup he and Mrs. Lee gave you when you were born. I trust you will again this year. Even in the midst of war, we mustn't abandon our family traditions.

I remain,

Your loving husband and father

Lincoln at the Battle of Sharpsburg.

Winnie did set Emma's place with her birthday cup, but not in the dining room, which would require firewood to heat. Rather, she set it in the warming kitchen, where they gathered for a simple meal of grits and beans.

"I'm sorry there's no sugar for blueberry pie this year, Miz Emma Jane," Winnie apologized.

"Oh, Winnie, it's okay," Emma Jane replied sincerely, understanding well the scarcity of ingredients. "Just having you all here with Mama and me is enough . . . though it would be so good to have Papa and Zach here, too."

Through the cold winter months and into the spring of 1863, Sarah and Winnie frugally prepared meals from their dwindling food supplies. Clothes were mended repeatedly, and only essential staples and seed were purchased at Turner's Store, and then only if they were available.

"They's riotin' in Richmond," Moses announced after a trip to town in early May. "Folks took to the streets hollerin' fo' bread. Seems nothin's lef' fo' city folk to buy. Ever' bit of food is goin' to feed the army. And Mr. Turner say Union troops been rippin' up the Virginia Central Railroad. It don' sound good fo' the Confederacy."

Indeed, by the summer of 1863 things looked bleak for the Confederacy. Stonewall Jackson was wounded at Chancellorsville and died on May 10. In July, General Lee boldly advanced his forces into Union territory in Pennsylvania, but a three-day battle at the town of Gettysburg resulted in great loss of life on both sides, and Lee's army was pushed back into Virginia.

"How long, Mama? How long?" cried Emma Jane, as she helped her mother and Winnie preserve the last of the summer vegetables. "When will this horrible war end? How long before we see Papa and Zach again?"

"I don't know, Emma Jane. Only God knows," her mother answered despondently. "Your father's letters are so infrequent these days. But we do know he survived Gettysburg. We just have to trust that God has him and Zach in His hands."

Battlefield of Gettysburg and the seminary used for a hospital.

Emma's sixteenth birthday passed almost without mention that October. There was no birthday cup in spite of her father's encouragement to maintain the tradition. All efforts were focused on preparing for the coming winter months, knowing that the scarcity of food supplies would require careful rationing until harvest the following year.

The winter and spring did nothing to relieve the stresses of war. Faith and perseverance were tested on both sides. In late May, Emma Jane and her mother received news that VMI cadets had marched against Union troops at New Market and Zachary had been seriously wounded.

"He's comin' home, thank God, he's comin' home! My boy's comin' home!" Sarah Williams cried as she read the letter saying Zachary had been furloughed to recover from his injuries.

However, Zachary's homecoming was bittersweet. Like his father, his initiation to war had caused profound emotional changes. He no longer bothered to tease Emma Jane, and he shared his growing conviction that the Confederate cause was lost. News that Union troops had burned VMI in June and laid siege to Petersburg, south of Richmond, left little hope for Southern victory. By September, what little enthusiasm Zach held was completely dashed when news reached the farm of General William Tecumseh Sherman and the Union army's fiery march across the South.

Zach prayed for both the healing of the nation and the reconciliation of grieving families on both sides. Could such healing ever occur? Could a nation and families divided by war ever be reunited? His faith that God could bring healing waivered less than his confidence that He actually would. Emma Jane yearned for her father's return while her neighbors yearned for an end to the escalating conflict, not yet knowing the full extent of the suffering they were about to endure.

Farm house damaged during the Civil War.

In late September, Union forces were ordered to the Shenandoah Valley to burn its farms and mills so they would no longer be capable of providing food for the Confederate army.

"Mother!" Zachary shouted from the front porch early on the morning of September 23. "Get everyone into the house! Get Father's rifle. It's Union soldiers. They're torching the fields, and I see smoke risin' over yonder from the Hawthornes' barn."

Still weakened by his wounds, Zachary leaned against the porch railing holding the rifle at waist level. However, as a dozen mounted troops appeared and approached the house, he had no choice but to lower the rifle.

The captain of the small band of soldiers said, "I'm under orders to burn this house and its outbuildings. Is anyone inside?"

"Only the six of us," said Sarah Williams forcefully as she, Emma Jane, Moses, Winnie, and Hattie joined Zachary on the porch.

"I'm sorry to have to do this, ma'am, but orders are orders. Now move off the porch. And you, young man, lay that rifle down if you know what's good for you."

As everyone moved cautiously, Zachary glared at the enemy troops. "Mother," he whispered, "it's Cousin David. Look, it's David Johnston. I know it is!"

"Oh, Zach, it can't be."

But it *was* David. As Zachary continued staring, his cousin looked away before maneuvering his horse next to that of the captain.

"Sir," he said quietly, "I need to talk to you privately if I may."

For several minutes the two spoke in hushed tones before the captain spoke up again. "You men ride on ahead. I'll join you shortly. Spare neither house nor barn. Those are my orders."

As the troops spurred their horses and rode away, the captain ordered everyone on the porch into the warming kitchen. "I'm under orders to burn this house. But before I do, I suggest you fill your buckets with water and bring them into the kitchen. Then gather your old blankets. No questions, now, just do as I say."

Moses ran to the well and began filling their buckets while Winnie and Hattie hurried upstairs to get blankets. Zachary and Emma Jane stayed with their mother in the kitchen.

Union soldier.

"Captain," Zachary said, "we know the soldier who spoke to you. He's—"

"I know who he is," the captain said. "He told me that you're cousins and that he and his family visited here before the war. He also said your father's a doctor and has cared for the wounded on both sides. I can't in good conscience burn you out, but orders are orders. So I will start a fire. What you do about it is not my affair. May God help you. And may He bring an end to this war so we can all go home to our families."

With these words, the captain ordered everyone outside. Knocking the kerosene lamp from the long table to the floor, he stepped back into the doorway and tossed a match into the kitchen. As the flames exploded, he mounted his horse and raced away.

Moses quickly entered the kitchen and began beating the flames with blankets while the others doused the table and chairs with water. After making sure the fire was completely out, they went back outside while the smoke cleared.

Moses held Hattie close as she cried uncontrollably.

"We're safe, Hattie," Emma Jane said softly as she took Hattie's hand. "God protected us."

"Lord," Zachary prayed emotionally, "please hold David and all his family and ours in your protective care. And please bless the captain for his kindness to us just now."

That evening before going to bed, Emma Jane wrote in her diary:

September 23, 1864. Dear Father, I know that you protected us today. I know it was no coincidence that Cousin David was with the soldiers who came to burn our farm. Thank you for his bravery in speaking to the captain on our behalf. Help me not to doubt that this war will soon end and Father will come home. I know you hear our prayers and that only you can bring an end to this terrible conflict.

Unknown to Emma Jane, her prayers and the prayers of a broken nation would soon be answered.

THINK ABOUT IT

» Why is Emma Jane's father needed at the battlefront? Why do you think he says, "I couldn't turn my back on any soldier in need, Union or Confederate"?

» Why was there no sugar available for Winnie to make a blueberry pie for Emma Jane's birthday? Common ingredients and materials are often in short supply during wartime, both on the battlefield and at home. Talk with a grandparent or neighbor who lived during World War II and ask about the kinds of things people in America had to do without during the war.

» What did the Union captain do for the Williams family? Why? Why did he choose to start a small fire instead of simply leaving the house untouched?

THE BATTLE OF GETTYSBURG

On July 1, 1863, the Union and Confederate armies met at a little town in Pennsylvania called Gettysburg. The Confederate Army, commanded by General Robert E. Lee, had marched north through the Shenandoah Valley to attack Pennsylvania. The Union Army, commanded by Major General George Meade, had slowly followed with the intention of protecting Washington, DC. At first, neither army was at full strength.

This photo, taken days after the battle ended, shows the position of the Union troops' stronghold in the hills above the farms where the main fighting took place.

The first day of the battle saw a victory for the Confederate Army. They pushed the Union Army from Gettysburg's western hills all the way to the hills on the southeast side of town. Reinforcements helped the Union Army take control of Cemetery Ridge and formed a strong line to hold off the Confederates.

On the second day, the newly reinforced Confederate Army attacked the Union line at its weakest points. The soldiers fought all day among the farms south of Gettysburg, but the Union Army remained in control of the hills, thanks in part to a daring charge led by Colonel Joshua Chamberlain.

On the third day, General Lee decided to attack the center of the Union line. After bombarding Cemetery Ridge with cannon fire all morning, Confederate soldiers advanced up the ridge in an attack called Pickett's Charge, but they could not take the hill. The Union Army had won.

By nightfall, the Confederate forces were retreating. The bloodiest battle of the Civil War was over, claiming more than 46,000 casualties. Although the South's leadership believed Gettysburg was just a setback, the battle proved to be the turning point in the war. The defeat broke the Confederates' momentum, and General Lee's forces surrendered less than two years later.

WORDS YOU NEED TO KNOW

- » **The church:** All people who have become members of God's family and citizens of His holy nation by believing in God's only Son, Jesus, as their Savior and choosing to obey Him

- » **Fellowship:** Enjoying a relationship of harmony with others

- » **Disciple:** A believer, student, and follower of Jesus Christ

- » **Evangelism:** Leading others to faith in Jesus Christ

- » **Forgiveness:** A choice to love those who have been unkind to me

HIDE IT IN YOUR HEART

But you are a chosen people, a royal priesthood, a holy nation, a people belonging to God, that you may declare the praises of him who called you out of darkness into his wonderful light. (1 Peter 2:9)

Make allowance for each other's faults, and forgive anyone who offends you. Remember, the Lord forgave you, so you must forgive others. (Colossians 3:13, NLT)

WE ARE THE CHURCH

Jesus died on the cross during the Jewish feast of Passover the day after praying that His followers, present and future, would love one another as a family. Yet as He had promised, He was raised back to life by God the Father. Thereafter, Jesus spent several weeks teaching His disciples. As His time on earth drew to a close, He told the disciples to wait in the city of Jerusalem until God the Father sent a helper, the Holy Spirit, to fill their hearts and give them power from on high to share the truth about Jesus with people all over the world. On the fortieth day after Passover, Jesus was taken up into heaven. The disciples watched Him ascend into the clouds, and then they returned to Jerusalem to await the coming of the Spirit.

Ten days later, the feast of Pentecost arrived. Each year on this day, Israelites from many parts of the world came to Jerusalem to celebrate the harvest. They brought sacrifices to God's temple and thanked Him for blessing them with good crops. On that day, as the

Descent of the Holy Spirit on the Twelve Apostles by Urbini. Photo: Giovanni Dall'Orto.

disciples were meeting together, a sound "as of a rushing mighty wind" came from heaven, "and it filled all the house where they were sitting" (Acts 2:2, NKJV). Every one of them was filled with the Holy Spirit, and each one began speaking in a language he had never uttered before. When the visitors to Jerusalem heard the loud noise, they came running and were surprised to hear the men from Galilee speaking in the language of their homelands. Then the apostle Peter spoke to the crowd and explained what was happening. He told the people about Jesus, who had been crucified. He told them how God had raised Jesus back to life and made Him Lord over all. And He told them of the Holy Spirit whose coming had been foretold by the prophet Joel.

Traditional site of Pentecost as it appears today. Photo: Assaf Shtilman.

When the people heard Peter's message, about three thousand believed and were baptized, and they, too, received God's Holy Spirit. In the days that followed, these people remained in Jerusalem and spent their time learning more about Jesus from the apostles. They worshiped together, prayed together, helped each other, and grew as new believers in Jesus Christ:

> *Everyone was filled with awe, and many wonders and miraculous signs were done by the apostles. All the believers were together and had everything in common. Selling their possessions and goods, they gave to anyone as he had need. Every day they continued to meet together in the temple courts. They broke bread in their homes and ate together with glad and sincere hearts, praising God and enjoying the favor of all the people. And the Lord added to their number daily those who were being saved.* (Acts 2:43–47)

These were the first Christians, the first members of what Jesus called His **church** (Matthew 16:18). The church consists of all people who have become members of God's family by believing in Jesus Christ as their Savior and choosing to obey Him. Ever since the day of Pentecost, the church has continued to grow. Today, more than a billion people around the world are members of the church. They come from every land and every country. They are tall and short, rich and poor, young and old. And they are "all children of God through faith in Christ Jesus" (Galatians 3:26, NLT).

Remember, the first members of the church came to Jerusalem from all over to celebrate the harvest. They came from three different continents, spoke many different

languages, and grew up observing very different customs. And yet, as new Christians, they cared for each other as family. They opened their homes to one another, they ate together, and they shared everything they owned. That's because Jesus intended for His followers to love and serve one another, just as He had shown them:

"A new command I give you: Love one another. As I have loved you, so you must love one another. By this all men will know that you are my disciples, if you love one another." (John 13:34–35)

The Bible says that, no matter where we live or where we come from, as Christians we are all "members of God's household" (Ephesians 2:19). And as brothers and sisters in Christ, we are commanded to love one another (1 Peter 1:22), honor one another (Romans 12:10), serve one another (Galatians 5:13), bear one another's burdens (Galatians 6:2), comfort and encourage one another (1 Thessalonians 5:11), show hospitality to one another (1 Peter 4:9), teach one another (Colossians 3:16), and be at peace with one another (Mark 9:50). And when people see us serving one another in love, they will know that we are God's family.

MAKE A NOTE OF IT

Read Romans 12:10 and write it in your notebook. To honor someone means to show that person love, appreciation, and respect. For example, you honor your mother on Mother's Day (or any other day of the year) by giving her a card or gift or by doing her daily chores for her. Think of someone at your church whom you can honor. Why do you feel this person is deserving of honor? What can you do to honor this person? Plan a special visit to honor this individual in person. Be sure to take pictures!

FELLOWSHIP IS ABOUT MORE THAN DONUTS

Ever since the Fall, people have been unable to get along for any length of time. When sin entered the world, human relationships became marked by disagreement, distrust, dishonor, bitterness, and envy. However, God always had a plan to restore harmony in our relationships with others through a single, sacrificial act of love. At just the right moment in history, He sent His only Son to redeem His creation, making it possible for His children to love one another perfectly.

Now those who put their faith in Jesus Christ and choose to turn from their sins are adopted into God's family, and together we are made one in Him:

You are all sons of God through faith in Christ Jesus, for all of you who were baptized into Christ have clothed yourselves with Christ. There is neither Jew nor Greek, slave nor free, male nor female, for you are all one in Christ Jesus. (Galatians 3:26–28)

Despite our many races, nationalities, and denominations, the church is one body, which is also called the body of Christ (1 Corinthians 12:27). As members of God's family, each of us is to live in harmony with other believers. By living in harmony with one another, we show the world what life would be like if they, too, followed Jesus. In fact, when we live and work with unity of faith and purpose, we help the world to believe. Jesus prayed:

"May they experience such perfect unity that the world will know that you sent me and that you love them as much as you love me." (John 17:23, NLT)

Does this mean the family of God lives in perfect harmony? Not yet. Although we are all new creations in Christ (2 Corinthians 5:17), we have not yet been perfected (Philippians 1:6). We will have occasional disagreements, and sometimes we will even fight. But Jesus' prayer for unity is one we can help answer by loving one another and living in fellowship until we become "united in heart and mind" (Acts 4:32, NLT).

What is fellowship? **Fellowship** is enjoying a relationship of harmony with our brothers and sisters in Christ. Today we use the word *fellowship* to describe anything from a church picnic to bowling with the youth group to sharing hot chocolate and donuts after worship service. There's nothing wrong with using the word in this way; these kinds of gatherings are fun and help us get to know our church family better. However, the word as used in the Bible has a deeper meaning.

Biblical fellowship is about a relationship, not just an activity. When the first Christians "devoted themselves . . . to the fellowship" in Acts 2:42, they were not simply bringing food to a potluck dinner and then afterward playing a rousing game of *Trivial Pursuit: The Torah Edition.* They were totally committed to one another, and they shared everything including their interests and beliefs, their activities and labors, their

privileges and responsibilities, and their feelings and concerns. They built godly relationships based on their relationship with God the Father through His Son, Jesus. And they shared a common goal to tell the world about the love of God and His free gift of salvation.

Fellowship with God's family does not happen only on Sundays and Wednesdays or at special events. Fellowship is meant to be a way of life for believers in Jesus Christ. Every program and every activity we plan should celebrate and build our relationships with one another. We should *desire* to be in each other's company. And like any close-knit family, we should always be ready and willing to help and support one another both physically and spiritually:

> *Let the word of Christ dwell in you richly, teaching and admonishing one another in all wisdom, singing psalms and hymns and spiritual songs, with thankfulness in your hearts to God.* (Colossians 3:16, ESV)

> *Share each other's burdens, and in this way obey the law of Christ.* (Galatians 6:2, NLT)

> *Therefore encourage one another and build each other up.* (1 Thessalonians 5:11)

> *Now you must show sincere love to each other as brothers and sisters. Love each other deeply with all your heart.* (1 Peter 1:22, NLT)

The Bible makes it clear that God's children have a responsibility toward one another. Therefore, we should not neglect our Christian family or avoid church services. Hebrews 10:24–25 (NLT) says, "Let us think of ways to motivate one another to acts of love and good works. And let us not neglect our meeting together, as some people do, but encourage one another." You cannot have a relationship with God's family unless you spend time with them. How can you encourage—or be encouraged by—your fellow believers if you rarely see them? You might learn a lot from watching a preacher on television, but you can't really fellowship with the church unless you get off your couch, go to where they are gathering, and get to know them as brothers and sisters in the Lord.

Only by loving and supporting and depending on one another and joining together regularly to worship and pray and study the Word of God will we be built up "until we all come to such unity in our faith and knowledge of God's Son that we will be mature in the Lord, measuring up to the full and complete standard of Christ" (Ephesians 4:13, NLT).

> *The holiest moment of the church service is the moment when God's people—strengthened by preaching and sacrament—go out of the church door into the world to be the church.*
> **Ernest William Southcott**
> 1915–1976

MAKE A NOTE OF IT

When do the members of your local church usually meet together as a family? Why do you think the church has traditionally met on Sunday, the first day of the week? Why is it important for all members of the church to meet together each week? How does fellowship with other Christians bring glory to God?

WE ARE SALT AND LIGHT TO THE WORLD

Salt is required to maintain good health, a fact that was known long before science understood how the human body works. The ancient Greek poet Homer referred to salt as a "divine" substance. The salt industry apparently agrees, as it claims there are 14,000 known uses for salt. Perhaps the most common use for salt is to season, cure, and preserve meats and other foods. It's also used medicinally to treat sprains, earaches, and sore throats. Handy moms and dads use salt to remove rust, seal cracks, and purge stains from clothing. Salt can be used to melt the ice on your front porch in the winter or to make ice cream during the summer!

Today, we tend to take salt for granted. Advances in chemistry and geology have revealed that the earth contains huge underground deposits of salt. But until the twentieth century, salt was thought to be very rare and quite precious. And so when Jesus called His followers "the salt of the earth" (Matthew 5:13), they were probably startled that He was comparing them to something so highly valued. What they didn't know was that, within a few years, Jesus would pay the ultimate price to purchase them, body and soul, for His own (1 Corinthians 6:20). God's family is precious to Him indeed!

A Brief History of Salt

You may think of salt as nothing more than what you use to flavor your French fries, but this seemingly innocuous condiment has a long and surprisingly tumultuous history. In 2700 B.C., a Chinese writer described forty different kinds of salt and their uses. Salt is mined from underground deposits or dried from seawater and has been used for many centuries as a food preservative, a seasoning, a disinfectant, and as a unit of exchange. According to the ancient historian Pliny the Elder, we get the word *salary* from the fact that salt was used to pay Roman soldiers.

A valued commodity through the centuries, salt has played a major role in national economies, political movements, and military actions. Caravans once trekked the Sahara Desert to trade salt ounce-for-ounce for gold. The city-state of Venice fought a series of wars in the fourteenth century to protect its salt monopoly in the region. Mozart's home town of Salzburg, Austria, was named for its location on a river route important to the salt trade. Salt was a strategic objective in both the American Revolution and the Civil War, and the 1864 loss of the Confederate salt works at Saltville, Virginia, was considered a major blow to the South's dwindling resources.

In 1930, Mahatma Gandhi organized the Salt March, a peaceful demonstration that was a major turning point in India's struggle for independence from Great Britain. Gandhi said he chose the British salt tax as the basis of his protest because "next to air and water, salt is perhaps the greatest necessity of life."

Salt has played a vital part in religious and community rituals in many cultures, symbolizing health, friendship, hospitality, and incorruptible purity. There are more than thirty references to salt in the Bible, owing to the significance of salt in Jewish culture. Jesus told us we are the salt of the earth (Matthew 5:13). As Christians, we are to be a seasoning, a preservative, and a cure in a world full of sin and hatred toward the things of God.

However, when Jesus said we are the salt of the earth, He was not simply declaring our value as people. He was also saying something important about how we are to live as the family of God. For example, the Jews who heard Jesus speak would have known that the Law of Moses required that every grain offering to God be seasoned with salt (Leviticus 2:13). Paul would later write that believers are to offer themselves wholly to the Lord as "living sacrifices":

Therefore, I urge you, brothers, in view of God's mercy, to offer your bodies as living sacrifices, holy and pleasing to God—this is your spiritual act of worship.
(Romans 12:1)

As followers of Christ, we are not to hold back any part of our lives from Him. Rather, we are to declare Him Lord and Master over everything we say and do and own. But some Christians want to withhold control over certain areas of their lives. One person may feel the need to lie and cheat to get ahead in business, so he tries to keep his job separate from his faith. Another is determined to be seen in only the latest fashions, so she wants to make her own decisions about how she spends her money. Others figure they can spend their Saturday nights any way they like as long as they show up at church on Sunday.

God's family members are meant to change the flavor of the world for the better. We are to reach out to this spiritually dry society and make people thirst for the living water of Christ. But salt that is mixed with incompatible minerals or corrupted by certain chemicals will lose both its salty flavor and its life-giving properties, making it of no value to anyone. When we refuse to give Christ total control over our lives, when we insist on trying to live with one foot in the world and the other foot in the church, we place ourselves in danger of losing our "saltiness." We cannot chase after the deceitful riches and fame of this world or allow ourselves to be weighed down by its material concerns without becoming corrupted ourselves. Jesus said, "You are the salt of the earth. But if the salt loses its saltiness, how can it be made salty again? It is no longer good for anything, except to be thrown out and trampled by men" (Matthew 5:13).

This doesn't mean that we should cower from the world. Jesus doesn't want us to wrap ourselves in a Christian cocoon and simply wait in hiding for His return. He put us on this earth to make the world a better place! He redeemed His church and purified it, and then He sent us out into the world to spread the good news of salvation while doing good works in His name by the power of His Spirit. On the night before He was crucified, Jesus prayed for his followers:

> *"My prayer is not that you take them out of the world but that you protect them from the evil one. They are not of the world, even as I am not of it. Sanctify them by the truth. . . . As you sent me into the world, I have sent them into the world."*
> (John 17:15–18)

You see, we do not belong to this world any more than Jesus did. We are "a chosen people, a royal priesthood, a holy nation, a people belonging to God" (1 Peter 2:9). God calls us "children of the light and of the day" (1 Thessalonians 5:5, NLT), and we must no longer allow any portion of our lives to remain in darkness. However, Jesus has sent us into the world so that we will "declare the praises of him who called [us] out of darkness into his wonderful light" (1 Peter 2:9).

Our job as the church is to "bring praise and glory to God" (Ephesians 1:12, NLT), and one of the ways we do this is by being salt and light to the world through serving our neighbors:

"You are the light of the world. A city on a hill cannot be hidden. Neither do people light a lamp and put it under a bowl. Instead they put it on its stand, and it gives light to everyone in the house. In the same way, let your light shine before men, that they may see your good deeds and praise your Father in heaven."
(Matthew 5:14–16)

Jesus has given His church this important assignment: "Go and make disciples of all nations, baptizing them in the name of the Father and of the Son and of the Holy Spirit, and teaching them to obey everything I have commanded you" (Matthew 28:19–20). This is called **evangelism**—leading others to faith in Jesus Christ. A **disciple** is a believer, student, and follower of Jesus. How do we make disciples of people who don't know about

God? One way is to "pray for all people, asking God for what they need and being thankful to him. . . . This is good, and it pleases God our Savior, who wants all people to be saved and to know the truth" (1 Timothy 2:1–4, NCV). Another way is to show them His love by doing good works in Jesus' name.

But we must also share with these people the good news of God's eternal plan to redeem and restore His children through the life, death, and resurrection of Jesus. Paul says that an important part of this message is *how* we share it: "Let your conversation be always full of grace, seasoned with salt, so that you may know how to answer everyone" (Colossians 4:6). So be ready to explain your faith and hope in Jesus to others, but always do so with love, gentleness, and respect (1 Peter 3:15–16). Talk to a hurting friend about what God has done for you. Tell a neighbor what you learned today about God. Don't be shy about sharing His love with others. For when Jesus told us to go and make disciples of all nations, He made this comforting promise: "I am with you always" (Matthew 28:20).

As you and your brothers and sisters in Christ carry the message of God's grace to the ends of the earth, you will see the hearts of individuals and nations turn to God, and the angels will rejoice in heaven (Luke 15:7).

[Scripture says] "Everyone who calls on the name of the Lord will be saved." How, then, can they call on the one they have not believed in? And how can they believe in the one of whom they have not heard? And how can they hear without someone preaching to them? And how can they preach unless they are sent? As it is written, "How beautiful are the feet of those who bring good news!" (Romans 10:13–15)

MAKE A NOTE OF IT

What did Jesus mean when He said you are the "light of the world"? What does this tell us about our job as Christians? How are you worshiping God when you do a good deed? Write about or draw a picture of one way you have recently "let your light shine before men."

WHAT SHOULD I DO?

Forgiveness is a choice you make to love those who have hurt you or been unkind to you. Although the members of God's family are "all one in Christ Jesus" (Galatians 3:28), we do not yet live in perfect harmony. We are still growing as individuals in Christ, and so we will sometimes disagree or even fight. Sometimes we will carelessly say or do something that hurts someone's feelings. So how should you respond when a member of God's family has hurt you or offended you in some way? The Bible says you must follow God's example and forgive that person (Matthew 18:21–35). Sometimes you will find it hard to do this, but remember what it cost God to forgive you. He paid a terrible price in order to purchase your freedom. The least you can do is to give up your pride and your hurt feelings in order to forgive the person who offended you.

> *It may be that the day of judgment will dawn tomorrow; in that case, we shall gladly stop working for a better future. But not before.*
> **Dietrich Bonhoeffer**
> 1905–1945

A PRAYER

Dear God, thank you for adopting me into your family. Help me to love my brothers and sisters in Christ, and show me how I can best serve them. Help me to grow your church by telling others about you and the wonderful things you've done for me. Help me to be brave and to remember that you are always with me. In Jesus' name I pray. Amen.

ENCOUNTERS WITH JESUS

SIMON AND THE CROSS

Simon was glad to walk on firm ground again. The three-week voyage from Cyrene, on the northern coast of Africa, had been perilous because of spring storms, even though the passenger ship rarely left sight of land. A man of imposing size with little tolerance for the sea, Simon didn't like traveling the Mediterranean this early in the season, but this was a special occasion. This year he was taking his teenage sons Alexander and Rufus on the thousand-mile pilgrimage to Jerusalem to celebrate the Passover as men.

Caesarea Maritima in the early 1900s.

The ship had sailed eastward along the African coast, stopping at the Egyptian seaport of Alexandria for supplies before making its way north along the curving coastline of Palestine. Although the nearest port city to Jerusalem was Joppa, the ship was too big to navigate the treacherous reefs surrounding the city. So instead they had docked at Caesarea Maritima, newly built by Herod the Great. The harbor itself was a feat of Roman engineering, as huge blocks of concrete had been sunk into the sea floor to create a massive breakwater to shelter ships.

Now safe on land, the boys and their father gathered their belongings and set off for the marketplace. A prosperous merchant, Simon had brought some of his wares with the intention of exchanging goods for local currency. Among the items he carried was a box of expensive *silphium* resin. Silphium, which grew chiefly in the hills near Cyrene, was prized throughout the Roman Empire as a condiment and a medicine. After some feisty bartering with a spice merchant, Simon exchanged the silphium for a heavy bag of Palestinian coins. Simon gave a coin to each of his sons to spend during their travels.

They spent the night at an inn on the outskirts of Caesarea, waking early the next morning to begin the final leg of their journey. With only three days to walk more than sixty miles, they would have to make good time if they wanted to reach Jerusalem before Passover.

The road was filled with other pilgrims heading for the Holy City, as well as merchants with goods from every corner of the empire, eager to profit from the festival. Roman troops passed by regularly, patrolling the road. Such blatant evidence of Israel's occupation made Simon's blood boil. Even in Cyrene, which was loosely governed by a Roman appointee, the minority Jewish population often chafed under the yoke of Roman rule.

The journey took them through Samaria and into Judea, gradually gaining elevation as they climbed from the sea to the mountains. The higher they climbed, the greener the countryside grew, and as the pilgrims neared their destination they began singing psalms.

Jerusalem in the early 1900s.

A few miles outside of Jerusalem, the path rose out of a valley and the Holy City was revealed in all its splendor. Perched on a high plateau and surrounded on three sides by deep valleys, the city of David shimmered as the afternoon sun highlighted the layers of tightly-packed structures and skimmed along the tops of the walls encircling the city. At its highest point stood the Temple, glistening like a jewel with its marble walls and gleaming decorations of gold. Simon and his sons stopped, breathless from the climb, to take in the beauty of the scene.

Outside the walls of the city, Simon led his boys into Bezetha, a village that had sprung up to accommodate the growing population of Jerusalem. Pilgrims were everywhere, renting rooftops for the week or camping out in the countryside. Simon confidently navigated the tangled streets, leading his sons to the house of his cousin, Isaac, where they received a warm welcome and a tasty meal. Since Isaac had already rented the flat roof of their house to a small group of pilgrims, Simon and his sons would sleep on the floor of the common area inside.

The next morning, the eve of the Passover, Simon and his sons went with Isaac to the Temple to sacrifice their lamb. Isaac had purchased a one-year-old lamb for the Passover feast, and it had been living with his family for a few days while they verified that it was without blemish. The lamb rested quietly on Isaac's shoulders while they waited outside the closed gates of the Temple for the group ahead of them to finish.

As head of the household, Isaac was personally responsible for sacrificing the lamb. The blood was collected by the priests in bowls and poured out at the base of the altar. Then the animal was cleaned and the fat and kidneys burned on the altar as an offering to God. The family then took the lamb back home to roast for the Passover meal in remembrance of how the children of Israel had been protected on the very first Passover night more than a thousand years earlier, when Moses had commanded the Hebrews to put the blood of a lamb on the doorposts of their houses as a sign that they belonged to God. At this sign, the Angel of Death passed over them when he came to kill the firstborn sons of Egypt.

Returning to Isaac's house, Simon helped his cousin roast the whole lamb on a spit of pomegranate wood in the courtyard. Throughout Jerusalem families were doing the same, making the air heavy with the smell of roasting meat.

While the lamb was being prepared, everyone hurried to get ready, dressing in their finest clothes and setting out a lavish table. The wine was properly watered down and set into braziers to warm. (Everyone would be required to drink four cups of wine during the Passover ceremony, so each host made sure he had enough.) The low table was lined with plenty of cushions for the guests to recline on.

By sunset, the lamb was ready. A hush fell over the city, as people gathered to begin the celebration. Jerusalem held its collected breath, then a trumpet sounded from the Temple. Passover had begun.

With a smile, Isaac gave thanks to God for delivering their ancestors long ago and for blessing his family today. Then everyone drank the first cup of wine and washed their hands, symbolically purifying themselves for the feast. In accordance with tradition, Isaac then explained the significance of the elements of the Passover ceremony: bitter herbs, to remind them of the hard life the Hebrew nation had once known as slaves in Egypt; the roasted lamb; and unleavened bread, to remind them of their rapid departure from Egypt. Each person then took some of the bitter herbs, dipped them in salt water, and ate them, tasting the bitterness of slavery and the salt of tears.

Then it was time for the history lesson, in which the youngest boy at the table had the responsibility to ask four questions. This year, that task fell on Rufus. Nervously clearing his throat, Rufus began: "Why is this night different from all other nights?" Gravely, Isaac answered the ritual questions, telling the family how God had blessed the nation of Israel throughout history. The familiar recitation warmed Simon's heart. When Isaac was finished, everyone drank the second cup of wine.

After rinsing his hands again, Isaac broke some of the unleavened bread into pieces and thanked God for providing bread and other good things to eat. Then he made little bites of lamb, bitter herbs, and unleavened bread (called the "sop") and passed them around to each person at the table.

At last, it was time to eat dinner! Solemnity forgotten, the table was quickly covered with dish after dish of delectable food. The room was filled with the sounds of eating and laughter and stories as the food slowly disappeared. Surrounded by family, with his sons close at hand, Simon felt richer than a king. When only fragments were left and everyone was too full to eat anything more, Isaac raised his cup and spoke a blessing. Then they all drank the third cup of wine.

The final portion of the evening was spent singing songs of praise. All Jerusalem seemed to resonate with joy. Finally, Isaac prayed and they all drank the last cup of wine. That night they all slept soundly.

The next morning, Simon woke early and roused his sons. In just over an hour the gates of the Temple would open, the trumpets would sound, and the priests would offer the morning sacrifice. The daily morning and evening offerings of an unblemished lamb gave the nation of Israel access to the presence of God and were special times of prayer and reflection. Simon wanted Alexander and Rufus to be able to witness this sacrifice as part of their Jerusalem experience.

Christ Carrying the Cross by von Raigern.

As the sun rose above the city, Simon led the way out of Bezetha and up the slope into Jerusalem. His sons followed close behind, eager to take in everything. When they reached the gate leading into Jerusalem, however, they were forced to stand aside for a procession of prisoners going the other direction. Guarded by four Roman soldiers apiece, each of the three prisoners struggled to exit the city under the weight of a heavy wooden beam.

"What's going on?" Rufus asked.
Simon signaled for his son to be quiet, for it was best not to attract the soldiers' atten-

tion. "Those men are going to be executed," he said under his breath.

Suddenly, the first prisoner collapsed, blocking the gateway and bringing the procession to a halt. Simon saw that he had been brutally beaten. The soldiers tried to get the man back on his feet, but it was useless.

The centurion in charge of the procession was clearly annoyed by the interruption. Looking around at the crowd, his gaze fell on Simon. "You!" the centurion said. "Carry this man's cross."

Simon froze. Touching an instrument of death, especially one streaked with another man's blood, would make him unclean. He would not be allowed to enter the Temple to watch the sacrifice or even eat the Sabbath meal that night. Besides, the task would be extremely humiliating, as if Simon were the one condemned to death.

The centurion's hand closed around the hilt of his sword, and Simon felt the danger extend to his sons. He stepped forward, not looking at the children, and slowly removed his outer garment.

With a jerk of his head, the centurion ordered the prisoner to be untied from the beam. But even without the weight of the crosspiece on his back, the man could barely stand. Irritated, the centurion grabbed the man by the arm and lifted him to his feet.

In the moment of stillness, mourners crowded around the prisoner, wailing and beating their chests as if he were already dead. The cries of the women echoed eerily off the stone of the gateway, raising the hairs on the back of Simon's neck.

But instead of accepting their pity, the prisoner raised his head and looked at the women. "Daughters of Jerusalem, do not weep for me," he said, "but weep for yourselves and for your children. For the days are coming when you will say, 'Fortunate indeed are the women who are childless.' The time is coming when this and worse will be done. For if these things are done when the tree is green, what will happen when it is dry?" Then the man turned his head and looked into the eyes of Simon.

Simon stared at the man in amazement. Despite his weakened condition, inner strength seemed to emanate from him. The man did not seem a victim, even though he was walking to his death.

Simon turned to one of the soldiers and asked, "Who is this man?"

The soldier threw him a sideways glance, then muttered under his breath, "He is called Jesus. A Galilean."

Simon was startled. "The rabbi Jesus?"

The soldier shrugged. "He's some kind of rabble-rouser, turned over to Pontius Pilate by the priests. Pilate tried to let him go, but they insisted he be executed."

Before Simon could inquire further, the centurion motioned the procession forward again. Lifting the wooden beam onto his broad shoulders—it was as heavy as one of his sons—Simon slowly followed Jesus, reeling at the implication of the soldier's news. If this truly was the man whose fame had reached even Cyrene, then he was a healer and teacher, not an insurrectionist. Why then had the priests turned him over to their enemies?

As they headed toward the execution site, Simon looked at his sons and mouthed the word *follow*. Alexander gave a short nod and put his arm around his younger brother. Simon knew they were smart boys; they would be fine.

The ascent up Golgotha, or Skull Hill, passed slowly, as the man they called Jesus struggled with each step. The execution site was far enough outside of the city to satisfy Jewish law, yet prominent enough to satisfy the people's love of spectacle. Every pilgrim coming into or out of Jerusalem would see the crosses and fear the power of Rome.

The centurion pointed at the center post in a group of three. "Put it down there. Then you can go."

Simon carefully lowered the crosspiece to the ground, then moved back several steps to avoid attracting the centurion's attention again. But he found himself unable to look away, even to search the crowd for his sons. Pale with exhaustion, Jesus stood without complaint. A servant approached the prisoners with a sponge soaked in a mixture of cheap wine and myrrh.

Traditional place where Simon of Cyrene began carrying Jesus' cross.

The mixture would act like a sedative, dulling the pain—a gift of mercy paid for by some of the influential women of Jerusalem. But Jesus refused.

Simon watched as the soldiers efficiently removed Jesus' outer robe, girdle, sandals, and headgear. Jesus' hands were then nailed to the crosspiece, which was raised with ropes and secured high on the center post, then Jesus' feet were nailed to the post. Climbing a ladder placed against the cross, a soldier nailed a *titulus* to the post above Jesus' head. On this board, where the condemned man's crimes were written, were the words "This is Jesus, the King of the Jews."

As the soldier finished, Simon heard Jesus say, "Father, forgive them, for they do not know what they are doing."

Simon's heart was pierced through. Tears streaming down his cheeks, he sank to his knees as the morning sky turned suddenly dark. He remained there for some time until a touch on his shoulder brought him back to his senses. Lifting his head, he saw that it was Alexander and Rufus, who had followed the procession at a distance.

"What does it all mean?" Alexander asked.

At that moment a trumpet sounded from the Temple, from within the walls of Jerusalem, marking the ritual sacrifice of the unblemished lamb, the sacrifice Simon and his sons thought they had missed.

TAKE A CLOSER LOOK

» Read the biblical account of these events in Matthew 27:32–54, Mark 15:21–38, and Luke 23:26–49 and compare them to the story you've just read.

» Why was Simon taking his sons to Jerusalem? Why do you think the Jews considered it special to observe Passover in the Holy City?

» Why was the lamb an important part of the Passover meal? Why do you think the lamb had to be perfect in order to be sacrificed? Now read John 1:29 and 1 Corinthians 5:7. Who is our Passover lamb? Why did Jesus have to live a perfect life without ever sinning?

» Read Romans 16:13. We cannot know for certain, but this passage could be a reference to the son of Simon the Cyrene identified in Mark 15:21. What do you think Alexander and Rufus experienced that day on the outskirts of Jerusalem? How do you think they felt seeing their father carry a cross? What do you think it was like seeing Jesus crucified?

» In the days following these events, how do you think Simon felt when he came to understand whose cross he had carried?

» How did Jesus serve *you* in this story?

WHY DOES THE CHURCH NEED ME?

BE ENCOURAGED AND KNIT TOGETHER BY STRONG TIES OF LOVE.

COLOSSIANS 2:2, NLT

THE BIG IDEA

In the 1939 movie *The Wizard of Oz*, Dorothy and her dog Toto escape a Kansas twister only to find themselves transported to a wondrous land where trees talk and witches come in both good and evil varieties. Oz is a breathtakingly beautiful place, but Dorothy wants nothing more than to get back home to her family. She learns that only one man in Oz is powerful enough to send her home, a great wizard who lives in the Emerald City that lies at the end of the Yellow Brick Road.

Dorothy and Toto set out for the city alone but soon fall in with three companions who could also use the talents of a wonderful wizard. The Scarecrow wants a brain, the Tin Man wants a heart, and the Cowardly Lion needs some courage. When they arrive in Emerald City, the four friends manage to gain an audience with the wizard. However, he tells them they must first prove their worthiness. The wizard dispatches Dorothy and her friends on a mission to capture the broomstick of the Wicked Witch of the West. Only when they return with this prize will he consider granting their requests.

When the Wicked Witch learns of their approach, she sends her minions, a host of flying monkeys, to intercept them. Their assignment is to capture Dorothy—and the ruby slippers she is wearing—at all costs. The intrepid seekers have just entered the witch's haunted forest when the flying monkeys descend upon them. After the monkeys make off with Dorothy and Toto, the Tin Man finds they have made a mess of the Scarecrow. "What happened to you?" the Tin Man asks. The disassembled straw man reports, "First, they tore my legs off, and they threw them over there! Then they took my chest out, and they threw it over there!" Undaunted, the Lion and Tin Man quickly begin piecing the Scarecrow back

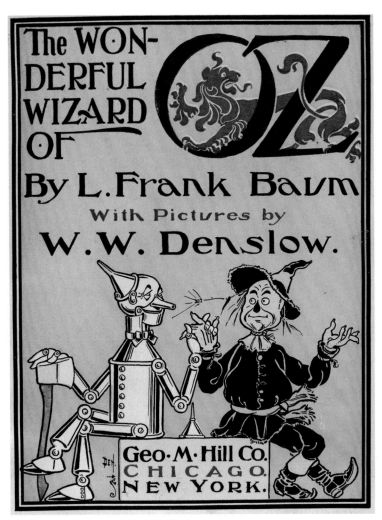

Title page from the 1900 edition of the book.

together so that they can proceed to the witch's castle to rescue Dorothy. After being attacked and his parts scattered hither and yon, the Scarecrow is able to carry on for one reason: A community of true and trusted friends put him back together again.

Like the Scarecrow, we all could use a little help now and then. Sometimes life's challenges can leave you feeling discouraged and disjointed. Other times the demands of home, schoolwork, church, and relationships will make you feel as if you're being pulled in several directions at once. And if you think you're being unjustly attacked, you just might come away feeling like the stuffing's been knocked out of you.

At times like these, it's good to know there's someone you can turn to for help and encouragement. This is just one of the wonderful benefits of being a member of God's family.

God has given us one another to love each other, help each other, comfort each other, and encourage each other. Galatians 6:10 says, "As we have opportunity, let us do good to all people, especially to those who belong to the family of believers." We are commanded to love and serve all people who are in need, but our first priority is to care for our hurting brothers and sisters.

The Scarecrow's plight also reminds us that, as members of God's family, we are one body made up of many parts. Each of us has a particular part to play in the body of Christ, and the body cannot function properly unless all of us are fulfilling our responsibilities. Each of us has been uniquely gifted by God to serve our brothers and sisters in Christ, and only when we are all using our talents and abilities as God intended will the body of Christ be healthy and effective in reaching the world with the gospel.

One final lesson we can take from the Scarecrow and his companions: Don't take your marching orders from the world and its wizards of dubious credentials. Instead, look to God's Word and His Son for your instructions on how to live and love and serve others. Remember, "God has put all things under the authority of Christ and has made him head over all things for the benefit of the church. And the church is his body" (Ephesians 1:22–23, NLT).

WHAT YOU WILL DO

» You will recognize the church as the body of Christ.
» You will understand that the body of Christ is made up of many individuals with Jesus as its head.
» You will begin to identify the role you have been chosen to play in the life of God's family.
» You will learn that God seeks and gives grace to those who are humble.

ROBERT E. LEE

Robert E. Lee is one of the most respected leaders in American military history. Known for his brilliant tactics as commander of the Southern forces in the Civil War, Lee proved himself a formidable opponent for the Northern armies.

Born in Virginia in 1807, Robert Edward Lee was the son of famous Revolutionary War colonel Henry "Light-Horse Harry" Lee. He graduated from West Point in 1829 without having earned a single demerit during his four years, a feat that has never been matched. Lee distinguished himself in the Mexican-American War, earning several field promotions. In March 1861, he was appointed colonel of the First Cavalry regiment.

One month later, following Virginia's secession from the Union, Lee made the difficult decision to resign from the United States Army. Although he didn't want to take sides and hated the thought of a civil war, his loyalty was to his home state. On April 23, 1861, Lee took command of the Virginia forces and was eventually named General-in-Chief of the Confederate Army.

Outmanned and outgunned by the Union Army, Lee nevertheless won stunning victories in several battles by using superior tactics. After defeat at Sharpsburg in 1862 and the disaster at Gettysburg in 1863, Lee nevertheless did his best to halt the advance of the Union Army, but he was handicapped by insufficient supplies and low morale among his remaining troops. On April 9, 1865, Lee surrendered unconditionally to General Ulysses S. Grant on behalf of the Confederacy. The Civil War was over.

After the war, grateful to leave his military career behind, Lee became president of what was later called Washington and Lee University. He helped work toward peace between both sides and gained the respect of all who knew him.

ANOTHER BOOK, BELL, AND CUP

"They've lost everything," Sarah Williams said as she and Winnie carried pillows and bedding into the guest bedroom. "I don't know how long the Hawthornes will need to stay with us, but I want them to be as comfortable as possible."

"I knows, Miz Sarah. They jus' like so many folk in this here valley. But I don' know how we's goin' to feed all the wounded soldiers Dr. Williams carin' for here and the Hawthornes, too. Our supply of cornmeal, beans, and hard tack is dwindlin' fast."

"We have to trust that God will provide what we need, Winnie. We still have a roof over our heads, and we can at least share that with others."

Dr. Williams had just returned home that October after witnessing the crushing Confederate defeat at Belle Grove. He had converted the dining room and parlor into a makeshift hospital to care for many of the valley's wounded. In the midst of this turmoil, Emma Jane's seventeenth birthday came and went with only a hug and a birthday wish as she and her parents, along with Moses, Winnie, and Hattie, worked long days aiding the wounded and the homeless.

"Emma Jane, please bring me the chloroform and be ready to assist. And we'll need more bandages," Dr. Williams said quietly as he wiped the brow of a feverish soldier.

"Yes, Papa," Emma Jane replied, knowing that the request for chloroform meant either an amputation or the removal of a deeply embedded bullet.

Standing by her father's side, Emma Jane averted her eyes as he leaned forward to make an incision. Surgical instruments and medical supplies were spread out on the dining table, which had been moved to one side of the room. Emma Jane fixed her eyes on the table and tried to recall happier times. She imagined the sound of the dinner bell that had so often called family and guests to Winnie's delicious meals. Her eyes were drawn to the top shelf of the now cluttered and dusty china cabinet where her silver cup, though tarnished, still occupied the same place it had for seventeen years. She smiled briefly, thinking of her father's ties to the Lee family who had given it to her parents when she was born. She remembered with fondness sharing the cup with Hattie on her tenth birthday and their secret meetings by the creek with the McGuffey's Reader.

Her father's kind but urgent command brought her quickly back to the present. "Emma Jane, forceps, please. Emma Jane?"

"Oh, Papa, I'm sorry. I must've been daydreamin'." Emma Jane obediently handed her father the forceps and ended her brief escape from the ugliness, odors, and grief of war that had for the unknowable future invaded the walls of her family's home. She forced herself to focus on her father's work, silently praying for him and for the wounded soldier.

An early snow fell that November, covering the scorched and battle-scarred landscape with a clean, white blanket. "The snow makes everythin' look so peaceful," Hattie said as she and Emma Jane filled buckets of water at the well, beginning another long day of caring for those who had taken refuge at the Williams farm. "I wish a snowfall was all it took t' cover up all the ugliness o' war and bring peace."

"I do, too," Emma Jane said wistfully. "I overheard Papa and Mr. Hawthorne talkin' last night. They were sayin' that Lincoln wants to bring a quick end to the war.

Papa says General Lee's defendin' Petersburg and Richmond, but his men are weary of war and there's hardly any supplies left, so Lincoln might just get his way. Papa thinks the South can't hold on much longer."

"Emma Jane," Hattie asked, "do you think once this war's over white folk and Negro folk will live side by side in peace? I mean, even if all the slaves is freed, do you think it's possible? I don' think there's no laws can really make that happen. Only Jesus can change folks' hearts and bring 'em back together again."

"I do believe you're right, Hattie," Emma Jane replied as the girls carried their buckets into the cook house and emptied them into a large copper kettle for boiling. "And that's what we've got to keep on prayin' for."

The ruins of Savannah in 1865.

The early November snowfall melted soon after, leaving roads muddy and rutted and exposing once again the scars of war. News arrived in late December that General William Tecumseh Sherman had captured Savannah. His March to the Sea, as the offensive came to be known, so crippled the Confederacy that there was little doubt in the minds of Dr. Williams and most Shenandoah Valley residents that the end of the war could not be long in coming.

Throughout the early months of 1865, the Williams farm continued to serve as a hospital for the wounded and a way station for the displaced. By the end of March, however, food and medical supplies were in such short supply that Dr. Williams was forced to send Zachary and Moses on a dangerous and potentially fruitless mission to Turner's Store.

"We should be home by early evenin'," Zachary said to his father as Moses hitched the horses to the wagon. "Even if there's nothin' to buy, Mr. Turner may have received word whether Richmond has fallen. If it has, well, in my opinion, there's nothin' left for General Lee but to surrender. Supplies are almost nonexistent, and many of us just don't have much heart for the cause anymore. And we just can't keep fightin' a war under these conditions."

"Just remember," Dr. Williams replied, "there's lots of folks up to no good on the roads these days, so be careful." Then he hurried back to the house to attend to his patients.

As twilight fell, Hattie lit four candles in the dining room and parlor, providing just enough light for Emma Jane and Winnie to distribute bowls of grits and beans to the soldiers still remaining under Dr. Williams's care. As Emma Jane turned to fetch more bowls, Zachary burst through the door.

"Richmond's fallen to Grant, and she's a-burnin'!" he shouted. "President Davis and his Cabinet have fled the city. It's over, I tell you! It's over!"

But no one celebrated in the Williams house that evening. Instead, a quiet melancholy filled the air. The sadness was not so much a response to the news that their once proud capital had fallen, though indeed the news was distressing. Rather, this dispiritedness was more deeply felt, welling up out of knowing that the approaching end to the war—or victory, as some would see it—had come only at the cost of immeasurable suffering and loss on both sides.

That evening, Emma Jane again turned to her diary.

April 4, 1865. News of Richmond's fall causes all of us deep sadness. I cannot imagine the suffering in that city. I grieve for the people there who must endure this loss so personally. I pray for General Lee and President Davis and for the people on both sides of this unbearable conflict who have fought bravely for what they believe. I do pray the war is finally over.

Less than a week later, on April 9, General Lee's Army of Northern Virginia surrendered to General Ulysses S. Grant at the courthouse just outside of Appomattox, Virginia. News of Lee's surrender spread quickly through the valley.

"Is it really over, Papa? Does General Lee's surrender mean the war is over?" Emma Jane asked hopefully.

"Oh, the fightin's mostly over, I reckon, or soon will be. But I'm sure the war won't be over in the hearts of many a Southerner for a long time to come. As for what lies ahead for this nation, only God knows."

Union soldiers in front of the Appomatix Courhouse, April 1865.

As news of the Confederate surrender spread throughout the North, victory celebrations and expressions of hope for reuniting and rebuilding the war-torn nation ran high. And although most Southerners had little to celebrate, glimmers of hope for a new beginning slowly surfaced. But only six days after General Lee's surrender, all celebration ended suddenly.

"How did it happen, Papa?" Emma Jane asked tearfully.

"Who killed him?" Zachary shouted angrily. "I don't care which side he stood for, it's wrong. This whole country's gone mad."

"News is still sketchy," Dr. Williams replied calmly. "Telegraph messages say only that Lincoln was shot at the theater on April 14 and died the following day. There's a manhunt on for an actor named John Wilkes Booth, who's been identified as the assassin."

Winnie, who with Moses and Hattie had been listening to Dr. Williams's report, fell to her knees and wept. "Oh, blessed Jesus, have mercy on us. Have mercy on this nation. Oh, blessed Jesus!"

Dr. Williams continued her prayer. "Do show us thy mercy, Lord. Extend thy comfort and peace to President Lincoln's family. Please do not let this tragedy lead to further division in our land. Help us to be instruments of thy healing. Make us one, O merciful Father."

John Wilkes Booth in 1865.

The assassination of Abraham Lincoln profoundly affected both the people of the North and the South. Northerners were distraught, and Southerners were stunned. Both sides worried how his death might affect the rebuilding of the nation. Yet rebuilding did begin.

"Why, I declare," Winnie said one June morning, "must be half o' Augusta County over at the Hawthornes raisin' them a new barn. That's a pretty sight, a pretty sight indeed. And jus' look at that new cabin. By nex' year I's guessin' a new house be standin' right where the old one stood."

"You're such an optimist, Winnie," Sarah Williams said, smiling weakly. "I'm just not sure I see things as brightly as you. Either way, we need to make short work of gettin' the dinin' room and parlor put back together. A bit more order in this house might just improve my outlook."

Though life on the Williams farm would never be quite the same as before the war, old routines and small pleasures slowly began to return. Dr. Williams began making rounds once more to treat his patients in the valley, while Moses and Zachary plowed and planted a few of the fields and began repairing the barns and fences. Emma Jane was happily surprised when Winnie again began ringing the dinner bell to call the family together for meals. Many food staples were still in short supply, but the family was grateful for God's provision.

One evening after supper, as Emma Jane cleared the dining table, she overheard her parents deep in conversation, each expressing strong convictions.

"I know, Sarah," Dr. Williams said firmly but kindly. "But I also know this is somethin' I must do, at least for a little while. And I want you, Zachary, and Emma Jane to go with me."

"But you've done your part as a surgeon on the battlefield. Why, we even turned our house into a hospital! Wasn't that enough?" she pleaded tearfully. "Goin' to Richmond to offer your services, even for a short time, seems well beyond your call of duty."

Thomas Williams took his wife's hands in his. "It'll be for a short time only. I only know that for some reason, God protected that school and brought it through the war. Now I have this opportunity to share with other surgeons what I've learned in the field. I truly believe I can be a part of God's plan for rebuildin' our nation."

"And just how do you propose we all travel to Richmond?" Sarah asked, dreading the thought of traveling through a war-torn landscape.

Virginia Medical College in Richmond, 1870.

"We'll take the train," Dr. Williams said. "The federal government has already repaired the Virginia Central Line from Staunton to Richmond."

"Excuse me, Papa," Emma Jane said respectfully as she entered the parlor. "But I couldn't help but overhear your conversation. Do you mean we're all goin' to Richmond? Isn't the city in ruins?"

"There is great devastation, but the medical college still stands, and that's where I can be of most use right now. I've found a boardin' house where we can stay at first. I expect we'll be there only a short time—a month or so at most."

As the train climbed slowly over the Blue Ridge Mountains, tiny black cinders drifted through the open windows, landing on the passengers' clothing and hair. "The mountains are so lovely," Emma Jane murmured to her mother, absently dusting the cinders away.

"Yes," her mother agreed, letting the natural beauty of the landscape quiet and refresh her heart. "Though I doubt we'll see much beauty once we arrive in Richmond."

When the train reached the city early that evening, the lingering summer light revealed the vestiges of destruction.

"We'll take a carriage to the boardin' house," Dr. Williams said as they disembarked amid the burned-out ruins of Richmond's industrial plants and once vigorous railway. "We should be there before dark."

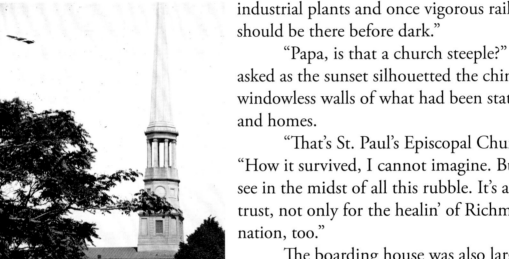
St. Paul's Episcopal Church in 1865.

"Papa, is that a church steeple?" Emma Jane asked as the sunset silhouetted the chimneys and windowless walls of what had been stately buildings and homes.

"That's St. Paul's Episcopal Church," he replied. "How it survived, I cannot imagine. But it's a joy to see in the midst of all this rubble. It's a sign of hope, I trust, not only for the healin' of Richmond but for the nation, too."

The boarding house was also largely undamaged and was a welcome sight for Dr. Williams and his family. Before going to sleep, Emma Jane wrote in her diary of their exhausting day of travel and her first impressions upon seeing the former capital of the Confederacy.

June 22, 1865. My first glimpses of Richmond have shown me beyond anything I could have imagined the utter destruction this war has imposed on our nation. Our suffering in the valley has been horrible (and many there suffered far more awful things than we did), but it pales in comparison to what I saw today among the rubble of this great city. I wish Hattie were here—not that she should have to witness this suffering, but because I know her faith that Jesus can heal any kind of brokenness would greatly encourage us today.

The next morning, Dr. Williams found his way to the medical college, where he was greeted warmly by Dr. Hunter McGuire, chairman of the department of surgery.

"It's a pleasure to finally meet you, Dr. McGuire. I've heard of the excellent medical services you provided for General Jackson and of your unselfish commitment to the medical needs of our soldiers in the field."

"Thank you, Dr. Williams. I appreciate your kind words. I likewise have heard much about your battlefield service, and I want to express my appreciation for your sacrifice."

"I could do nothin' but serve, Dr. McGuire. But tell me—how did you hear about my work?"

"From General Lee. I've conversed with him often during the war and learned that you are longtime friends."

"Our friendship goes back to the Mexican War. And that was a very long time ago, indeed."

"Well, he greatly respects you, and after I informed him that you were coming to the college today, he has made plans to see you."

"I'm delighted! Or I should say I'm nearly speechless," Dr. Williams replied. "I haven't seen the general since Sharpsburg. Where and when shall we meet?"

"Come to my office at three o'clock this afternoon. Barring any unforeseen events, he will meet us there."

"How wonderful to see you, Thomas, my good, good friend!" General Lee exclaimed, extending his hand. "I'm sorry we must meet in such trying times, but thank God the war is over. Now tell me, how are Sarah, Zachary, and your dear Emma Jane?"

"The family is well," Thomas responded, noting that his friend's face bore the marks of aging and the stresses of war. "Zachary has recovered from his wounds, and the whole family has come with me to Richmond."

Over tea, the three men shared memories of the past and dreams for the future, each expressing his desire to see the nation healed and unified. After what seemed only moments to Dr. Williams, General Lee rose reluctantly to leave.

"Thomas," he said warmly, "why don't you bring your family to the service at St. Paul's this Sunday? I would so enjoy meeting them."

"And they would be delighted to meet you, General Lee, especially Emma Jane, who continues her birthday tradition of usin' the silver cup you and Mrs. Lee gave her at her birth."

Early Sunday morning, the Williams family walked the dreary Richmond streets toward St. Paul's. As they drew near, the church bells rang out.

"Papa," Emma Jane said softly as she slipped her arm through his, "I do love the sound of church bells. When I hear them, I sometimes think of Winnie ringin' our dinner bell."

"How's that?" her father asked, chuckling. "They hardly sound alike."

"Oh, I know, and maybe I'm just sentimental. But both kinds of bells invite people to stop their work and come to a meal, don't they? They're just different kinds of meals."

"Why, Emma Jane, you never cease to amaze me," her mother remarked. "That's a beautiful thought. The Lord knows how much we all need spiritual sustenance in these difficult days."

As the Williams family entered the church, they were immediately aware of the stark contrast between the smoky ruins in the streets outside and the hushed reverence of the beautiful nave filled with worshipers, some kneeling in prayer. When they were seated, they too knelt in prayer.

Dear Father, Emma Jane prayed silently, *We thank thee for the peace and beauty that fills thy church. May we honor thee in worship, and may these worshipers and this city find peace and healing in thy great mercy and love.*

"And in this book," the rector said, lifting the pulpit Bible, "we find healin' words of life for our city and for a divided nation. But these words are not just words on a page. They are the livin' Word, who is our Lord and Savior, Jesus Christ, in whom we find the peace and reconciliation we so desperately seek after these painful years of war. As we come forward to share in the holy Eucharist, may we never forget the price our Savior paid for our reconciliation to God and thus to one another, His broken body and shed blood."

Standing before the congregation, the rector invited members and visitors to come to the altar to receive the bread and the wine. Quietly but deliberately, a well-dressed black man stepped into the aisle from a pew in the rear of the church reserved for slaves and freedmen. He walked decisively to the altar and knelt alone at the rail. No one else moved as gasps and hushed whispers spread throughout the astonished congregation. Emma Jane glanced at the faces of the bewildered parishioners near her. Even the rector stood indecisively, looking first at the black man kneeling at the altar, then at the rest of the congregation.

Just when it seemed to Emma Jane that nothing could dispel the uneasiness within the nave, a distinguished gray-headed white man stood up, slipped into the aisle, and walked to the altar. There he knelt beside the black man. Again, soft murmurs filled the church as people strained to identify the white man who was defying both church and social tradition.

"It's General Lee," whispered Dr. Williams.

"Oh, my," Emma Jane gasped softly before putting her hand to her mouth to muffle her spontaneous expression of surprise. Then she leaned slightly forward in the pew, hoping to see more clearly the man she and her family had so long admired.

"Come," Dr. Williams said quietly as he stepped into the aisle and motioned for his family to follow him to the altar.

Kneeling at the rail, Emma Jane reflected quietly on the humble gesture of reconciliation she had just witnessed. Then, as she had at every Communion before this, she reverently received the bread from the rector's hand and the wine from the silver cup he held to her lips. But on this morning she wept quietly as she heard the familiar words "the body of Christ broken for you" and "the blood of Christ, the cup of salvation, shed for you." She now understood more fully the price Jesus had paid to reconcile people not only to God, but also to each other.

Returning to her pew, Emma Jane caught a glimpse of the black man returning to his pew at the back of the church. And she yearned deeply to see Hattie—to share with her what she had just seen—and to assure her dear friend that it was indeed true: Only Jesus can change folks' hearts and bring our families and our nation back together again.

The interior of St. Paul's Episcopal Church in 1900.

THINK ABOUT IT

» What kinds of bells are heard throughout this series of stories? What do you think the different kinds of bells mean to Emma Jane and her family?

» Eucharist is another name for Communion, or the Lord's Supper. What is Communion? What does it symbolize? How is Communion observed at your church?

» The story of Robert E. Lee and the black man is based on an actual incident that took place after the war. Why do you think the people of the church are so surprised when General Lee kneels to take communion with the black man?

FREDERICK DOUGLASS

Born a slave, Frederick Douglass became one of the most well-known men in America in the nineteenth century. He was famous as an orator, writer, and abolitionist.

Born Frederick Bailey in 1818, he was taught to read by the wife of one of his owners. Although these lessons were short-lived, Frederick continued reading everything he could and even teaching other slaves to read. Mistreated and beaten by his masters, he eventually escaped to New York with the help of his fiancée, Anna Murray. Frederick and Anna were married eleven days later, taking Douglass as their last name.

While in New York, Frederick became involved in several abolitionist organizations and was asked to tell his story. At the age of twenty-three, Frederick began lecturing about his life as a slave and quickly gained fame for his engaging speaking style. Worried that his owner would recapture him, friends urged Frederick to leave America for a tour of Ireland and Great Britain, where he was treated as a man rather than a slave. While there, supporters raised enough money to buy his freedom.

Upon returning to America, Frederick started his own abolitionist newspaper, the *North Star*, and became an active supporter of women's rights as well as black rights. He believed that all people, regardless of gender or race, deserved to be treated equally. He published his first autobiography, *Narrative of the Life of Frederick Douglass, an American Slave*, in 1845.

Douglass continued his abolitionist work throughout the Civil War, fighting for the rights of black soldiers in the Union army. His work was known to Abraham Lincoln, and the two became good friends. After Lincoln's assassination, Mary Todd Lincoln sent the president's favorite walking stick to Douglass as a gift. In thanking the First Lady for her kindness, Douglass assured her that he would treasure the cane, not only for himself, but also because of Lincoln's "humane interest in the welfare of my whole race."

After the war, Douglass continued working to better the lives of black Americans. He held several political positions and helped pass the Fifteenth Amendment, which gave black men the right to vote.

WORDS YOU NEED TO KNOW

» **The body of Christ:** Every member of God's family functioning together as one body

» **Teamwork:** A group of people working together to achieve something that none of them could accomplish as separate individuals

» **Edify:** To build up and strengthen our brothers and sisters in Christ

HIDE IT IN YOUR HEART

Now you are the body of Christ, and each one of you is a part of it. (1 Corinthians 12:27)

For the eyes of the LORD run to and fro throughout the whole earth, to show Himself strong on behalf of those whose heart is loyal to Him. (2 Chronicles 16:9, NKJV)

WE'RE ALL IN THIS TOGETHER

What are you doing at this very moment? You might say you're reading a book or listening to someone read aloud. Perhaps you're even writing or drawing in a notebook. But even as you sit there quietly, a great flurry of activity is taking place inside you. For example, without thinking about it, you're breathing in and out around twenty times per minute, inhaling fresh air and exhaling carbon dioxide. Meanwhile, your heart is beating about seventy-five times each minute, receiving a rush of newly oxygenated blood from your lungs and pumping it to your fingers, your toes, your brain, and your organs. In addition, your mind is processing and storing the information in this book even while the brain is actively sending commands and signals to every other part of your body. Meanwhile, your body is busy burning fuel, regulating its own temperature, repairing itself, and performing numerous other vital tasks in a symphony of harmony and precision.

The Bible calls the church the **body of Christ**, and as in the human body, much of the everyday life of the church happens outside the spotlight, unseen, unknown, and often unrecognized. Most people who attend your local church probably know the names of the church's senior pastor, the youth pastor, the children's ministry director, and the worship leader; their names and photographs probably appear in the bulletin or on the church's website. But what about the kindly older woman who has a hug for everyone who walks through the door? Or the man who directs traffic in the church parking lot? What about the person who cleans the restrooms after services? Or the volunteers who stuff envelopes, print bulletins, and answer the church's phone during the week? Or the people who visit the sick, invite their neighbors to services, and pray every day for their local church and their community? Every one of these people is required for the body of Christ to function as God intended both in your community and around the world.

You know that your body is made up of many parts, each of which serves a very different function. Your heart cannot do what your liver does, nor can your liver step in and act as a substitute for your heart. Your lungs need your brain in order to function and vice versa. Indeed, you must have a working heart, liver, brain, and at least one lung just to survive! Each part of your body performs a unique function, and each part and its function is important for your well-being. The Bible tells us:

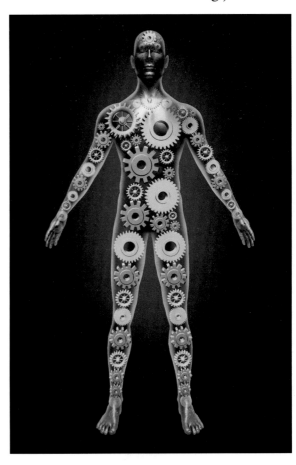

If the foot should say, "Because I am not a hand, I do not belong to the body," it would not for that reason cease to be part of the body. And if the ear should say, "Because I am not an eye, I do not belong to the body," it would not for that reason cease to be part of the body. If the whole body were an eye, where would the sense of hearing be? If the whole body were an ear, where would the sense of smell be? But in fact God has arranged the parts in the body, every one of them, just as he wanted them to be. If they were all one part, where would the body be? As it is, there are many parts, but one body. The eye cannot say to the hand, "I don't need you!" And the head cannot say to the feet, "I don't need you!" (1 Corinthians 12:15–21)

Likewise, the church is one body made up of many individuals, each of whom has been given talents and abilities by God in order to fulfill a role that meets the needs of the church as a whole:

Just as our bodies have many parts and each part has a special function, so it is with Christ's body. We are many parts of one body, and we all belong to each other. (Romans 12:4–5, NLT)

Many of us have been told growing up, "You can do anything you put your mind to." Whether spoken by a parent, a teacher, or a pastor, these words of encouragement sound great in theory. But God never meant for any of us to rely solely on ourselves. Sure, we

THE GREAT RACE OF MERCY

The Iditarod Trail Sled Dog Race is one of the most physically demanding races on the planet. From Anchorage in south central Alaska to Nome on the western coast, each team of twelve to sixteen dogs and its musher, or driver, cover more than a thousand miles in as little as ten days. The annual race commemorates an event from Alaska's colorful past, when part of the Iditarod Trail became a highway of life for an epidemic-stricken community.

During the winter of 1925, a deadly diphtheria epidemic broke out in Nome, and the only doctor in the area did not have enough medicine to treat the disease. The nearest supply of diphtheria antitoxin was in Anchorage, but winter weather prevented it from being transported by ship or plane. So the medicine was taken by train as far as Nenana, and a dog sled relay was set up to carry the life-saving antitoxin the rest of the way to Nome.

Traveling through blizzards, in temperatures ranging from –20 degrees to –60 degrees, twenty mushers and their teams raced to cover the 674 miles between Nenana and Nome. Each team carried the serum about fifty miles before handing it off to the next team in line.

One brave team, driven by Leonhard Seppala and led by the sled dog Togo, started from the opposite end, racing from Nome to meet the serum halfway. After traveling for five days through the most treacherous portions of the Alaskan wilderness, Seppala and Togo met up with the sled team carrying the serum. They immediately turned around and took the serum on the next leg of its westward journey, traveling another ninety-one miles before handing the serum off to the next team.

Four hours later, the serum was given to Gunnar Kassen and his lead dog, Balto. They pushed through a fierce storm to cover the last fifty-three miles and deliver the serum to Nome. Normally, the 674-mile journey would have taken twenty-five days to complete, but these intrepid mushers and their faithful, hard-driving dogs made the run in just five and a half days. Thanks to their cooperation and dedication, the epidemic was stopped and hundreds of lives were saved.

Photo: by Frank Kovalchek.

can achieve some personal goals through sheer determination and hard work, but God has something much bigger in mind for His children—a higher standard, a greater calling. We have been commissioned for nothing less than the daring rescue of a world in distress, billions of lives held captive by an enemy bent on their destruction.

The truth is, you can never become everything God created you to be without the help and support of your brothers and sisters in Christ. Nor can they be at their best without you! We all belong to each other, and we need each other. Just as we call upon even the smallest body parts during our daily activities, so the church needs all the talents and abilities that each person brings to the body of Christ. None of us is capable of going it alone and achieving all that God set us on this earth to do. The message of the gospel spread through much of the known world in the first century because the members of the early church were interdependent. They took care of each other, and they relied on one another for help and encouragement. They loved God and each other, and they exhorted one another to love and care for the people around them.

Perhaps you think you're too young to contribute anything to the family of God. Maybe you're afraid to share the gospel with your neighbors because you worry that no one will listen to you. Maybe you think you're not knowledgeable or charismatic or well-spoken enough to influence others. Just remember that the first disciples didn't look like much to the rest of the world either. They were uneducated, unmannered, and uncultured. They weren't particularly mindful of the things of God (Matthew 16:23). They weren't humble (Mark 9:34) or sensitive (Luke 9:54), and their loyalty left much to be desired (Mark 14:72). And before the Holy Spirit took hold of them, they weren't even terribly dependable (Matthew 26:40).

The apostle Paul wrote to the early believers:

Remember, dear brothers and sisters, that few of you were wise in the world's eyes or powerful or wealthy when God called you. Instead, God chose things the world considers foolish in order to shame those who think they are wise. And he chose things that are powerless to shame those who are powerful. God chose things despised by the world, things counted as nothing at all, and used them to bring to nothing what the world considers important. (1 Corinthians 1:26–28, NLT)

God loves to take ordinary people and do extraordinary things through them. Every member of God's family, past and present, was once a broken individual, defiled by sin and

> *Alone we can do so little; together we can do so much.*
> **Helen Keller**
> 1880–1968

separated from God. But Jesus called each of us—He called you—out of the crowd, cleaned us up, filled us with the Holy Spirit, and then wove us together into a colorful tapestry of love made beautiful by His truth and grace. Empowered by the Spirit and equipped to serve, the first disciples took the world by storm. Today, you and I are empowered by the same Holy Spirit and equipped by the same God, and we, too, have been called to reach this world for Christ.

MAKE A NOTE OF IT

A person who's feeling particularly clumsy might say, "I'm all thumbs today." But have you ever tried to go a day without using your thumbs? Try this exercise: Place a pen or pencil between your index finger and your middle finger and, without using your thumb, write the following phrase in your notebook: We are many parts of one body. Now try writing it again. This time you can use your thumb, but you must first cover your eyes with a blindfold. Just for fun, now try writing by holding a pencil with your foot!

TEAMWORK IS NOT JUST A BUZZWORD

There's a lot of talk about teamwork these days. The word itself is only about two hundred years old. **Teamwork** is simply a group of people working together to achieve something that none of them could accomplish as individuals. In the world of business, it's often said that the acronym TEAM stands for "Together Everyone Achieves More." Teamwork and unity are the keys to effectiveness: If we want to achieve "more," then we must work "together." Yet many teams aren't teams at all but merely collections of individuals who have been hired by the same organization. Too often, instead of working toward a common goal, each member of the organization competes with the others for the most power, the biggest contract, the best equipment, and the greatest prestige.

This is often true in professional sports where selfish play and expressions of individuality have become something of an art form. What

CANADA GEESE

Canada geese are very common in North America and are easily identified by their black heads, brownish bodies, and white "chinstraps." These geese are perhaps best known for the way they travel, flying in a V-shaped formation. The V formation greatly boosts the efficiency and range of the flock, particularly during long migrations. In this pattern, one bird flies at the point and two lines of birds spread out behind, right and left.

The V formation works because of a scientific principle called wingtip vortices (VOR-tih-sees). During flight, small upward air currents are created by the tips of each bird's wings. The Canada geese receive a lift from these air currents, riding on them like invisible floatation devices so that they use less energy while flying. Overall, the savings in expended energy enables a flock of twenty-five birds in formation to travel seventy percent farther than a single bird flying on its own! Of course, this means the bird at the front must work harder because it does not have these currents to ride on. So when the lead goose gets tired, it falls back into the formation and another goose takes the point for a while.

Flying in a V formation also allows every goose to see where it's going while still keeping watch over the others. If one bird gets sick or is injured, two others will fall out of formation and follow the struggling bird to the ground to help and protect it. They will stay with the injured bird until it's able to fly again, and then they will work together to catch up to the flock.

One other beneficial aspect of the V formation is that it allows for effective communication among the members of the flock. The geese at the rear of the formation are the ones who do the honking we so often hear. This is their way of encouraging the geese up front and letting them know that all is well at the rear of the formation.

Of the many lessons we can learn from Canada geese, maybe this one lesson stands out above the others: It's the natural instinct of geese to work together. Whether it's rotating duties, giving a lift to the others, helping those in need, or simply calling out encouragement, the flock is always in it together, and this enables them to accomplish what they set out to do.

so many of today's pro athletes fail to realize is that wearing the same shirts doesn't make a group of people a team. In most professional sports—football, baseball, basketball, soccer, hockey, cricket, rugby, even curling—championships are won by *teams*, not individuals. Even a professional golfer must work closely with a caddie, a swing coach, a fitness trainer, and a business manager in order to reach the upper echelons of the sport.

Not long ago, a pastor in Hawaii wrote a book titled *Doing Church as a Team*. In it he tells the story of the time he and five members of his church were invited to compete as a team in an island canoe race. One of the most popular sports in Hawaii is canoe paddling. In this sport, there are six paddlers in a canoe, or *wa'a*, which has a balancing arm called an *ama*. The pastor and his friends were inexperienced paddlers, so they went to a local club and took lessons from a canoe instructor. After showing them how to hold their oars properly, the instructor said to the novice crew, "We're going to paddle our first stretch of water. It will be an eighth-of-a-mile sprint. When I begin the stopwatch and say 'Go,' just paddle as fast and as hard as you can. When we cross the finish line, I'll notify you. That's when you can stop paddling. Got it?"

The instructor shouted "*Ho 'omakaukau? I mua!*"—meaning "Ready? Go forward!"—and the crew began paddling furiously. They thrashed the water with their oars on either side of the canoe. Each paddler would frantically switch sides when one arm got tired, often

whacking the person in front of him with the oar. After what seemed like hours, the canoe was half filled with water, the paddlers' lungs were on fire, and their arms felt like lead. Finally, the instructor yelled, "Okay, stop!" Then he checked his stopwatch. "One minute and forty-two seconds," he said. "Pretty sad."

The exhausted crew began profusely apologizing to each other for the scrapes and wounds they had inflicted with their flailing paddles. Then they bailed the water out of their canoe, which had begun to resemble a torpedoed submarine more than a sleek racing vessel.

Photot: Bianca Henry.

The instructor then gathered the whimpering novices together, and after sharing a few basics about safety, he taught them how to paddle as a team. Each paddler was instructed to mirror the one in front of him, and everyone was to move in time with the lead paddler. They learned how to switch their paddles to the opposite hand without injuring each other. Then they practiced again and again until their strokes were smooth and rhythmic as a metronome.

"All right," said the instructor, "let's try that same eighth-of-a-mile stretch again. Only this time, I want you to stroke as if you were taking a leisurely stroll through the park. No sprinting. Just mirror the person in front of you as you were taught. Stroke as a team and don't try to break the sound barrier this time, okay? *Ho 'omakaukau? I mua!*"

This time their oars silently entered the water, coordinated in perfect time. The lead paddler called out, "Hut!" In perfect chorus, the others answered, "Ho!" and they were off. The canoe cut through the water like a knife through warm butter. They switched sides without skipping a beat, each mirroring the movements of the rower in front of him.

Before they knew it, the instructor was yelling, "Okay, stop paddling!"

Their sooner-than-expected arrival at the finish line had caught them all by surprise.

"Anybody tired?" the instructor asked. They all shook their heads no. Then the instructor held up his stopwatch for all to see. "You beat your last time by twenty-four seconds!"

No one had been injured, and the canoe was practically dry inside. The crew had expended far less effort yet had beaten their previous time handily. They congratulated each other, gave a few victory shouts, exchanged leis, and took pictures. They had accomplished something together because they had paddled as a team. What an amazing feeling!

The church is one body with one head who is Jesus Christ (Ephesians 1:22–23), and we must work as a team to be effective in a world that is hostile to the things of God. No matter how much effort we are willing to put forth as individuals, if we don't all pull in the same direction at the same time and with the same destination in mind, we won't get very far. And we certainly won't get there very quickly. If we all insist on doing our own thing, however good our intentions, our flailing about will result in hurt feelings, mixed signals, and ineffective ministry. But if we will learn to work together as a team, we'll be astonished at how much further we get—and with fewer injuries!

ONE BODY, MANY GIFTS

God does something very special for every member of His family. He gives each person a gift—a spiritual gift. There are many different gifts, and each one is necessary for the body of Christ to accomplish the will of God. As a member of God's family, you have been given at least one of these gifts, and God wants you to use it to build up your brothers and sisters in Christ and to bring others into His family. Although some believers will discover their gifts and God's call on their lives at an early age, you will likely begin to recognize and understand your gift and abilities as you increase in age and wisdom.

God has equipped you with this gift to help you serve others. Paul wrote that Christ gifted pastors and teachers and others "to prepare God's people for works of service" (Ephesians 4:11–12), and he made it clear that "a spiritual gift is given to each of us so we can help each other" (1 Corinthians 12:7, NLT). The apostle Peter wrote, "God has given each of you a gift from his great variety of spiritual gifts. Use them well to serve one another" (1 Peter 4:10, NLT). When you discover your gift and use it to help others, you will find tremendous joy and satisfaction in doing God's will and His work!

So what are these gifts God gives His children? Our God is generous, and He gives many gifts through the Holy Spirit. Let's take a look at just a few of these gifts as described in Romans 12:6–8.

THE GIFT OF PROPHECY

The apostle Paul wrote to the believers in Rome, "If God has given you the ability to prophesy, speak out with as much faith as God has given you" (Romans 12:6, NLT). Prophecy is a gift that allows a person to clearly speak God's Word in order to comfort and encourage believers, to correct those who are in error, and to **edify** the body of Christ. The word *edify* means to build up and strengthen. This spiritual gift enables the church to grow, mature, and move forward according to the will of God. "Follow the way of love and eagerly desire spiritual gifts, especially the gift of prophecy . . . so that the church may be edified" (1 Corinthians 14:1, 5).

THE GIFT OF SERVING

Paul wrote, "If your gift is serving others, serve them well" (Romans 12:7, NLT). Although God commands all Christians to serve one another, some people have a gift for serving in special ways at all times. Sometimes called the gift of "helps" (1 Corinthians 12:28, KJV), the gift of serving enables a believer to work gladly behind the scenes by investing in the life and ministry of other members of the body. People who have this gift enjoy knowing that by fulfilling everyday needs and responsibilities, they are freeing up others to do what God has called them to do.

THE GIFT OF TEACHING

Paul wrote, "If you are a teacher, teach well" (Romans 12:7, NLT). People with the gift of teaching have a special ability to clearly explain the truths of God's Word so that others learn and understand. Whether they are teaching children, youth, or adults, people with this gift inspire their students to obey God's commands and to live and serve more like Christ. Teachers are passionate about sharing biblical truth with others, and they enjoy seeing "the lights come on" and people come alive as they gain understanding. The gift of teaching also helps Christians grow in their faith and reach out to others in their community.

THE GIFT OF ENCOURAGEMENT

Paul wrote, "If your gift is to encourage others, be encouraging" (Romans 12:8, NLT). All Christians are commanded to encourage one another, but some have a special ability to give comfort, hope, and reassurance to their fellow believers. People with this gift come alongside those who are discouraged, weary, or spiritually weak and help them to trust and hope in the promises of God. When Barnabas visited new believers in Antioch, he "encouraged them all to remain true to the Lord with all their hearts. He was a good man, full of the Holy Spirit and faith, and a great number of people were brought to the Lord" (Acts 11:23–24).

THE GIFT OF GIVING

Paul wrote, "If [your gift] is giving, give generously" (Romans 12:8, NLT). The gift of giving enables some believers to cheerfully give of their time, abilities, and resources without thought of receiving anything in return. Again, all Christians are commanded to give, but people with this gift are quick to recognize God's blessings in their lives and share those blessings with others who are in need. They trust completely in God's provision. Some who have this gift also have a special ability to make money so that they may use it to further God's work and advance His kingdom.

THE GIFT OF LEADERSHIP

Paul wrote, "If God has given you leadership ability, take the responsibility seriously" (Romans 12:8, NLT). People with the gift of leadership have a special ability to provide direction and guidance to God's people. Leaders set a good example and motivate others to perform to the best of their abilities. They are able to set goals in accordance with God's will and then communicate those goals in a way that inspires God's people to accomplish His purposes for His glory.

THE GIFT OF MERCY

Paul wrote, "Whoever has the gift of showing mercy to others should do so with joy" (Romans 12:8, NCV). As we have talked about throughout this study, every Christian

should have compassion for those who are suffering. But some have a special gift for caring for people who are in physical or emotional distress. People who have the gift of mercy are quick to respond in times of crisis with acts of love and compassion, offering grace and restoring dignity to those who are hurting. These people recognize the needs of the lonely and forgotten, and they concern themselves with addressing social issues that impact people in their community and around the world. They often serve in difficult or unpleasant circumstances, and they do so cheerfully.

MAKE A NOTE OF IT

First Corinthians 12:31 tells us to "eagerly desire" the best gifts of God. If you could have anything from God that would help you to help others, what would you ask for? The gift of prophecy? A great singing voice? Leadership? Generosity and money to give to the poor? Write about or draw a picture of yourself using this gift. Now read 1 Corinthians 13:1–13. What does the Bible say is the greatest gift you can give to others?

WHAT SHOULD I DO?

As God's children, we have been given special gifts and abilities, and sometimes we might be tempted to look at our abilities and think we are somehow greater or more privileged than others. Yet we do not have any gifts that were not given to us by God (James 1:17). Paul wrote to members of the church at Corinth, "Who says you are better than others? What do you have that was not given to you? And if it was given to you, why do you brag as if you did not receive it as a gift?" (1 Corinthians 4:7, NCV).

Instead of boasting about our gifts, we need to follow Christ's example and, with humility, use our gifts to help people and point them toward the Giver of all good gifts. Humility is an attitude that says, "I am not better than anyone else, and I am willing to do whatever is necessary to help." The Bible says, "God opposes the proud but gives grace to the humble" (James 4:6). Indeed, He is actively looking for humble men, women, boys, and girls whom He can work through to show His power and might:

> *"This is the one to whom I will look: he who is humble and contrite in spirit and trembles at my word."* (Isaiah 66:2, ESV)

> *For the eyes of the LORD run to and fro throughout the whole earth, to show Himself strong on behalf of those whose heart is loyal to Him.* (2 Chronicles 16:9, NKJV)

Just think of it: A humble attitude acts like a magnet drawing the gaze of our wonderful heavenly Father. He has promised to support the efforts of those who are humble, and the grace He gives to the humble heart is indescribably bountiful. As Jonathan Edwards wrote in his diary, "The pleasures of humility are really the most refined, inward, and exquisite delights in the world."

A Prayer

Dear God, I want people to see how big and wonderful you are. I want them to know that with you anything is possible. Help me to do my part in caring for the family of God. Help me to discover the gifts and abilities you have given me, and show me how to use them to build up the church and serve others. I ask these things in the name of your Son, Jesus. Amen.

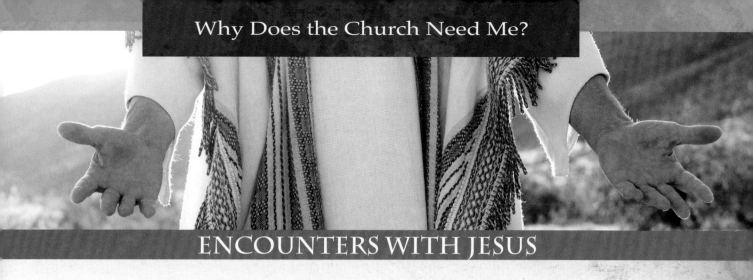

ENCOUNTERS WITH JESUS

THE STRANGER

Cleopas passed through the Western Gate as he departed Jerusalem. Now that the Sabbath was over and he could travel again, he was relieved to be going home. Moshe trudged along behind him, mirroring Cleopas's grief and sadness. Cleopas and Moshe had been friends since childhood, as close as brothers, so it was only fitting that they share this sorrowful day.

Jesus was dead. He had been betrayed by one of his closest friends, falsely accused by the religious leaders in Jerusalem, and handed over to the Romans for execution. The memory still turned Cleopas's stomach. He knew he couldn't stand by as the Teacher was nailed to a cross like a thief, so that dark day he had remained in a locked room, far from Skull Hill.

Cleopas picked up the pace, eager to free his mind from the confines of the city walls and put behind him the events of the past few days. It felt good to stretch his legs, as if the exertion could ease his heartache. The village of Emmaus was only a couple of hours away— about sixty stadia, as the Romans measured it. They had gotten a late start, but Cleopas hoped to make it home before sunset and begin a new day by sharing the evening meal with his family.

A short time later, they reached the edge of the plateau upon which Jerusalem stood. Behind them lay the great city shining in the late afternoon sun, its walls painted gold by the western light. Before them the road wound downward through a series of hills as the rocky plateau gave way to lush countryside. Tucked away in a cool, green valley was the small village of Emmaus, important only to those who had grown up there. Perhaps there, Cleopas thought, they would find the peace they were now lacking.

For the past two days, Cleopas and Moshe and the followers who remained loyal to Jesus had huddled together, keeping inside as much as possible with all the doors and windows shut and bolted. Many of them had been frightened that the Sanhedrin would arrest all of Jesus' followers in order to wipe out any remnant of his teachings. Some were more ashamed at their cowardice in denying their Lord. But all were deeply saddened by Jesus' death and horrified by his crucifixion.

During the first lonely hours they had argued and debated Jesus' teachings, sifting through the pieces of his life and ministry to make sense of his ignominious death. Yet no satisfactory conclusions had been reached. Then, earlier that morning, Mary Magdalene and two other women had returned from visiting Jesus' tomb, bringing with them a strange tale of angels speaking and the huge stone that covered the opening to the tomb being rolled away. They said the tomb was empty, that Jesus' body was nowhere to be found. Even after Peter and John had gone to the tomb to investigate, no one knew what to think. Their best guess was that Jesus had ascended into heaven, like Enoch or Elijah. But the women kept insisting that Jesus was alive.

Even now, Cleopas couldn't bring himself to believe that Jesus had come back from the dead, despite the fact that he had witnessed Jesus bring Lazarus back to life. Cleopas sighed. How could they have been so wrong about him? He knew that Jesus had been nothing less than a great prophet. After all, only a prophet could do the things he had done, feeding multitudes, healing the sick, and casting out demons. But they had believed him to be so much more. Cleopas himself had been certain that Jesus was the One who would deliver the children of Israel from their oppressors and bring peace to the entire Jewish race.

Roads around Jerusalem in the early 1900s.

"All the signs pointed to him being the Messiah," Cleopas burst out, unable to keep silent any longer.

Moshe sighed. "We *all* thought he was the One." He kicked at a stone on the road, sending it clattering off to the side. "I mean, all the miracles he did, all the people he healed."

Cleopas forced a smile. "Remember when he entered Jerusalem, how the people lined the road with palm branches and called him Lord? I felt sure that was the day he was going to proclaim himself king."

Moshe put an arm across his friend's shoulders. "His words and miracles prove that he was a great teacher. We'll just have to be content with that and look elsewhere for the Messiah."

Cleopas nodded. "I just don't know what to do now. I don't know what I'm supposed to believe anymore."

Moshe looked out over the valley in front of them. "We continue to follow Jesus' teachings and do the best we can. Then we hope it is enough."

Cleopas started walking faster, the downhill slope increasing his speed. Words and thoughts tumbled over one another in his mind until he launched into another round of debate about the details of Jesus' life, trying to see if the pieces added up any differently this time. Moshe joined in passionately. Their sadness and anger and shame and regret boiled over. All of it had been said before, but it felt good to talk about it, to let it all out here in the open.

They didn't realize how loudly they were arguing until they came to a crossroads dotted with other travelers trying to reach home before dark. After a few strange looks from the others, Cleopas and Moshe decided to refrain from further discussion, at least until the road was clear again.

As they left the crossroads, heading deeper into the hills toward Emmaus, a stranger approached them. "What were you talking about along the road?" he asked.

Cleopas assumed he was a pilgrim on his way home from celebrating the Passover feast in Jerusalem. The stranger must have overheard their loud debate. Cleopas stopped and turned to face the man.

"Are you really the only pilgrim in Jerusalem who doesn't know about the things that have happened there the last few days?" Cleopas felt like the whole world should have stopped turning when Jesus died, and he was shocked to hear that it hadn't.

The stranger considered Cleopas's words and countenance. "What things?"

Cleopas started walking again, his heart heavy as the memories came flooding back. "The things about Jesus of Nazareth," he answered. "He was a prophet who did powerful miracles, and he was a mighty teacher in the eyes of God and all the people." Emotion choked off the rest of his answer. Telling someone who was unfamiliar with what had happened made it real all over again, as if his hopes lay freshly shattered about his feet.

Moshe, seeing his distress, took up the story. "The Sanhedrin handed him over to the Romans to be crucified, like a criminal." He clenched his jaw, staring resolutely into the distance. "We had hoped he would be the One to liberate Israel."

Swallowing, Cleopas said, "This happened three days ago. Then this morning, some women who were among his followers came back from his tomb claiming that Jesus was alive. Some of our men ran out to see and found that indeed his body was gone, just as the women had said. Now we don't know what to think."

The stranger gave them a look of deep pity. "Foolish men! Why do you find it so hard to believe everything the prophets spoke? Didn't the Scriptures say that the Messiah would have to suffer all these things before entering his glory?"

Cleopas stared at the pilgrim. What did this man know that they didn't know? He was suddenly hungry to learn any scrap of information that might revive the barest hint of hope.

Was there something in the Scriptures that they had missed?

"Please, tell us what you know," Cleopas begged.

And so he did. For the next hour or so, the stranger walked with them and taught them about the prophecies concerning the Messiah. Beginning with the writings of Moses, the stranger explained all that the Scriptures said concerning the Messiah, how he must suffer and how he would ultimately triumph. Although Cleopas had heard all these Scriptures, he had never understood them as fully as when this stranger explained them.

Cleopas stopped. He felt as though the world had been turned on its head. These truths had been in the Scriptures all along, and he had missed them! No wonder his hope had faded away to nothing at Jesus' death. He had been so focused on his desire for political freedom that he had been blind to the truth of what Jesus had come to do. Cleopas felt like he had been living in a dark cave and then stepped out into the bright sunlight. His heart burned within him, as if it were too small to contain so much knowledge and joy.

He turned to Moshe and gripped his shoulders, too excited to speak. Moshe looked as stunned as he felt, tears falling unheeded down his face. Cleopas was sure his own cheeks were wet too. Joy bubbled up in him like a spring. The pieces fit now. His faith in Jesus made sense once more. Yet in the last hour it had grown so much that yesterday's faith was but a pale shadow in comparison.

Wiping the tears from his eyes, Cleopas saw that they had reached Emmaus. He started up the path toward home, but the stranger didn't follow. Instead, he looked as though he were preparing to continue down the road.

The road to Emmaus in the early 1900s.

Cleopas ran back to him. "Please, sir, come and stay with me tonight. It is almost sunset, and you won't be able to walk very far in the dark."

Moshe pleaded, "Yes, you cannot leave us just yet."

The stranger looked at them for a long moment, as if gauging their sincerity. Finally, he nodded, accepting their invitation.

Relieved, Cleopas led the stranger to his house where he treated him with every courtesy.

After greeting his family and washing the dust of the road from the feet of his guests, Cleopas invited Moshe and their new friend to join him in the dining room. Reclining there, they continued talking while they waited for the food to be prepared. Outside the window, the sun set in a riot of pinks and oranges and purples brushed lavishly across the sky.

Christ at Emmaus by Rembrandt.

When the meal was ready, Cleopas's family joined the men at the table, and Cleopas offered the stranger the honor of saying the blessing. Taking a piece of unleavened bread, the man spoke a blessing, broke the bread into pieces, and handed them around the table.

In that instant, Cleopas knew. Exactly how he knew escaped him, but he knew. *The stranger was Jesus, alive and well.*

At the same moment, Moshe gasped. His eyes met Cleopas's, full of wonder.

Cleopas didn't know how they could have missed it. The man before them was definitely Jesus, yet changed in a subtle way, as if no longer part of this world and its cares. It was almost as if they had been blinded to prevent them from comprehending the true nature of the man as they walked together on the road.

But before either man had time or wit to say anything, Jesus suddenly vanished. One moment he was there, as real and solid as the table they reclined at or the bread they held. The next moment, he was gone.

Rising quickly, Cleopas and Moshe stared at each other and at the empty place where Jesus had been. This couldn't have been a vision or a spirit. Cleopas had washed the man's feet, and Jesus had broken the bread.

"Didn't you feel it while he was talking?" Moshe asked. He put the palm of his hand on his chest. "My heart was burning as he taught us along the road!"

Cleopas put a hand on his own chest, trying to catch a full breath. All the doubts and fears and despair he had felt only hours ago had melted away. Jesus was alive, just as the women returning from the tomb had said.

Without realizing what he was doing, Cleopas started for the door, followed closely by Moshe. This news was too important to keep to themselves; they had to run back to Jerusalem and tell the disciples as soon as possible.

Strapping on their sandals and throwing their cloaks around their shoulders, Cleopas and Moshe took up torches and headed into the twilight. They gave no thought to the dangers of the night, nor of the seven-mile walk in front of them. Jesus was alive, and nothing would keep them from delivering the good news to anyone who would listen!

TAKE A CLOSER LOOK

- Read the biblical account of these events in Mark 16:12–13 and Luke 24:13–32 and compare them to the story you've just read.

- Why was Cleopas so disheartened as he left Jerusalem? Why do you think he wanted to go home to Emmaus instead of staying with Jesus' other followers?

- Why did he no longer believe that Jesus was the Messiah whom God had promised to the Jewish people?

- A Greek *stadion* was a unit of measurement equivalent to about 600 feet. Approximately how many miles would sixty *stadia* cover? Could you walk this distance in two hours?

- Why do you think Cleopas and Moshe did not recognize Jesus when they met Him on the road? Why do you think they suddenly recognized Him when He blessed the bread and gave it to them?

- Do you think Cleopas and Moshe were with the disciples on the day of Pentecost? Why or why not?

- How will you recognize Jesus when He returns for His followers?

THE HOUSE OF TRUTH: THE TWELFTH PILLAR

You have learned that followers of Christ can experience relationships of harmony and oneness with other members of God's family. During the last two lessons, you erected the fourth and final pillar in your Servanthood Wall:

BIBLICAL TRUTH 16:

Jesus died to bring me into a new family of harmony called the church.

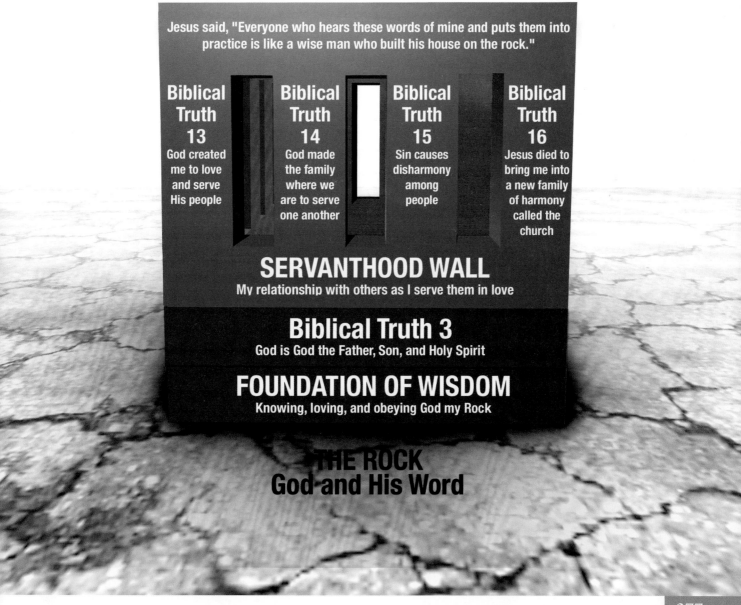

Jesus said, "Everyone who hears these words of mine and puts them into practice is like a wise man who built his house on the rock."

Biblical Truth 13
God created me to love and serve His people

Biblical Truth 14
God made the family where we are to serve one another

Biblical Truth 15
Sin causes disharmony among people

Biblical Truth 16
Jesus died to bring me into a new family of harmony called the church

SERVANTHOOD WALL
My relationship with others as I serve them in love

Biblical Truth 3
God is God the Father, Son, and Holy Spirit

FOUNDATION OF WISDOM
Knowing, loving, and obeying God my Rock

THE ROCK
God and His Word

ACKNOWLEDGMENTS

Our gratitude and appreciation go out to several individuals, without whom this book could not have been written. Thank you, as always, to John Stonestreet of Summit Ministries and Davis Carman of Apologia Educational Ministries whose vision and commitment to worldview studies made this series possible.

Thank you to Zan Tyler, director of Apologia Press, for her unwavering support and tremendous encouragement. You are a joy to work with.

Thank you to our loving wives, Nancy and Peggy, for their invaluable assistance and remarkable patience during the writing of this book. We greatly appreciate your reading and re-reading of the text. Nancy, you have a remarkable eye for catching the smallest typographical error and graciously correcting our grammar. Peggy, thank you for compiling the index and contributing to the notebooking journals and Teacher's Helps.

Thank you to Tanya Dickens, Harry Hanger, Delreece Moore, and Hal Young for your invaluable contributions to the Civil War stories.

Thank you to Doug Powell, not only for his outstanding creative design work, but also for his insights into Christian apologetics and the Greek lexicon.

And our very special thanks to Amanda Lewis, architect of the Encounters with Jesus stories. Your imagination and creativity brought our vision to life!
Soli Deo Gloria!

INDEX

"WHO AM I, O LORD...THAT YOU HAVE BROUGHT ME THIS FAR?"

1 CHRONICLES 17:16

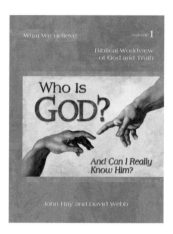 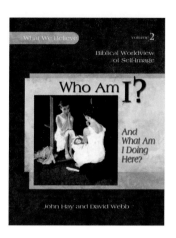 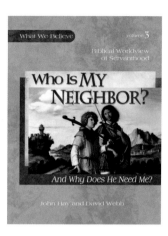 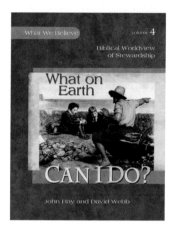

Volume 1	Volume 2	Volume 3	Volume 4
Who Is God? (And Can I Really Know Him?)	**Who Am I? (And What Am I Doing Here?)**	**Who Is My Neighbor? (And Why Does He Need Me?)**	**What on Earth Can I Do?**
Biblical Worldview of God and Truth	Biblical Worldview of Self-Image	Biblical Worldview of Servanthood	Biblical Worldview of Stewardship
ISBN 978-1-935495-07-9	ISBN 978-1-935495-08-6	ISBN 978-1-935495-09-3	ISBN 978-1-935495-10-9

PARENTS LOVE THE
WHAT WE BELIEVE SERIES

"Apologia has successfully produced another awesome curriculum which exceeds our expectations, and for that, we in the homeschool community are grateful!"
Marissa Leinart
Emmy-winning news anchor

"An excellent resource that our family will be using to guide our worship times!"
Timothy Paul Jones, Ph.D.
Editor of *The Journal of Family Ministry*

"A 'moral flashlight' to illuminate the source of truth for young people everywhere. Get it and read it with your kids. I am."
Chuck Holton
Homeschooling father and best-selling author

"A wonderful tool for families!"
Leanna Ellis
Homeschooling mom and award-winning novelist

Visit www.apologia.com or call toll-free 1-888-524-4724

CELEBRATE YOUR CHILD'S SPIRITUAL JOURNEY

The What We Believe Series is a wonderful way to build a foundation of faith. Now your children can personalize and capture what they learn along the way in a keepsake they will want to revisit as they grow in Christ. These beautiful spiral-bound notebooking journals from Apologia include lesson plans, study questions, artful graphics, imaginative writing and drawing prompts, puzzles, activities, and full-color mini books. There's even a place on the cover for the child to write his or her name as the author of the journal!

NATURE'S FOOTPRINTS

Read a book about tracking animals, then plan a nature hike with a parent. Bring equipment to draw or photograph any animal prints you find. Record your findings here.

MAKE A NOTE OF IT
WHY DID GOD MAKE ME THIS WAY?

In the story "Sasha's Choice," Sasha learned that he was created by God to be unique and that neither his birth nor his lame foot was an accident. What is it about the way you were made that you've sometimes wished you could change? Have you ever considered thanking God for making you this way?

Notebooking Journal

Who Am I?

And What Am I Doing Here?

Written By

LET WISDOM BE YOUR GUIDE

WORD LIST

King Kong	anger	Judas
King Solomon	deceitful	Salt Lake City
The Last Supper	Gethsemane	genealogy
impulse	Vulcan	temple recommend
fisherman	psalm	polygamy
Ichthus	grief	tithing
emotions	Lazarus	Mormon Church
anxious	tempest	

ACROSS

1. The Christian "fish" seen on millions of car bumpers
7. Put on "a garment of _____ instead of a spirit of despair" (Isaiah 61:3)
11. Giant ape who "fell" for an actress
13. Leonardo da Vinci's famous mural of Jesus and His disciples
14. He betrayed Jesus to the authorities
15. Deep sorrow usually brought on by the loss of a friend or loved one
16. Profession of Peter, James, and John
17. Star Trek planet where inhabitants are taught to suppress their emotions
18. "The brain is _____ above all things" (Jeremiah 17:9)
19. Also known as the Church of Jesus Christ of Latter-day Saints

DOWN

2. You must have this special pass to enter a Mormon temple
3. The study of a family's history
4. "Controlling your _____ is better than capturing a city (Proverbs 16:32, NCV)
5. The practice of giving ten percent of your income to your church
6. Olive grove where Jesus prayed the night of His arrest
8. A sudden or spontaneous urge to do something you hadn't planned to do
9. He wrote that there's "a time to weep and a time to laugh" (Ecclesiastes 3:4)
12. Ellie's home town
13. The practice of having more than one wife or husband
15. "Do not be _____ about anything" (Philippians 4:6)
16. The Lord is "slow to _____ and rich in love" (Psalm 145:8)
18. They're a gift from God
20. Jesus wept at the death of this brother of Mary and Martha

---

ENCOUNTERS WITH JESUS
THE WEDDING FEAST

1. Read the biblical account of the wedding at Cana in John 2:1–11 and compare it to the story you've just read. What did the authors of your book add to the story as told in the Bible? Did they leave out anything important? How would you have told the story differently?

2. With Miriam getting married, what do you think it home will be like for her sister Rachel?

3. Why do you think hospitality was such an important part of a Jewish wedding?

4. Why was Miriam so distressed that the wedding party was running low on wine? What might people have said if the wine had run out so early in the festivities?

5. According to the apostle John, this was the first of the miraculous signs Jesus performed. So why do you think Mary came to Jesus with this problem? Why do you think she expected Him to do? Why?

6. Although the time for Jesus to reveal Himself to the world as the Son of God had "not yet come," He chose to turn the water into wine. Why do you think Jesus made this decision?

7. How did Jesus serve this young bride? What need did He meet? Whom else did He serve through this miracle?

8. What is your favorite story from the life of Jesus? Why?

Notebooking Journal

Who Is MY NEIGHBOR?

And Why Does He Need Me?

Written By

MAKING A DIFFERENCE

```
S H M A K E A D I F F E R E N C E J I Y
A Q E Z B R H F B T L N F C A R G O O I
F V L J V J O Z K W I J P V T I H G Q N
E O F H O R P I X O O B Y C Q Y R W H T
T F R E L C X Y N A Z F A M T R I U N E
Y G E L L C M X U R C R G P K W N T O R
I Y I P E A X S L E S E P F J P A F U D
N D G E Y Q Z D X B E B T W O B Y T W O P
N L H R B V N G D E T H E S Q I J X B C E
U U T J A L L T H A T Y O U C A N B E J F A D
M B E A L L T H A T Y O U C A N B E P N
B B R A L E L X A E S S M D E E J F A D
E U F O G Q U I B S R C F K H R G N N E
R B U D D Y S Y S T E M C T D A S P
S F X S O C I A L H X E G F C L W S O C
H M D R C L X V A H O O E D T D A S P
I J M X S E R V A N T H O O D T D A S P
T R U S T I N G G O D B G F A H S R H B
Z H W A C H I N A N N S Q O R Q R F I S
Y U K K C H A N G E T H E W O R L D P O
```

volleyball	interdependence	buddy system	two are better than one
China	servanthood	NASCAR	be all that you can be
cargo	trusting God	make a difference	change the world
freighter	companionship	two by two	mustard seed
social triune	helper	safety in numbers	

Notebooking Journal

What on Earth

CAN I DO?

Written By

I Know What I Believe, Too

Introducing What We Believe coloring books for those who learn best when their hands are active! These 64-page coloring books are lovingly illustrated by award-winning artist Alice Ratterree. Every drawing depicts a story or teaching from the companion textbook, so even the youngest member of the family can follow along!

IMAGE LICENSE INFORMATION